ENTERPRISING
WOMEN

Race in the Atlantic World, 1700–1900

*Published in Cooperation with the Library Company of Philadelphia's
Program in African American History*

SERIES EDITORS

Richard S. Newman, *Rochester Institute of Technology*
Patrick Rael, *Bowdoin College*
Manisha Sinha, *University of Massachusetts, Amherst*

ADVISORY BOARD

Edward Baptist, *Cornell University*
Christopher Brown, *Columbia University*
Vincent Carretta, *University of Maryland*
Laurent Dubois, *Duke University*
Erica Armstrong Dunbar, *University of Delaware and
the Library Company of Philadelphia*
Douglas Egerton, *LeMoyne College*
Leslie Harris, *Emory University*
Joanne Pope Melish, *University of Kentucky*
Sue Peabody, *Washington State University, Vancouver*
Erik Seeman, *State University of New York, Buffalo*
John Stauffer, *Harvard University*

ENTERPRISING WOMEN

Gender, Race, and Power in the Revolutionary Atlantic

KIT CANDLIN
AND
CASSANDRA PYBUS

The University of Georgia Press
Athens

Paperback edition, 2018
© 2015 by the University of Georgia Press
Athens, Georgia 30602
www.ugapress.org
All rights reserved
Set in Adobe Caslon Pro by Graphic Composition, Inc.

Most University of Georgia Press titles are
available from popular e-book vendors.

Printed digitally

The Library of Congress has cataloged the
hardcover edition of this book as follows:

Candlin, Kit.
Enterprising women : gender, race, and power in the revolutionary Atlantic /
Kit Candlin and Cassandra Pybus.
x, 241 pages ; 24 cm. — (Race in the Atlantic world, 1700–1900)
Includes bibliographical references (pages 215–230) and index.
ISBN 978-0-8203-4455-3 (hardcover : alk. paper) —
ISBN 0-8203-4455-9 (hardcover : alk. paper)
1. Racially mixed women—Caribbean Area—History—19th century.
2. Women, Black—Caribbean Area—History—19th century.
3. Businesswomen—Caribbean Area—History—19th century.
4. Social stratification—Caribbean Area—History—18th century.
I. Pybus, Cassandra. II. Title.
HQ1501.C35 2014
305.40896'9729—dc23
2014011856

Paperback ISBN 978-0-8203-5387-6

O brave new world, that has such people in it!
—Miranda in Shakespeare's *The Tempest*

>

CONTENTS

Acknowledgments ix

INTRODUCTION. Elisabeth and Her Sisters 1

CHAPTER ONE. The Free Colored Moment
War and Revolution in a Brave New World 15

CHAPTER TWO. Bars, Brothels, and Business
Rachael Pringle Polgreen and Rosetta Smith 32

CHAPTER THREE. By Labors and Fidelity
Judith Philip and Her Family 57

CHAPTER FOUR. A Lasting Testament of Gratitude
Susannah Ostrehan and Her Nieces 80

CHAPTER FIVE. The Queen of Demerara
Mrs. Dorothy Thomas 103

CHAPTER SIX. By Habit and Repute
The Intimate Frontier of Empire 126

CHAPTER SEVEN. Uncertain Prospects
Mixed-Race Descendants at the Heart of Empire 147

Conclusion 169

Notes 181

Bibliography 215

Index 231

ACKNOWLEDGMENTS

THIS BOOK HAS REQUIRED extensive research in far-flung places that would not have been possible without generous grants from the Australian Research Council, which also provided a five-year professorial fellowship for Cassandra Pybus and a four-year postdoctoral fellowship for Kit Candlin.

We owe a huge debt of gratitude to independent researchers Chris Rathbone, John Wilmer, and David Alston, who have unstintingly shared research with us that has proved invaluable. Equally invaluable has been the generous assistance we received from Curtis Jacobs of the University of the West Indies in Grenada. We cannot thank these people enough.

We are also indebted to the *Legacies of British Slave-Ownership* team working at University College, London, under the direction of Catherine Hall, and in particular we want to acknowledge the help we received from Nick Draper. Over the years we have been encouraged and stimulated by discussions with numerous scholars and especially wish to acknowledge Gad Heuman, Barry Higman, Lucy Frost, Jerry Handler, Daniel Livesay, Peter Hulme, Catherine Hall, Richard Drayton, Rebecca Scott, Maya Jasanoff, Marcus Rediker, and Richard Newman.

We have been more than fortunate to work in an outstanding intellectual environment in the School of Philosophical and Historical Inquiry at the University of Sydney, and we are grateful for the support we have received from the school and from Maria Cortes and Cam Pham in particular. Special thanks are due to Andrew Fitzmaurice, the head of the Department of History, and to our colleagues in the research support group: Penny Russell, Kirsten McKenzie, Clair Lowry, Blanca Tovias, Ann Cuthoys, Richard White, Mark McKenna, Judy Keene, and Cindy McCreery.

For their personal support and their generous offers of accommodation, we thank Jo Pearson, Adam Low, Peter Hulme, and Tain and Grace Tompkins. For their research and editoral assistance, we thank Darien Rozental, Justine Greenwood, Sarah Crawford, and Keren Lavelle.

Archives were indispensable to this book, and we are more than grateful to the staffs of the National Archives of the United Kingdom, the National Archives of Scotland, the Family Record Center of the Church of the Latter-day Saints in Utah, the Liverpool Record Office, Special Collections at the University of Virginia, the National Archives of Trinidad and Tobago, the Department of Archives of Barbados, the Barbados Museum and Historical Society, the Supreme Court Registry of Grenada, the Harry Ransom Center at the University of Texas, the London Metropolitan Archives, the British Library, the Nottingham Library's Special Collection, and St. George's Church, Benenden.

ENTERPRISING WOMEN

INTRODUCTION

Elisabeth and Her Sisters

ELISABETH SAMSON, a spinster aged forty-nine, had set her sights on becoming the wife of the organist of the Dutch Reformed Church in Paramaribo, the tiny capital of the colony of Suriname.[1] To this end, she had instructed her solicitors in the Netherlands to petition the Dutch States General, the highest authority for colonial affairs, requesting permission to marry. The year was 1764. The Political Council of Suriname had already refused her permission because eighty years earlier a ruling of the Suriname Company, which ran the place, had prohibited marriage between Europeans and Africans. Back in 1685, when the Suriname Company first sought to curtail the practice of Dutch men marrying their enslaved concubines, the principals would not have imagined that an African woman would seek to marry a Dutch man. Now this was exactly what Elisabeth Samson proposed, proudly affirming in her petition to the States General that she was "a freeborn Negress." She wanted to be married to the man of her choice and was not about to be denied.

Elisabeth Samson could buy and sell most of the Political Council of Suriname. She was a black woman, but she also was one of the wealthiest planters in the Atlantic world: the owner of a number of substantial properties in and around Paramaribo, including a very large mansion situated on prime land, six massive plantations, including one that was over a thousand acres, and many hundreds of slaves. Having personally visited the Netherlands, she knew Dutch law and understood the way the Dutch colonial system worked. To her great satisfaction, the Dutch States General declared that Dutch law did not prohibit interracial marriage and their ruling overrode that of the Suriname Company. The only problem was that the legal deliberations had taken three years, during which time her fiancé had died. Unperturbed, she promptly fixed upon another Dutch man, to whom she was married at her mansion in December 1767.

Elisabeth Samson was born in 1715 to an African woman called Nanoe, who had been enslaved but was manumitted on the death of her owner in 1713, along with her two mulatto children, Maria and Charlo. Nanoe had six other children with her enslaved African husband, and these children remained in bondage even when she was freed. Her last child, Elisabeth, was born free in 1715 because her mother was then a free woman. The manumitted son, Charlo, became a carpenter, and he purchased the six other children from his father's widow, then progressively manumitted his siblings over the next decade until the whole family was emancipated. Elisabeth grew up in the household of her half sister Maria, who married a wealthy Swiss planter and, after his death, a German merchant. Elisabeth was highly literate and was trained by her brother-in-law in business matters, at which she proved remarkably adept.

By nineteen she had begun to accumulate property, and by her mid-twenties she was the owner of two small coffee plantations. Sometime in her twenties she acquired a business partner who was also her lover, a German army captain named Carl Creutz. He received a grant of one thousand acres in 1749, and with Elisabeth Samson's capital and her two hundred slaves, the couple created a large and successful coffee plantation, which they called "Clevia." "Clevia" was registered in their joint names, as were a second plantation, "La Solitude," and two large houses they owned in the town. The slaves, however, were clearly demarcated as the property of Elisabeth Samson alone, and she retained sole ownership of her original plantations. It was she who controlled the operation of the plantations, managed the household, and transacted all the business, while Creutz attended to political matters and went off into the jungle to do battle with the Maroons.

Despite living on the frontier, the couple lived in grand style, occupying a lavishly furnished mansion in Paramaribo that was staffed by forty-four slaves and filled with a cornucopia of luxury goods, including hundreds of bottles of wine and nineteen dozen Japanese porcelain teacups. The inventory of their household filled more than thirty folios. Elisabeth Samson and Carl Creutz wanted for nothing, unless it was legitimacy. Creutz was a member of the Political Council, so he knew that the local law of Suriname prohibited marriage between Europeans and Africans, but that did not restrain him from ostentatiously flaunting his relationship with a black woman as his lover, his business partner, and his social equal. The governor grumbled about the couple in his private diary but did nothing about it, given that Carl Creutz was his good friend and Elisabeth Samson was very rich.

In 1762 Creutz died at the age of forty-seven. He had no children, so his will left his half of their joint estate to Elisabeth Samson for her lifetime, after which it would go to his brothers. Within two years Elisabeth Samson had paid the Creutz brothers in Germany the considerable sum of 155,000 guilders in order to consolidate the property as her own in perpetuity. That accomplished, she then proposed marriage to her tenant, a Dutch man many years younger than her who lived above the stables on the adjoining block. Christopher Brabant was merely the church organist, so he had no political status to uphold and protect. Presumably, he was keen to marry Elisabeth Samson and move into the luxurious mansion next door to enjoy the fruits of her vast wealth, but it was she, not he, who initiated the official request to marry. The Political Council upheld the law against such a marriage, even though it acknowledged there were favorable circumstances in this particular case. As the governor explained to the authorities in The Hague, the marriage of Elisabeth Samson to Christopher Brabant meant that he would become her legal heir, and "the wealth the young man will inherit in due time will," the governor argued, "come into white people's possession." This was a very good thing for the governor, since it was "not recommendable [that] the black people are rich and have possessions ... and become high and mighty like white people are."[2] Although this was an attractive proposition to the Political Council, it was not a sufficient inducement to break its own law.

During the legal deliberations in The Hague it would scarcely have slipped the notice of the Dutch authorities that this black woman was past fifty and most unlikely to have any children, so the marriage would ensure that her fortune flowed into Dutch hands. Although Brabant died during the three years it took the Dutch authorities in The Hague to allow the marriage, Elisabeth Samson soon found another young Dutch man to marry. When she died in 1771, Hermanus Zobre inherited all of her properties and possessions, making him a millionaire at the age of thirty-three. If he was grateful to his late wife he gave no sign of it, not even bothering to erect a tombstone in her memory. In little over a decade, Elisabeth Samson's carefully managed wealth would all be frittered away on her husband's ill-conceived projects and high living. All her money was gone and the property was taken for debt by the time he died in 1784.

Elisabeth Samson had an unworthy husband and no children to preserve her memory. Until the twenty-first century, she remained little more than a colorful piece of local folklore in Suriname and otherwise was entirely unknown in the history of the Dutch empire, despite a large amount of material relating to her residing in the Dutch archives. It is thanks to the painstaking research of Suriname writer Cynthia McLeod that we know about her impressive life.[3] Growing up in Suriname, McLeod knew about Elisabeth Samson from local history, but assumed that she must have been a slave concubine who had been manumitted on the death of her master, who then left her his fortune. What other narrative could there be to account for a fantastically rich black woman in the early eighteenth century? That she was a self-made entrepreneur was inconceivable. It was when McLeod went looking for Elisabeth Samson in the Rijksarchief in The Hague, as well as searching archives in Amsterdam, Rotterdam, and Germany, that she found a very different story from the one she had received from Surinamese history. It was highly gratifying, she reports, that her research was able to "have salvaged the remarkable person of Elisabeth out of the sphere of 'the helplessly forlorn and pitied black mistress' who inherits the fortunes of her industrious white master."[4]

Certainly the micro-biography of Elisabeth Samson is intriguing, but is it of any real use to historians of the Atlantic world? Surely this black woman is sui generis, a historical anomaly of passing interest for her enterprise and audacity? Can this exceptional case tell us anything meaningful about race and gender in the eighteenth-century Atlantic world? We took the view that it could. The mere knowledge that the daughter of two enslaved Africans could be an independent agent and amass her own personal fortune in the middle years of the eighteenth century complicated and challenged much of what we had understood about race and gender in slave colonies. More important, it gave us a tantalizing glimpse of what was possible for a free black woman to achieve in the Atlantic slave world. We might have dismissed her extraordinary circumstances as particular to unique features of the Dutch empire, with no relevance to the Anglo imperial sphere, were it not for having stumbled upon evidence of another fabulously wealthy black woman, this time from a British colony, who had demanded that the Colonial Office in London overturn a colonial law that discriminated against her as a free woman of color.

That woman was Dorothy, or Doll, Thomas, born a slave on Montserrat around 1756, who went on to establish business interests across the British colonies of the Windward Islands and the South American littoral. Her existence was uncovered by chance by Cassandra Pybus while undertaking research on a project entirely unrelated to the British Caribbean.[5] At the same time that the biography of Thomas began to reveal itself, Kit Candlin discovered other such women in the colony of Trinidad.[6] This book builds upon this initial research and published findings, but greatly expands the detail and implications, as well as making inevitable corrections to some of our earlier errors and assumptions.

One would search in vain for any mention of these women in the historiography of the British Caribbean, or even in local histories of the colonies where they did business; they simply disappeared from view. These women were largely illiterate and left no family papers, no letters, no diaries, and no oral history. To look for their life stories might seem an impossible task, but our excavation of colonial archives, newspapers, parish records, and contemporary travelers' accounts yielded a rich trove of materials that complemented what we had learned about Elisabeth Samson. Along the way we were hugely surprised to find quite a few more entrepreneurial black women in the archives we consulted, and even more surprised to find that they were comparatively wealthy. This was so unexpected that we felt it was crucial to reconstruct these contradictory colonial lives to provide much-needed nuance to the historiography and to give greater texture to the story of the Caribbean slave colonies.

The idea was born that we should excavate the colonial archives to find other enterprising black women in the British Caribbean colonies in the long eighteenth century. We understood this would be something of a Herculean task, but it could be done. Since the groundbreaking manifesto of Carlo Ginzburg and Carlo Poni in 1979,[7] the intensive archival research needed for the recovery of the lives of forgotten people has been transformed by digital technology. Each year the capacity to find minute information grows exponentially with the digitization of a vast range of archival sources plus sophisticated search engines, not to mention the indefatigable work of genealogists and family historians, who proved to be invaluable for this project.

GIVEN THE BREADTH OF EXPERIENCES we found among free women of color across the British Caribbean, as well as the complexities presented by the many different Caribbean archives, we felt that a study that incorporated the entirety of the Caribbean would have been a task at once too large and too diffuse. What we needed for our project was a region of the Caribbean where we could intensively search the archives and still keep the project cohesive. Certainly it had to be transcolonial, given that the women we had already found were particularly adept at crossing borders and boundaries, rather than spending their whole lives in just one colony. One of the significant features we were able to discern was their capacity to make or remake themselves in a variety of different situations, and their ability to exploit the gaps in a fluid political and racial climate. We wanted to highlight the transcolonial and transcultural aspect of these women's lives, and so looked for a region of the British Caribbean that was particularly multicultural and fluid during the Age of Revolutions. We chose to concentrate on the southern Caribbean, including the colonies of Grenada, Trinidad, and Demerara, which were important late colonies for the British and places that were contested and fought over to a far greater degree than other territories.[8] The imperial insecurity of the region would have likely profoundly influenced the lives and the choices of the women, and we also suspected that such political insecurity may have produced a number of such women by the end of the eighteenth century.

During this time the British Caribbean was changing markedly as island colonies adjusted their imperial connections. While there was nothing to quite equal the extraordinary swap that saw the British exchange the wilderness of Suriname for New York, colonies such as Grenada, Dominica, Tobago, and St. Vincent, known as the "ceded islands," were easy pickings from France as a result of the Seven Years' War. These imperial acquisitions were followed at the end of the century by the takeover of Dutch Demerara by the British in 1796 and Trinidad from Spain in 1797, as part of the renewed war with France. These were forgotten places, barely imaginable in the metropolitan capitals of Europe, undeveloped and sparsely populated, filled with the flotsam of the Atlantic. This was a liminal world where complex, multiracial communities numbered in the hundreds, not thousands, and the African slaves were hardly counted. Most of these colonies, at the time of cession at least, were poor and marginal, with virtually no investment in infrastructure or defense.

Aspiring and established planters looking for new opportunities, many of them with slaves, flocked to the ceded islands, seeking to build or rebuild their fortunes on the edges of the Atlantic. Alongside these planters came others, rich and poor, who also sought the freedom and anonymity that might be found there. Smugglers and privateers, many of them heavily involved in illicit trade with the Spanish American colonies on the mainland, made this region their home, while the predatory navies of Europe and America sought to defend slippery, ever-changing interests. As with frontiers everywhere, these islands and the sea between them became synonymous with insecurity and danger.

But there were advantages to be found here. The ceded islands became destinations of desire not just for whites, but for free Africans and their descendants, who sought the sanctuary that an undeveloped frontier might offer. These southern islands had been mainly colonized in the last waves of Caribbean expansion by a mixed bag of Europeans other than Britons and were unique in their liberties within the British sphere. Older possessions like Jamaica had strict racial laws, but these new colonies were less secure, and the British colonial authorities made concessions to French, Spanish, and Dutch colonists who took a less absolute view of race. This made the ceded colonies attractive to free Africans and their descendants. Cooks, cleaners, washerwomen, nursemaids, tradesmen, storekeepers, and hoteliers all took the opportunity to refashion their lives in the region.

All these arrivals radically changed the ethnic profile of these places. On Grenada and St. Vincent, numbers both white and black increased almost exponentially. In just ten short years from 1788 to 1798 the free population of Trinidad jumped from three thousand to twelve thousand, the majority free colored, while the number of slaves rose even more dramatically. These raw, volatile colonies were just the kind of places where an enterprising free colored woman could thrive. By the beginning of the nineteenth century just under half the slave owners on Grenada, Tobago, and Trinidad were women, and many of them were women of color. The business records that survive from these colonies are filled with the petty transactions of such women, often with other women, buying slaves and other property, owning shops and trading goods.

By the late eighteenth century, the southern Caribbean presented a particular phenomenon of fluid, contested colonies with a history of insurrection, even while located in the cockpit of British colonial efforts in the Atlantic world. As the Age of Revolutions spread war throughout the region, colonies changed hands repeatedly or descended into chaos. In the transient insecurity that this world engendered, some free colored women were able to reach dizzying heights of success in comparison to women not just in the Caribbean but anywhere in the British world.⁹ The freedom that could be found in an insecure frontier society provided marginal subjects with many more opportunities than those in the metropole, and the free colored women who are the subject of this book grabbed these opportunities with both hands. To understand how they thrived in this world we need to scrutinize the social milieu of these colonies and shift the focus from the white male elites and their traumatized, degraded slaves, and seek out the women who found distinctive advantages there in the turbulent years between 1763 and 1840.

So this book is about wealthy free colored women in a frontier world, some of whom grew powerful enough to affect colonial justice, make demands of white men, possess many slaves, and own hundreds, sometimes thousands, of acres of the most valuable farming land in the world. Of course, there were free colored women who rarely experienced a life beyond the petty world of prostitutes, hucksters, and washerwomen, who would never own any land or slaves and who would not acquire a share of the hefty compensation paid by the British government for emancipating the slaves. Nevertheless, the ebullient, enterprising colonial subjects we have chosen to research present an extraordinary story that has yet to be fully told in the context of Atlantic history.

This is a uniquely southern Caribbean tale. As a site of inquiry, the British colonies in the southern Caribbean hold advantages for our research other than the numbers of free colored women. Because of their geographical position it is possible to compare and contrast the newer ceded colonies with the long-established colony of Barbados, which was settled by the British in 1627. Barbados was an important node for the empire in the region; it was, as visitors observed, "the London of the West Indies." A much older and comparatively more stable colony than its neighbors, it was also where some of the women in this story were born or was a place they passed through. Focusing our research in the region that surrounded Barbados makes it possible to examine the comparative dynamics between that pivotal British colony and more recently acquired territories.

The newer colonies, as Barry Higman has argued, represent the second and third stage of colonies in the Caribbean, yet they have received far less scholarly attention than places such as British Jamaica, Spanish Cuba, or French St. Domingue.¹⁰ The colonies of Grenada, Trinidad, and Demerara, near to and feeding off Barbados, are a highly appropriate location for exploring the transient, and transnational, lives of our subjects. We wanted to see if the multicultural and trans-imperial experience of these colonies had any bearing on the lives and the self-fashioned choices that these women made. We knew from our previous work that the ceded colonies of the southern Caribbean, together with the South America littoral, had a greater degree of transience and opportunity in the Age of Revolutions than much older, more stable places, such as Barbados. So the southern Caribbean appeared likely to provide an almost perfect location for this project. If we were going to find micro-biographies of enterprising women of color, we reasoned, the southern Caribbean, with the stable colony of Barbados and the volatile ceded colonies nearby, together with a polyglot population, was where we were likely going to find them.

FROM THE OUTSET OUR RESEARCH was informed by the existing scholarship, and we sought to address what we saw as a gap in Caribbean historiography with regard to free women of color. To be sure, there have been a number of important works on free people of color, including histories of individual colonies and histories with comparative scope, and several focus on free women, notably *Engendering History: Caribbean Women in Historical Perspective*, edited by Verene Shepherd, Bridget Brereton, and Barbara Bailey; *Women in Caribbean History*, also edited by Verene Shepherd; and *Beyond Bondage: Free Women of Color in the Americas*, edited by David Barry Gaspar and Darlene Clark Hine. But even though successful free women of color were consistently remarked upon by contemporary observers, they have been treated in somewhat cursory fashion by historians. With the exception of contributions by Pedro Welch and Paulette Kerr, most Caribbeanists have focused their attention on free women's economic marginality and their closeness to slavery, rather than on their interactions with networks of white power.[11] However, as historians wrestle with the complexity of the position of free people of color in Atlantic slave societies, the picture has become more multifaceted with a surge of biographical studies situated within the "black Atlantic," taking the lead from Paul Gilroy's pioneering work *The Black Atlantic*, which set in motion a new interest in cross-currents and transnational movement. We were especially encouraged by the project of Rebecca Scott and Jean M. Hébrard to recover the life of the emancipated slave Rosalie and her descendants in Haiti, Cuba, New Orleans, and France.[12]

We have been disconcerted by a decidedly masculinist bias in the historiography of the British Caribbean, wherein men are consistently seen as dominating economic transactions and power relations. We feel this bias has distorted the historiography, focusing the attention of historians engaging with issues of race, gender, and power on the exploitation of women with dark skins by economically dominant white men. In this narrative, free women of color, who have long been an acknowledged presence in Caribbean colonies, are confined to a marginal role in a narrow sphere of activity: as the dependent concubines of the white male elite. Our research has yielded another narrative where white men certainly feature in the lives of free colored women, but in much more nuanced ways.

The interaction of race and gender is the key issue here. In the twenty-first century we have seen a deepening awareness among scholars of the Anglo Atlantic world that race is historically contingent, politically inflected, and culturally malleable. There has been an explosion of scholarship on the contingencies of race in the United States, producing what the cultural theorist Homi Bhabha calls "a blizzard of whiteness studies."[13] This scholarship has in turn fostered an interest in the construction of race in the British imperial sphere. It is a pity, however, that most of this scholarship on race, gender, and empire has drawn on evidence from the latter part of the nineteenth century, best exemplified by Catherine Hall's work and that of Antoinette Burton, as evidenced in their chapters in *The Oxford History of the British Empire: Gender and Empire*. In this influential collection, edited by Phillipa Levine, nine out of thirteen essays focus on aspects of Britain's imperial world in the last decades of empire. In *Gender and Empire*, edited by Angela Woollacott, the emphasis is almost entirely on the later empire and the focus is on white women. Similarly, *Gender and Imperialism*, edited by Clare Midgley, has only one contribution, by the distinguished Caribbean historian Hilary Beckles, that deals with the late eighteenth and early nineteenth century. Yet the prominence of free women of color in the local economies of colonies as diverse as Demerara and Barbados testifies to the powerful position to which some daughters of enslaved Africans had risen by the end of the eighteenth century. In many cases their economic standing had little or nothing to do with white men. Wealthy in their own right, these women needed no white male in order to be a significant player and source of influence in the business culture. They may have cohabited with imperial powerbrokers, but they were independent, articulate, and entrepreneurial women who were often able to manipulate economic circumstances and personal situations to their own advantage in order to self-fashion their existence.

The women we have uncovered were savvy and socially mobile, maintaining networks of contacts and associates (many of whom were other free colored women) to secure themselves and each other in shifting times. They were careful to have their children well educated. While researching the lives of their children and grandchildren, we were again surprised to find large numbers of mixed-race children sent to Britain to be educated, either privately with tutors or in boarding schools financed with money from the Caribbean. With some capital behind them, and often boasting a high level of education, these mixed-race offspring, both male and female, were successful in penetrating deep into British society, their personal biographies carefully constructed to obscure any hint of miscegenation. This little-known byproduct of empire has provided us with invaluable insight into what Ann Laura Stoler refers to as the "tense and tender ties" of empire: that social and cultural space where sexual and affective transgressions of the taxonomies of race and power were enacted.[14] Our research has also yielded important evidence for the argument that British racial identity was not fixed in the eighteenth century and remained malleable and contingent well into the nineteenth century.[15]

For the children and grandchildren of our subjects, legal and racial legitimacy became their primary focus as they sought to navigate the world of empire against the currents of race and class. Some of them, particularly the daughters, followed their mothers into entrepreneurial successes in the Caribbean, often capitalizing on their mothers' business achievements, while others rejected the choices made by their mother and achieved professional success in the metropolitan heart of the empire. Indeed, we would argue that free people of color were some of the most dynamic in the nineteenth-century imperial world. A colonial governor, a surgeon general in the British army, and a colonial mayor all feature in this story, the descendants of African slaves who found a place and considerable success in imperial service. There were other descendants who established their legitimacy by laundering themselves successfully into the British middle class, becoming merchants, doctors, country parsons, and lawyers.

This aspect of our research sheds more light on the interconnected world of empire, adding a further dimension to the work of scholars like Miles

Ogborn, who has traced individual lives as subjects crisscrossed the empire in the early modern era.[16] The life stories of transient individuals are crucial for the study of mobilities in empire, and it has been encouraging to see historians turn their gaze on the transients of the African diaspora. Excellent micro-biographies of such colonial travelers have emerged from research in the Dutch, French, and Iberian empires, beginning with Jon Sensbach's pathbreaking study, *Rebecca's Revival: Creating Black Christianity in the Atlantic World*; Rebecca Scott and Jean M. Hébrard's *Freedom Papers: An Atlantic Odyssey in the Age of Emancipation*; and James Sweet's *Domingos Alvares, African Healing, and the Intellectual History of the Atlantic World*. However within the anglophone imperial sphere there has been next to no attention to the agency and mobility of ex-slaves and their descendants and the ways that such people were insinuated into imperial networks. The outstanding exception that proves the case is the almost obsessive focus on the life of Olaudah Equiano, who published his remarkable autobiography in 1789, which has spawned several biographies.[17]

It is a truism of archival research that you do not see what you are not looking for. Given that the exclusion of Afro-Caribbean people as active historical agents is endemic in the historiography of the British Caribbean in the long eighteenth century, it is perhaps unsurprising that historians continue not to notice them. Emma Rothschild's *The Inner Life of Empires* is a case in point. This impeccable study of the imperial networks of the Scottish Johnstone family has shown us how micro-biography can allow the historian to explore the connections between the life stories of individuals and the wider socioeconomic-political events of which they were a part. Her book should stand as a fine example of the way the nitty-gritty of individual lives illuminates the macro-history of empire; however, Rothschild has undermined her own argument on this point because a strand of the micro-history of the Johnstone family is absent. What is missing in her telling is the very stuff that has the capacity to challenge the way we understand the life of empire, at both the micro- and the macro-level.

Crucial elements of the Johnstone family's experience are not explored in the book because, as Rothschild ruefully acknowledges, this Scottish family kept secrets about the mixed-race family members whose existence they never publicly acknowledged. These were the children of the supposed bachelor Alexander Johnstone, whose large slave plantation in Grenada was inherited by his siblings and became the foundation of their subsequent wealth and enhanced social standing. Rothschild found evidence of Alexander's mixed-race descendants in the family papers, but apart from a couple of bemused references, she ignores these Afro-Caribbean Johnstones and makes no attempt to pursue their lives in the Caribbean and Britain. Her choice to focus solely on the white Scottish family as agents of empire is more than a disappointing oversight. Micro-biographies of the clandestine family have the capacity to tell us something new and important about the macro-history of empire. To incorporate the excluded, disenfranchised, and disinherited Afro-Caribbean family members would be to tell a very different story and provide a window into a much more problematic imperial story.

Despite the limitations, Emma Rothschild's micro-biographies of the Johnstone family members provide a new approach to imperial history. The white family members traveled very great distances and experienced diverse colonial conditions, so their personal stories can be read as a history of diverse legal conditions and social classes that extends across the frontiers of historical inquiry to encompass the histories of economic life, of politics, of slavery, and of family relationships. For much the same purpose, we chose to construct serial micro-biographies of enterprising free women of color. We believe that micro-biographies provide insight into the connections between historical events and individual experience, which allows for an intimate exploration of the multiplier effect of empire. By privileging the agency of Afro-Caribbean women we seek to challenge the white and masculinist focus of the historiography of economic life, slavery, and family relationships in the Anglo imperial world of the Atlantic in the eighteenth and early nineteenth century.

We have also chosen to construct micro-biographies because this form provides a narrative structure that is not tethered to the inevitable limitations of our fragmentary evidence. Telling life stories allows us to capture something of the intelligence, ebullience, and sheer audacity of our subjects. Each biography serves as a particular case study of the macro-history of the times. By examining the trajectory of an individual life, we are best able to explore personal agency in the push and pull of historical forces and to resist the homogenizing impulse inherent in macro-historical accounts.

A CRITICISM MIGHT BE MADE that this book is concerned only with a minority of elite women who were enthusiastic supporters of the colonial project and who profited by it through the ownership of slaves. We accept that this is indeed the case, and we welcome the micro-biographies of enslaved Africans and subaltern free people of the Caribbean slave colonies. With one exception, the women we have researched have not been the subject of historical inquiry, yet each led a remarkable self-fashioning life that challenges and complicates our understanding of gender, race, and power in Caribbean slave society.

Recovering the remarkable life stories of these enterprising women has been a cumulative revelation, given that everything we had read on the dynamics of race, gender, and power in the British imperial sphere had either ignored or underplayed their significance. Each of the micro-biographies presents a singular life, yet at the same time provides us with a unique window into the experience of the descendants of enslaved Africans in the Caribbean slave colonies. Placed together, the various biographies reinforce each other to provide a compelling picture of the strategies of survival of emancipated slaves and their descendants in the eighteenth and nineteenth centuries, at the same time that they illustrate the shifting constructions of race.

By examining the role of entrepreneurial women of color as key actors in the contested, multinational colonies of the southern Caribbean, this book challenges the current understanding of the dynamic between gender, race, and power in the Atlantic world during the Age of Revolutions. Recovering the life stories of these women and piecing together the networks of power that sustained them positions free women of color as an integral part of the wider Atlantic economy, situates them in the social and cultural life of the Caribbean, and demonstrates how their influence reached right into the heart of empire over several generations. We argue, more broadly, that such women were part of a highly successful and economically tenacious group, and that they were a particular feature of the region from which they came. Intrinsic to this book, therefore, is a fuller understanding of the factious insecurity of development in the southern Caribbean during a period of imperial uncertainty, when allegiances to Spain, France, the Netherlands, and Britain were in a state of flux. This was a multicultural world and a region that was characterized by transience and transcolonial migration. The contestation of empire shaped the lives of these women, while they and their children in turn helped to shape the imperial project in the Atlantic world.

CHAPTER ONE

The Free Colored Moment
WAR AND REVOLUTION IN A BRAVE NEW WORLD

WHILE THE SEVEN YEARS' WAR raged across the Atlantic world, a motley collection of British speculators, financiers, merchants, and other hopefuls bided their time. With the ink on the Treaty of Paris of 1763 barely dry, they fell over themselves to divide the spoils from defeated France. Bringing great fortunes and even greater credit to bear, they inundated the British government with proposals, suggestions, and advice in order to secure a share in the new prosperity.[1] Provinces in India, the whole of explored Canada, the Floridas, and four brand-new colonies in the Caribbean: the Seven Years' War had been good for Britain, and the metropolitan moneymen could barely contain themselves.

With the East India Company ruling its share of the subcontinent jealously, popular attention turned to Atlantic gains.[2] Most eyes were on the Caribbean. In the age of King Sugar, it was an easy choice to make. Over the next fifty years slavery would loom even larger in the account books of empire, and slave-grown produce throughout the world would almost double, but the 1760s were the planters' golden age and a nadir for humanity.[3] Fine ladies took their well-dressed chattel for walks through fashionable London, and hardy sea captains in Liverpool and Lancaster counted out the body spaces on newly minted slave ships. If they thought about it at all, few could even conceive of a world without slaves or the things slaves labored to grow. And if anyone did stand up and say something, there were over fifty MPs in the British Parliament—the West India lobby—who would tell them to sit down again.[4]

By far, the most sought-after new land therefore was to be found in the windward Caribbean territories of Grenada, St. Vincent, Dominica, and Tobago, which became known as the ceded islands. The Lords Commissioners for New Lands was set up partly in response to the rush, while new governors in the region complained of the workload and the effort that went along with these new conquests. From his base on Grenada, Robert Melvill,[5] the ceded islands' first governor, went so far as to "ease the expense" of settling newcomers by using his own money, while his subordinates on lesser islands, like St. Vincent and Dominica, struggled to prevent the new arrivals from encroaching on Indian land. The collective history of these colonies forms the Caribbean backbone of our story of women.

The imperial gains of 1763 began the second phase of British expansion in the Caribbean, pushing the power base out from colonies like Jamaica, Antigua, Montserrat, Nevis, and St. Kitts in the north and Barbados in the south and filling much of the space in between. By the end of the eighteenth century, under external pressures from war, revolution, and migration, this second phase of Caribbean growth led to a third and final phase, when the frontier colonies of Trinidad and Demerara, at the very bottom of the archipelago, were conquered and occupied in the 1790s.[6]

For the most part, these ceded islands were comparatively undeveloped frontier spaces that had experienced isolation and a lack of investment prior to the British arrival.[7] In contrast to the deteriorating soils and oversubscription of the older colonies, however, the opportunities they represented seemed boundless. Domestic British broadsheets and magazines—particularly in Scotland—were full of descriptions of the potential of this new territory. An article in *Scots Magazine* waxed lyrical about the "abundant fertility of the soils," which, the magazine argued, would "raise genteel fortunes" for anyone who went there.[8] In Ireland a young Edmund Burke was incredulous that anyone could disparage such a fruitful settlement, the glorious product of "English valour."[9]

Unsurprisingly, after 1763, offers of land in the ceded islands were eagerly taken up. Concerned that just a few magnates would buy up too much land, a limit of three hundred acres for every application was imposed to help diversify the people who would come to the new territories.[10] On Grenada, legislation was even proposed to financially assist poorer newcomers to partake in the Caribbean bounty.[11] New planters were so rapacious on St. Vincent that within two years of formal British control, settlers acting without the sanction of the London government had forcibly seized three thousand acres of land previously designated as Indian space.[12]

Free people of color also found this region attractive, and they flocked to the Windward Islands from the 1760s onward. Relegated to the margins of white society, these people had a precarious existence in the older colonies. Tales of stolen free colored patrimony, of forced separation, and of capricious whites only too happy to let free people of color fall on hard times are staples of Atlantic world history.[13] For stateless and vulnerable free colored people relocating from colonies such as French St. Domingue, Martinique, and St. Lucia, the southern Caribbean was compelling. Little is known about the communication channels between free colored populations, but it seems likely that people heard that the British imposed far less strict regimes in the fledgling colonies of the ceded islands than in their older possessions.[14] Free colored people in the new colonies could buy land, often without caveat, and there were no restrictions on their movement, on whom they could marry, or on whether they could gather in numbers or carry weapons. In the years following the takeover, free colored men could even become officers in the militias of Tobago and Grenada—something the paranoid Assembly of French St. Domingue had found unthinkable.[15]

There were also comparatively large numbers of free colored people in these islands already. Many had been manumitted by their former owners or had been born from unions between isolated French or Spanish planters and their slaves in the early part of the century. These were habits that many British migrants readily adopted, and many slaves continued to be freed throughout the eighteenth century. The existence of societies of free colored people throughout the new British colonies made assimilation for others much easier. So great were the numbers that by 1783 free people of color on Grenada were 53 percent of the total free population. The majority of these free colored people were women.[16]

As the effusive writing in *Scots Magazine* suggested, many of the new arrivals from Britain came from Scotland, and they would play an important part in the story of free colored women. For years the Scots had played second fiddle to the English, and antipathy toward the Scots remained a virulent stream in English culture.[17] Certainly there were large numbers of Scots on Jamaica, and Scottish firms had sewn up the trade of St. Kitts and Nevis, but many more Scots were poised to take advantage of the new conquests. With Lord Bute as the first Scottish prime minister of a unified Britain, the end of the Jacobite wars, and the highland clearances in full swing, there was little to stop many Scots from migrating to the Caribbean. In doing so, these opportunists easily turned the fortunes of the Seven Years' War into what was undoubtedly the eighteenth century's Scottish moment. Scots were appointed throughout the new dominions. Robert Melvill was the ceded islands' first governor, Archibald Campbell became governor of Jamaica, James Grant became governor of East Florida, while George Johnstone was governor over the border in West Florida. James Murray was awarded Quebec, and just a few years later John Murray would become governor of New York. The imperial opportunities presented to Scots in the middle years of the century were exploited with enthusiasm.[18]

The Scots tended to form close-knit groups connected by marriage, birth, and kin. They operated in tight networks, they were notable for aggressive acquisition and savvy business sense, and, in an age of patronage, they promoted each other unreservedly. Competing with the English for the spoils of empire, they had to use clannishness as a way to survive.[19] Robert Melvill was particularly ready to plant his compatriots in the councils and assemblies over which he held control. In Dominica, Tobago, and Grenada, Melvill made sure that new councils were stacked with Scots.[20] These interloper appointees highlighted the fault lines in imperial rule by exacerbating the bitter disputes between the Crown and elected assemblies. In myriad ways political tensions riddled the southern Caribbean.[21]

The Scots knew how to play the game. Hand in glove with their hard business sense came a social permissiveness and a forward-looking, can-do attitude. Coming from cosmopolitan and almost exclusively military backgrounds, many governors encouraged this approach.[22] Melvill used his power to buy up, through proxies, not only the three hundred acres he was allotted on Grenada and St. Vincent, but a further thousand on Dominica. When questions were raised over this portfolio later in his life, he had a tract written that absolved him from any guilt since his purchases, it was argued, were made only as an enthusiastic "example" for his fellow planters.[23] He was only one of many Scots to aggressively work the system in their favor.

Unlike the early settlers on Jamaica in the seventeenth century, there were no years of experimentation for those arriving on the ceded islands. Planters came with a fully developed sense of the planting system and its pitfalls. They knew which crops to grow, how to grow them, and in which soils they worked best. Most knew about hurricanes and the climate, and how best to mitigate their effects. Numerous popular books and almanacs were eagerly read, helping the colonists to learn about dangerous diseases and the ever-present threat of insects. Thanks largely to the existing colonies, the new men also knew how to manage and control their slave workforces.[24]

Using existing networks of Scots across the Atlantic world, new settlers arrived in the southern Caribbean with a colonial support structure in place. Merchants, factors, and agents—many of whom were closely tied by marriage or kinship—were only too ready to take a share of the enterprise. Friends in older partnerships, trusts, and corporations, who brought considerable prior experience and expertise to bear, often formed new merchant companies and partnerships. Mcdowell and Millikin, Bartlett and Campbell, and Telford, Norton and Co. were just three of the many successful Scottish firms that were created out of older combinations. This activity was coupled to substantial home-based industries, such as the law, dominated by families like the Baillies, the Houstons, and the Campbells. From Aberdeen to London, the ports of greater Britain could all be harnessed by Scottish firms and utilized for everything from merchant marine enterprises to shipbuilding, from storage to distribution.[25]

Born of conquest, the new colonies formed the last Caribbean frontier, a deep space filled with competing loyalties and mixed populations. Without clear borders and between empires, these colonies were sites of contestation where more often than not colonial governors had to negotiate their authority against a backdrop of threats and unrest. Even when war did not threaten, planter assemblies would regularly fall into disputes between the nominated representative of the Crown and their own sectional interests. Landowners argued incessantly in a constant stream of property claims and counterclaims.[26] Looming over these internal disputes was the threat of slave revolt—especially as the number of slaves brought into these colonies completely dwarfed those arriving in the older possessions. Pressures were compounded—especially on St. Vincent and Dominica—by a series of debilitating wars with black Caribs.[27] With resident French Catholic populations in all of these new islands, and well-populated French dominions like Guadeloupe and Martinique just a short sail away, British governors also found themselves embroiled in bitter contests over religion and custom.[28]

Despite the insecurity and the administrative problems, these colonies were overwhelmingly places of fortune and possibility. These themes, which marked the region in the last decades of the eighteenth century, created a unique atmosphere where sustained social control was difficult to achieve for distracted governors, and where populations were mixed to a level that seriously undermined the smooth running of the colonies. In this space of compromise and accommodation, a comparatively level and highly permissive culture arose. Taking advantage of this permissiveness were free people of color, some of whom began to inherit from their European fathers or partners.[29] As they grew in wealth, free colored people also grew in stature, and as the century progressed whites found that they no longer enjoyed an exclusive hold on land tenure, slave ownership, and influence.

This was a fluid, frontier world, however, where new British conquests sat uneasily beside the other great empires in the region. More than once would these islands change hands as wars, revolutions, and revolts tore across the Atlantic world. The American Revolution, followed closely by the French Revolution, triggered a series of lesser but no less disruptive colonial revolutions fought largely around the Caribbean Sea. The French retook Grenada, St. Vincent, and Tobago during the American War of Independence, along with the Dutch colony of Demerara, accelerating the animosity between the earlier French inhabitants and newer arrivals from Britain. But with the British destruction of the French fleet in the Caribbean in the closing stages of the American Revolutionary War and with mounting financial difficulties at home, France was forced to return these colonies in the peace of 1783.[30] Every time a colony changed hands like this, a new group of people would be unsettled by the conflict. This transience made the southern Caribbean—with the close interconnectedness of its islands—an ethnic polyglot, very different from the homogeneity of the older European possessions.

Despite all the drawbacks, the southern Caribbean in the eighteenth century continued to be a place for new men and women, be they Scots migrants or free people of color. Here, on the edges of America, such people could exploit the gaps in the imperial framework and draw on a strong community of support. By the 1780s the new people in the region were making their presence felt in the wider world.

The peace of 1783 that followed the end of the American Revolution did nothing to ease the tensions between the French and British, who took back the ceded island colonies with renewed vigor and a sense of righteousness. Tensions were most pronounced on Grenada—the most prosperous of the new British colonies in the southern Caribbean. The arrogant and uncompromising behavior of the British settlers and administrators who arrived in the colony, especially after it was reclaimed from the French in 1783, ensured that Grenada remained at the center of the conflict between the two empires for the next twenty years. Law after law was aimed at the complete disenfranchisement of any French settlers who chose to remain in the colony.[31] Eventually, with so few European French left, the attacks on the rights of the francophone Catholic community fell squarely on the francophone free colored people, whose success was jealously coveted by new settlers from Britain.[32] Further laws began to emerge that attempted to curtail their influence in society and their prominence in the commercial life of the colony. By insulting this emergent community, however, the British were playing with fire. Their imperial hubris would have an enormous cost.

IN FEBRUARY 1787, in the district of St. Marks, Grenada, British authorities arrested a thirty-four-year-old woman, referred to in the documents as Marie Rose Cavelan. Her crime was to be a free woman of color, and the authorities were so dismissive of her that they did not even use her married name, even though she was well known as the wife of a prominent free colored planter, Julien Fedon. She and her husband owned the "Lancer" estate, a moderately sized plantation, and at least a dozen slaves.[33] The couple had inherited money from their white fathers to which they had steadily added over the previous ten years. Later, they would purchase the plantation "Belvidere" in a private transaction involving the prominent attorney James Campbell.[34] They were a young couple, well liked and respectable.

The law under which Marie Rose Fedon was detained had been enacted the year before. It required every free colored person on the island—over two thousand people—to prove their free status to the authorities in the capital, St. George's. Those who did not would be arrested and, after six weeks, any people who could not prove their liberty were to be sold into slavery.[35] As a French-speaking plantation owner, Marie Rose Fedon was contemptuous of such laws. Descended from a French man who had come from Martinique in the 1750s, she had lived almost her whole life on the island as a free woman. Like many francophone free colored women of standing, she was educated and took a very active part in the couple's business transactions. Marie Rose's signature is on all the documents between the couple and the authorities, and she appears to have been as involved in the finances as her husband was. Her family, the Cavelans, was a well-established one. She understood the law and its implications, but she was proud of her French heritage and the liberties she had previously enjoyed. She saw no reason to travel the fourteen or so miles from "Lancer" to the capital to prove who she was to the Anglo interlopers.

The law in question was yet another vagabond law introduced by Governor Melvill and extended by his Scots successors, all of which were aimed at curtailing the prominence of a rapidly growing community that was free, colored, and Catholic.[36] Oppressive and discriminatory laws of this kind had, initially, been predominantly anti-Catholic and anti-French in intent rather than being aimed at free colored people. While often virulently against Catholicism, many of the Scots who made the law lived with free colored women, regardless of their religion. As a result, Marie Rose Fedon and her Catholic family had always managed to work within their dictates, however demeaning. In one such legal wrangle, Marie Rose and Julien Fedon had been forbidden to marry in a Catholic ceremony. They chose in 1775, however, not to follow many other francophone people and leave the island for French territory, but to remain and submit to the quiet indignity of an Anglican wedding ceremony. When the French briefly reoccupied the island between 1779 and 1783, they went to the trouble of expunging the British sacrilege and getting married again, this time by a Catholic priest.[37]

After 1783 the British reoccupied Grenada with a renewed sense of purpose, determined to send a clear message of racial superiority and religious intolerance. Prominent free people of color were a deliberate target. The strike at Marie Rose Fedon threatened a whole group of interconnected families, as the authorities must have been well aware. Her two sisters had married the brothers of Julien Fedon, and all three couples were at the heart of the free colored community in the island. It was a tight social circle that included many other relations, godparents, brothers- and sisters-in-law, and business partners; the group represented most of the biggest and wealthiest free colored families on the island.[38] The new ruling was a profound insult and an outrage, but it was also an attack on her as a woman.

The law was enacted against the free colored community, but it was enforced against women. Julien was as prominent as Marie Rose was, and yet he did not have to prove himself. This was enforcement designed for maximum humiliation. It also betrayed the increasing levels of unease among some elements of the white community, who felt threatened not only by the prominence of women like Marie Rose Fedon but by the complicated patterns of miscegenation that had developed over the previous half century. By striking at women in this way, conservative elements in the white Grenadian society emphasized free colored people's racial inferiority and second-class status. It also sent a clear message to the many white men in the society who had transgressed racial boundaries and taken up with free women of color or with slaves.[39] The colonial indulgence of Europeans earlier in the century had now become a clear problem for some in the British community.

Given that she was not in a relationship with a white man, and being far from a vagrant or "vagabond," Marie Rose probably thought this was a law she could ignore. Neither she nor her husband could have anticipated that this time the British were serious. They came and forcibly took her to St. George's. Unable to stop the arrest, Julien Fedon must have been frantically worried about what would happen. His wife had just six weeks to prove that she was a free person or face enslavement. Her plight was made even more unnerving because Marie Rose was born on French Martinique; her baptismal record, which could prove her free status, would have to be brought from the French colony and it might not be found in time.

Rather than risk that time-consuming process, Marie Rose and Julien Fedon drew on their connections and their reputations to secure her liberty. The best man at their wedding, Joseph Verdet, and a wealthy white planter, François Philip, testified and swore oaths as "credible freeholders" to the authorities in St. George's that she was free.[40] Even so, Marie Rose stayed incarcerated for several weeks while her husband and family tried to get her released. They were fortunate that the justice of the peace, Dr. John Hay, a man who could have made things very difficult for the couple, chose not to demand a record of her birth. No doubt to the couple's relief, he accepted the word of Philip and Verdet, and signed her Certificate of Freedom.[41]

Hay's small act of kindness was something that Marie Rose and Julien Fedon would not forget, any more than they would forget the degrading trauma of her incarceration or having to be married by a Protestant vicar. Within just a few years this couple would be at the heart of one of the bloodiest revolutions to ever strike the British empire, a revolution that would destroy the jewel of the ceded islands and forever bear their name: the Fedon Rebellion.[42] When the revolution erupted in 1795, Marie Rose Fedon was in the thick of the action, standing firmly beside her husband, her active and engaging presence well attested to by eyewitnesses. She was said to look on with "a cold indifference" when her husband decided to execute the colonial governor and forty-five other British prisoners.[43] But she remembered John Hay and his kindness. When his turn came to face the firing squad, the couple repaid their debt and spared his life.

THE FEDON REBELLION WAS THE most violent expression of conflict that erupted between revolutionary France and Great Britain in the Caribbean between 1793 and 1815. It would only be surpassed in magnitude by the revolution on St. Domingue.[44] But the experience of the Fedons and the violence of their rebellion were not unique. The war with France spawned several interconnected struggles that tore through the Caribbean during the Age of Revolutions. Most of the combat between the two nations occurred in the Windward Islands in the southern Caribbean. All of these subsidiary wars drew energy from pent-up anxieties and tensions similar to those experienced on Grenada during the previous decade. At their heart were men and women just like Marie Rose and Julien Fedon, who had gained much from the development of the ceded islands. The war would prove to be the turning point in the free colored world throughout the southern Caribbean and the catalyst of much of what was to come.

As the long wars with France played out in the Caribbean in the 1790s and into the nineteenth century, shifting alliances complicated matters; the fighting rapidly drew in other imperial allies and combatants who, in turn, dragged their colonies into the conflagration. With so many nations having colonies in such close proximity, the wars turned the Caribbean into a cauldron of invasions and counterinvasions, one small war leading to another. Whole armies were swallowed alive fighting republicans or royalists, fighting jungles and fighting disease, while waves of refugees and migrants wandered from island to island looking for opportunities or sanctuary. Often the administrations in the southern Caribbean barely functioned; the levers of metropolitan power were stretched to the limit and frequently broke.

War in the Caribbean took on a life of its own; no longer fighting just an imperial war between Britain and France, or an ideological war that pitted republicans against royalists, it was also a race war. Both sides of the ideological divide tried to gain the support of local populations, whether they were European, white creole, or free colored. The Revolutionary War provided unique opportunities for free people of color in particular, whose numbers had grown significantly by the start of the war. Many of them, like the Fedons, used the conflict to try and gain more power for themselves as white rule fractured around them. Adding immeasurably to the drama, both sides found themselves fighting on dangerous ground occupied by slaves, who proved only too willing to take advantage of the situation to take their liberty for themselves. And with offers of freedom for good service, all sides, royalist and republican, French and British, armed slaves in droves.[45]

The Revolutionary War, as it played out across the Caribbean, was also a war of ideas, the most basic of which was a new conception of the citizen and the implementation of the Declaration of the Rights of Man. This proclamation fundamentally struck at the heart of the slave regime. In 1793 the revolution in France had taken its radical turn: the Rights of Man were taken to their logical conclusion with an emancipation decree.[46] This decree greatly exacerbated the tensions in the Caribbean, splitting the French further. The Rights of Man naturally resonated strongly with free people of color. Emboldened by the new language of *égalité*, many joined in the war enthusiastically.[47] Conversion was greatly assisted by an explosion in propaganda and the printing presses that produced it.[48]

In the French dominions many planters remained steadfastly loyal to the old regime, not so much for any love of the king as for the sake of their livelihoods. The opportunistic British secretary of state for war, Henry Dundas, saw potential in this loyalty. Starting in 1793 he focused on France's wealthiest colony, St. Domingue, planning to link up with struggling royalist French planters there, reimpose slavery, and take the territory for the British. He intended to follow this up with a wider campaign in the southern Caribbean to conquer the French colonies of Martinique, St. Lucia, and Guadeloupe, which had evaded capture in 1763.[49] With France distracted by the European war and her colonies in disarray following the revolution of 1789, it all seemed easy.

It did not work out that way. In 1794 a large republican army arrived in the southern Caribbean to counter Dundas's efforts to grab the poorly defended French islands. The republican army was led by a thirty-four-year-old French commissioner, Victor Hughes, who had formerly been the inquisitor general of La Rochelle, where as a twenty-eight-year-old he had personally executed scores of counterrevolutionaries.[50] He brought his hardline attitude to the Caribbean, and from the moment he arrived the character of the war changed markedly. Within months he had executed hundreds of counterrevolutionaries on Guadeloupe.[51] Atrocities and violence escalated as the fighting grew more intense and the stakes grew higher. Hughes had no compunction about freeing and arming slaves nor in fermenting unrest and revolution across the Windward Islands. He was keen to exploit any group that bore a grudge against the existing order, be they disaffected French planters, slaves, or free people of color.[52] By the end of 1795 the British were losing, fighting a desperate rearguard action to retain and defend what they had gained the previous year.

By 1796 the situation for the British had become dire. Since the capture of St. Lucia in June 1794, the army of occupation had experienced deadly guerrilla fighting that intensified as the beleaguered garrison members were picked off by armed free colored "brigands" from the hills in the middle of the island. "The deaths on Morne Fortune have been dreadful," wrote the exhausted military governor. "Sixty to seventy a week." The situation was so fraught that after only four months, and suffering from yellow fever, he asked to be relieved.[53] This was also the case on Grenada, where the chief surgeon, a man named MacGrigor, described the mortality as "frightful."[54] From his base on neighboring Guadeloupe, Hughes spurred on the massive pro-republican insurrection led by the Fedons, which destroyed most of the island. Many whites were killed, estates burned, and towns ransacked, while slaves deserted their plantations en masse and joined in the fighting. Again encouraged by Hughes, another ugly war broke out on St. Vincent, with black Caribs, white republican French, and free colored people finding common cause against the British settlers. On Martinique the situation was little better than on St. Lucia, with the invading British holding back an increasingly aggressive insurgency, and on Dominica, unrest simmered in the streets after the arrival of a thousand refugees from the conflicts on neighboring islands and St. Domingue.[55]

As frightening and confusing as these troubles were for the British in 1795, the most alarming aspect of the Revolutionary War in the Caribbean was the awful mortality. Due to a deadly combination of yellow fever and malaria that swept through the archipelago in successive waves between 1791 and 1797, the British army lost seven hundred men a month, the worst casualty rate it had ever suffered.[56] The losses on St. Domingue were particularly ghastly, but all across the islands the death rate was very high. The destabilization of the colonies and the mass movement of people seeking to escape the violence intensified the negative impacts of disease and revolution. Between 1794 and 1795 the southern Caribbean had been turned into a nervous hotbed of conflict marked by sickness, cowardly local councils, poor discipline, and shocking levels of corruption and avarice, which plagued the

British campaign in particular. All of these factors crippled what once had promised to be a most sanguine British offensive to wrest France's Caribbean empire from the clutches of the Jacobins. With republican power on the ascendant, 1795 was a year that all British generals would sooner forget.[57]

FOR EUROPEANS SENT TO THE REGION to fight, the Revolutionary War was complex and shocking. The realities of failure were so great that combat easily wore down the morale of armies already under strain due to the frightening death rate. More than once British commanders in chief were replaced, and more than once officers were so unnerved by the cat-and-mouse war that they took their own lives.[58] A war that often involved fighting an unseen enemy who melted easily into the jungle took a drastic toll on men's nerves. Discipline was a constant problem, as was desertion. With abandoned plantations and vast stores of rum on all the islands, looting and drinking were rife.[59] In virtually every battle of the Revolutionary War, in every colony, looting, alcoholism, and desertion among the Europeans profoundly influenced the outcome.

It would take two more extremely costly expeditions to the Caribbean before the British effectively pacified their conquests from revolutionary France. In the process they not only managed to hold the islands of Martinique, St. Lucia, and St. Vincent, they were also able, eventually, to gather enough men to put down the Fedon Rebellion on Grenada. By the end of the eighteenth century the British also managed to wrest the frontier colony of Trinidad from the Spanish and take the South American coastal colonies of Demerara, Essequibo, and Berbice from the Dutch. Britain now controlled all the colonies in the Windward Islands. The colonies once seen as backward "ceded islands" had, by the end of the eighteenth century, begun a new life.

THE YEAR THAT THE BRITISH CAMPAIGN in the southern Caribbean faltered was a turning point in Atlantic history. After the arrival of Victor Hughes during the previous year, 1795 saw a new power emerge from a conflict between European rivals, a group hitherto only marginal in the history of the world. Up until that point free people of color were a statistic, occasionally showing up as bit players in the social demography of the Caribbean, or as walk-on actors in a drama centered on slaves and masters. They were always targets for discrimination and abuse, as Marie

Rose Fedon and her husband found on Grenada. But 1795 changed all that. During the Age of Revolutions the assertive nature of free colored people gained considerable strength. The upheaval of 1795 saw the restless energy of these people collectively flex its muscles in a hundred situations across the Caribbean. As Henry Dundas would discover to Britain's cost, nowhere was this energy felt more than in the insecure and contrary colonies of the southern Caribbean.

In every conflict pivoting on that year, free colored people took center stage. In 1795 they led the insurrection on Grenada and, in the same conflict, it was loyalist free colored people who played a central part in the ultimate failure of the Fedon Rebellion a year later.[60] Free colored people were also the black Caribs and "brigands" on St. Vincent who, led by Joseph Chatoyer, so unnerved the colonial troops sent against them.[61] On St. Lucia, free colored people led the fight against the British occupation in a dynamic guerrilla war, while on Martinique a crucial part of the republican general Rochambeau's defense was the large contingent of free colored people under the leader Bellgarde.[62] As the war progressed on different islands, large engagements took place in which there were virtually no white people fighting on either side. On St. Domingue, the fight for the world's richest colony took a dramatic turn when, in May 1794, Toussaint L'Ouverture switched sides, from royalist to republican, taking his thousand-man free colored army with him. In a war with many twists and turns, it was *the* decisive move, changing irrevocably the outcome.[63] In Jamaica, 1795 saw some of the oldest "free" communities in the Caribbean, the Maroons, begin another long campaign—centered on Trelawny and St. James parishes—to advance their rights as free men and women against the encroachment of planters.[64]

In part, the reason for this explosion in free colored people's prominence was opportunity, but this opportunity was driven by wider factors. The Age of Revolutions in the Caribbean was a time of demographic as well as ideological revolution. The strict racial divide across the British Caribbean was fracturing, driven by the contestation in the southern Caribbean and by the large numbers of francophone free colored people who had come there. Into this permissive world of interracial mixing created by the original French and Spanish settlers came the Scots, who adopted much of the same permissiveness, forming relationships with free colored wives and mistresses. This was inevitable. The Scots world in the Caribbean was a society of men, and the women in the colonies were almost entirely enslaved Africans and their descendants.

By 1795 the children of these unions had come of age to swell the ranks of free colored people everywhere, and the eventual British victory in this long war did nothing to curtail their prominence, despite the fact that vast numbers of free colored people had taken the republican side. Their active participation and their sheer numbers in the Windward Islands especially meant that the blatant discrimination seen on Grenada became an increasing rarity.

Free colored power was also given a boost by the anonymity and confusion provided by war and revolution. With the easy passage between the islands and with Europeans distracted by the Revolutionary War or, later, the wars of independence that rocked the Spanish empire, free colored people could readily slip into neighboring colonies and take on new identities. Julien Fedon could be one case in point. No one can be sure what happened to him because his body was never found. While Marie Rose Fedon may have died in the fighting, there is circumstantial evidence to suggest that her husband escaped their defeat on Grenada in 1796 and moved to Trinidad to be with his relatives already living there.[65] Given the disorganization of the Spanish government and the British takeover of Trinidad in 1797, the opportunities to start again were many.[66]

The Revolutionary War created opportunities for thousands of people, white and black, who became refugees, moving from island to island as conflicts washed over communities. Increasingly, the slave revolts that shook the Caribbean in the last years of the eighteenth century and the first decades of the nineteenth pushed people from one colony to the next.[67] Whether forced or voluntary, these migrations had a profound effect on the development of the colonies in the southern Caribbean. In the years following 1795, these colonies would remain not only some of the most unstable colonies in the Atlantic world but also the most multicultural.

After the 1790s, men and women of color, such as Marie Rose and Julien Fedon, keep appearing in the historical record to confound and confuse the narrative of Caribbean history. What had been a race war between slave and free, black and white, was complicated by their presence; a conflict for global domination between European rivals and their allies became a contrary war where not all French were republican and not all British subjects were loyalist. As generals sent to the region found, not all whites could be trusted and not all blacks were enemies. The appearance of the free colored community on the world stage therefore is not only a story of struggle against European colonial power, or a fight against slavery, or complicity in the colonial project; rather, it is about how free colored people confused, complicated, and upset the racial balance of the Caribbean. Free colored people blurred the boundary between race and servitude, and between politics and class. Their presence threw into stark relief the contradictions and hypocrisies of chattel slavery, and the strict racial lines began to fray.

By the beginning of the nineteenth century the free colored population had exploded to completely dwarf the white population in colonies such as Trinidad, Demerara, Grenada, St. Vincent, and Tobago. Even on Barbados, Britain's oldest colony in the Caribbean and the only colony to consistently have a majority of whites in the free population until the end of slavery, people of color still represented a third of the free population by 1829.[68] On Trinidad their numbers continued to grow from 4,000 in 1797 to just under 16,000 by 1829, while the white population of 2,000 merely doubled in the same period, making free colored people almost four times as numerous.[69] Even though many free people of color were removed from Grenada after the failure of the Fedon Rebellion, by 1829 Grenada had 3,786 free people of color while the white population was just 801.[70] In Dominica in 1830 it was a similar story: 703 whites lived alongside 3,590 free black and free colored people.[71] Even the aggressive development of Demerara's slave society at the end of the eighteenth century did not stop a rapid rise in the free population of color there. By 1830 the 3,000 whites in the colony were outnumbered by over 6,000 "free blacks."[72] The demographic story of the Caribbean from 1795 to the end of slavery is the story of free colored people; there is no getting around or ignoring them.

In the last years of the eighteenth century, waves of migrants, refugees, and opportunists flooded the southern Caribbean, while colonies repeatedly changed hands from one imperial power to the next. This fluidity gave this contested region a particularly pronounced multiculturalism; entrepreneurial free people of color were perfectly at home in this fractured world. Here was where Victor Hughes chose to strike Britain the hardest, and he relied on the free colored community in the region to be the central forces in that fight. Similarly, in defending their new colonies, the British were forced to rely on free people of color. Both sides responded to the demographic revolution in the Caribbean by trying to gain the loyalty of free colored people. There would be no going back.

From the moment that Scots and other British hopefuls pushed their way into the southern Caribbean, the valuable colonies of Dominica, Tobago, Grenada, St. Vincent, Trinidad, and Demerara became contested sites of imperial drama and engendered unique possibilities. The late settlement of these colonies created ample opportunities for increasingly large numbers of free colored people to buy land and slaves of their own. With women of color manumitted at a much greater rate than their male counterparts, and therefore a much greater presence in the freed community, it was free women of color especially who seized the moment. They and their children would be in the forefront of this brave new world.

CHAPTER TWO

Bars, Brothels, and Business

RACHAEL PRINGLE POLGREEN AND ROSETTA SMITH

EUROPEANS LIVING OR TRAVELING in the Caribbean during the Age of Revolutions encountered many enterprising women of color. Most were poor hucksters or washerwomen who laundered clothes; others ran shops or market stalls; but some were much richer, owned prosperous businesses, or lived on large estates. By the beginning of the nineteenth century, free women of color dominated the towns and urban spaces. From Bridgetown to Georgetown, St. Pierre to St. George's, the southern Caribbean was a place of enterprise.[1]

Entrepreneurial free women of color represented a serious challenge to white patriarchal power for some, while for others, including many merchants and other white business owners in the towns, such women could be both middling facilitators and business partners. They could just as easily be friends and acquaintances outside the realms of finance, money, and transactions. In this world, a black woman could lend a white friend money for his marriage or request a ship's captain to take a manumission application to England because it would be cheaper there.[2] However, this world has been largely hidden by the white people who held a monopoly on the written word.

The prominent women of color who grew up in the southern Caribbean at the end of the eighteenth century were targets for comments and criticisms at the time, whether these were prompted by fear, loathing, or desire. Being free, colored, and lighter skinned than most people of African descent, such women were designated, in print at least, always as objects. Sexualized free women of color were, by the late eighteenth century, ubiquitous in media from popular songs to whole novels as objects of disdain, and positive images are hard to come by. Objectified, commented on, and criticized, their lives were often caricatured to fit a predetermined mold. The stories that commentators took back to Europe created powerful stereotypes that have proven remarkably hard for historians to shake. Discounted and belittled, entrepreneurial free women of color were consigned to two broad character types.

The first and most prominent was the free colored mistress, a grasping, wily prostitute to power, a concubine to the white male elite. Liberal commentators eagerly recounted tales of procurement in ports and advised newcomers to take up with a free colored mistress. Conservatives, however, were alarmed by the breakdown in the slave order, which they read as creating a moral vacuum. They warned unsuspecting men to be wary of the charms of free colored women, lest a young man's prospects be destroyed by a domineering, grasping woman whose only ambitions were for herself and her (invariably illegitimate) offspring.[3] When the local publisher John Poyer wrote his *History of Barbados* in 1808, he made specific mention of the accession in 1794 of Governor George Ricketts, who lived at the governor's mansion with a free woman of color, Betsey Goodwin. He was disgusted that Ricketts should be so enthralled by this "sly and insidious female" and that, at her alleged suggestion, the governor allowed prisoners to go free.[4] The furor was so great that at the Colonial Office, Lord Portland openly censured the governor.[5] Poyer thought that Ricketts was setting a dangerous precedent. He argued that since the arrival of Goodwin there had been a visible change in the manners of the free colored people, who had "assumed a rank in the graduated scale of colonial society to which they had been hitherto strangers." In Poyer's mind, Ricketts undermined the racial order and threatened the stability of the island. Black prisoners, said Poyer, now "boasted of the impunity which they could obtain through the influence of Betsey Goodwin."[6]

Even some favorable accounts of free women of color were tinged with threat. John Waller was in Barbados for a year in 1807. In his *Voyage in the West Indies*, published in 1820, he wrote that "the natives cohabit with people of colour from a very early age and I have observed many instances of them being perfectly captivated by their free coloured mistresses who thus obtain their freedom and that of their children." While Waller thought he should "bear testimony" to the fundamental "immorality which prevails in this respect," he still believed that, but for these casual relationships, these women could be "chaste and virtuous." He thought that white women through their "apathy" were the most under threat from the influence of free women of color and their "indecent debauchery."[7]

The second stereotype was the infamous boardinghouse keeper. In this case, the implication of immorality was often unspoken, but almost always the stories were written in such a way as to imply that the women were nefarious madams out to fleece white men in the one economic area that was open to them. Writers like Poyer bemoaned the licentiousness and louche behavior in the southern Caribbean, and there is no doubt that taverns, bars, and brothels did a roaring trade throughout the Age of Revolutions. This was especially so in Bridgetown, Barbados, one of the largest ports in the Caribbean and the home of both the British Southern Command and the Royal Navy.[8] Whether they ran a brothel or not, free colored women were at once victims and perpetuators of racist power and patriarchy. They were the tainted ones; rarely did the taint fall on the men who frequented their establishments.

Dr. George Pinckard remarked in 1806 that "the hostess of a tavern is usually a black or mulatto woman who has been the enamorata of some Bukra man ... who now indulges in indolence and the good things in life, grows fat and feels herself to be of importance to society."[9] Fifty years later C. W. Day maintained the theme. "Those acquainted with Barbados," he opined, "its customs and above all its prices know how shockingly the poor passengers are generally plundered. There is no mercy shown them; all is extortion. Mulatto rapacity is far worse than Italian or even the Dutch." He claimed that items were "retailed to strangers at 500 percent above their value."[10] Anthony Trollope who, like Day, traveled through the Caribbean in midcentury, alluded to this stereotype, remarking that "there is a mystery about hotels in the British West Indies. They are always kept by fat, middle-aged ladies who have no husbands." He thought their knowledge of the "male frequenting hotel world ... [was] hardly compatible with a retiring maiden state of life."[11]

Even former slaves recounted stories of madams and hotels, especially in Barbados. When the memoirs of the former slave Jeffery Brace were written, he recalled his time on the island in the employ of a man named Welch and his black, brothel-owning mistress. Remembering the sadistic abuse he received at the hands of his former owners, he could barely contain his detestation, describing Welch's partner as a "large, fat, greasy guinea woman: flat nosed, thick lipped with teeth as white as snow."[12]

Pervading all these stories was the objectified sexuality of the woman of color, who was either an object of disgust for her sexual confidence, or a thrilling prospect because of her loose availability. Much of this invective came from earlier writers in the Caribbean, like the Jamaican planter Edward Long, who believed that black people were a race demonstrating "all the species of inherent turpitude." He was echoed by J. B. Moreton, who wrote that black women "from their youth are taught to be whores, and to expect their living to be derived from immoral earnings."[13] When F. W. N. Bayley visited Barbados in 1826 he repeated the sentiments of Long fifty years before. He thought that the free women of color who resided in the colony all preferred "living with white men in a state of moral degradation," and they were, he continued, "the cause of much of the immorality that prevails in the West Indies."[14] Yet peeking through all these negative accounts are glimpses of another world. Bayley could not help but notice the thoughtful kindness of his hostess, the famous Sabina Brade, a colored woman who owned Bridgetown's largest hotel in the 1820s. When he was leaving the colony, he observed "her great consideration" in sending her slave Matt out to his boat loaded with "cake and ten bottles of sorrel wine" to see him on his journey.[15]

Henry Nelson Coleridge, nephew of the poet, was a deeply religious man of the cloth. When he wrote about his "six months in the West Indies" in 1825, he thought there were too many bare-breasted slaves, who represented the potential for moral deviance, and thought the planters "ought to do something about it." Despite being unusually critical about the institution of slavery, he, like Bayley, reverted quickly to a well-worn theme when it came to free women of color. Coleridge's usually benign words hummed with sexual repression as he decried the appearance of free colored women. "We [the English] eat too much beef and absorb too much porter," he lamented, "for a thorough amalgamation of the tropical lymph in the veins of the black, hence our mulatto females have more of a look of very dirty white women than the rich oriental olive that distinguishes the haughty offspring of the half-blood of the French or Spaniard."[16]

With some important and notable exceptions, in both historiography and literature these two powerful tropes of the mistress and the madam have dominated since their initial appearance in books, novels, commentaries, and travelogues written in the first half of the nineteenth century. Contemporary trends in modern history rarely have questioned these popular themes. There are relatively few works that do not take as fact the understandings presented by these white men.[17] More often, research that explores the lives of enterprising free women of color does so by underscoring the perception of them as grasping, manipulative, and dependent, rather than contesting the premise of this perspective.[18] Another approach ignores the prominence of wealthy free women of color in the towns, in favor of stories of women who helped their free colored husbands petition for rights.[19] Some may think that a concubine to a white man, or a madam in a tropical brothel, do not offer an example of positive agency for black studies, Caribbean history, or gender history, and that such women are no more than a passing curiosity. We do not agree.

This chapter critiques the two dominant stereotypes by deconstructing the lives of two free colored women who each fleetingly became famous: Rachael Pringle Polgreen (1753?–91), a Barbadian hotelier, and Rosetta Smith (1780–1825?), the Trinidadian mistress of Governor Thomas Picton. On the surface, the biographies of these women appear to fall squarely into the circumscribed categories of madam or mistress, yet a closer analysis of their lives reveals a far more complex and textured picture. This picture is made even richer by placing the women within the context of the free colored community around them, rather than confining their story to the intersection with the lives of European men or the popular tales written about them.

Far from being just madams or mistresses, these were savvy, well-connected, and resourceful women who operated substantial businesses in a complex world of material wealth. It took skill to maintain the kinds of property portfolios that these women enjoyed, and even more skill to move in the circles that brought them opportunities they could use to their advantage. We do not discount the fact that both their biographies involved white men, nor do we overlook the fact that these women abused and exploited enslaved Africans. We do not set out to make these women heroines; rather, we seek to explore their complex lives and their entrepreneurial enterprises.

ON JULY 21, 1791, a middle-aged woman, "sick of body" but of "sound mind, memory and understanding," wrote out her last will and testament. Surrounded by lawyers and witnesses, she knew she had just days to live. For ten years, her business, the Royal Naval Hotel, had been the life of Barbados—the British sugar jewel in the southern Caribbean. Widely regarded as one of the finest hotels in the Windward Islands, if not the whole Caribbean, it was eagerly sought out by merchant sea captains and Royal Navy officers looking for some rest and relaxation. It was the place where she had conducted all her business and where she had managed her thirty-eight slaves, of whom more than half were children.

She was particular about her language and careful with the details. Although she was ill on that July day, she knew exactly what she was doing. After her death, her executors took charge of the inventory of her possessions, making sure everything was organized and itemized. On the list were numerous pieces of extremely rare and valuable mahogany: tables, chairs, sideboards, and bureaus. There were beds—some four-posters as well as simpler examples—and the corresponding bedsteads and bedding, spirit cabinets, card tables, gaming tables, Windsor chairs, washstands, two old rowboats, curtains, carpets, three trunks, and a chest, plus all the accoutrements of a large kitchen, such as copper kettles, pots, pans, waterstones, and scales. Along with this list came scores of other items from nine jars of green sweetmeats to nineteen bottles of castor oil. The thoroughness of her executors was first-rate. They made sure that nothing was missed and were particularly careful about the movable pieces of precious tableware: pewter plates and tankards, dinner china, glass lanterns, candlesticks, and no less than four cases of knives and forks. Naturally, the silver attracted their attention, especially the silver cutlery that she kept for special occasions.[20]

The pages of the inventory finally concluded with the main items: real estate and people. The first was a large house near the old fort with "the land on which it stands including the kitchen" valued at £1,000, along with an adjoining house and land valued at £100. There were also two other houses valued at £26 and £150, respectively. Of the thirty-eight people she owned only ten were valued at less than £40, and most of these were children and the ill or infirm. Most of the others were appraised at £60 each, which was a first-class rate for a slave on Barbados in 1791. Even the adolescents commanded £50. Clearly, this woman knew what slaves to buy, and how to look after them and her own interests. All in all, the total of the inventory came to £2,936, 9 shillings, and 4 1/2 pence. It was, the executors duly recorded, "a true and reasonable appraisement given freely under our hands this 13th day of August 1791."[21]

This list of property was just the kind of inventory one would expect of a wealthy white person in Barbadian society at the time, but in fact it was the inventory of Rachael Pringle Polgreen, a free woman of color. Having risen to prominence in the 1780s, Rachael Pringle Polgreen personified what was possible during the late eighteenth century's free colored moment. She was the first black hotelier to be noticed in Barbados. There could well have been others before her, but the records only come alive for many free people of color in the anglophone Atlantic in the third quarter of the century.[22]

ON HER DEATHBED, Rachael Pringle Polgreen freed six of her slaves and passed the rest on to white friends to whom she owed thanks. A young black woman named Joanna was freed and given her mulatto son Richard, along with an older black woman, Amber, who was most likely Joanna's mother. Also freed was a mulatto woman named Princess Samply, who was given "the house and land that she now resides in" and four mulatto children.[23] Interestingly, a mulatto woman named Betsey Goodwin, listed with the highest value of £60, appeared on the list, but she was not among the slave property specifically named as gifts to white friends. Presumably she was among the "residue and remainder of my estate, real and personal, here and elsewhere" to be divided between Polgreen's "good friends" William Firebrace and William Stevens, who were also her executors, and Thomas Pringle, a captain in the Royal Navy. Whatever process these worthy men used to deal with the estate residue, Betsey Goodwin was soon a free woman. By 1796 she was supposedly residing in the governor's mansion and sleeping in his bed. Poyer says of Betsey Goodwin that Governor Ricketts "brought with him from Tobago a mulatto woman," but we can find no evidence that was so, and apparently Betsey Goodwin was well connected to the free colored population in Bridgetown.[24]

Rachael Pringle Polgreen was neither unique nor exceptional in the urban environment in Barbados in 1791. Even by her early death there were several other industrious women from the free colored classes of Barbados. Within twenty years there would be still further free Barbadian women of color, including Polgreen's one-time property, Betsey Goodwin, who would echo, and even surpass, her success.

Mary-Bella Green, Nancy Clarke, Katherine Payne, and Hannah Gill were all colored women who, by the 1790s, owned several properties each in and around Bridgetown.[25] A second, slightly later cohort of women, centered around Sabina Brade, Betsy Lemon, and Betsy Austin, rose to prominence at the beginning of the nineteenth century. Later still would come Hannah Lewis, Caroline Lee, and Mrs. Roach.[26] These were all urban women, but Barbados was essentially a rural economy. Amaryllis Collymore was another free woman of color and a former slave, like many of them, who owned hundreds of acres of rural land and scores of slaves that she inherited from her white husband, Robert Collymore. Her skills as a planter over the succeeding years made her without doubt the richest free woman of color in pre-emancipation Barbados.[27]

It needs to be underscored that free colored people lived in a society that was as stratified and divided as the white society. Most of them did not inherit their manumission from a white father or partner, nor did they, like Amaryllis Collymore, live on a large estate. In fact, most manumissions in the late eighteenth century, especially in Barbados, came through white women, not men.[28] There were differences between those born free and those made free, between urban and rural, and between the radical and conservative elements of the free colored community. The differences between free colored men have received attention from scholars focused on the fight for civil rights and on the differences between groups of male activists in that fight. However, the stratification and complexity of female society has largely been passed over.[29] It is important to recognize that divisions were also found between free women of color.

The triennial slave registers from 1817 onward show definite stratification among free women of color. The free women who survived from the late eighteenth century to have their slave property listed in 1817 demonstrate that they were not all poor with a few wealthy women like Amaryllis Collymore, but there was a graduated spread, from free women of color who owned one slave to those who owned ten or more, like most demographic groups on the list. Interestingly, slightly more slave owners were women than men, and free women of color took their places among them at all levels from the richest to the poorest.[30]

Rather than being exceptions, women such as Rachael Pringle Polgreen were at the pinnacle of a complex hierarchy of power in a free colored and free black world that numbered some one thousand people by the 1790s. Slavery was intrinsic to this world; its presence leaked into every seam of Barbados, where the basic unit of property was a person, and owning slaves was not just a mark of status, it was fundamental to the economy. It should therefore be expected that black women could own people because owning slaves was the modus operandi of the free society. Scholars have investigated whether elite free colored slave owners operated differently than their white neighbors, and their research indicates that free colored people were no less harsh and no more inclined to manumit their slaves. A caveat to that finding would be that free women tended to be urban, not rural, where the conditions were harsher.[31]

Owning people on an equal footing with whites was a preoccupation for many people of color. Free men of color signed many petitions in the first decades of the nineteenth century for voting and assembly rights, but the one that received the most signatures on Barbados was an 1803 petition for equal rights as slaveholders.[32] It was a similar story elsewhere. For many free colored people, the right to vote ran a distant second to the right to own chattel. It can be assumed that the women in this broad community had the same aspirations. So we should not be surprised that a successful entrepreneur like Rachael Pringle Polgreen was the owner of thirty-eight slaves, nor that on her deathbed she chose to manumit only six of them.

WHAT ELSE DO WE KNOW ABOUT Rachael Pringle Polgreen? Despite her notoriety among contemporary visitors to Barbados, and more recent negative extrapolations about her, there is not much hard evidence about her life. Her archive begins fifteen years before she wrote her will, in the St. Michael rate books and tax assessments for Bridgetown in the late 1770s.[33] Apart from those records, which pertain to her property, there are also three notices she placed in the local paper in addition to her will and inventory. There exists a very short anecdote about her in early nineteenth-century accounts and a brief mention of her in the *Barbadian* from the 1840s.[34] The main sources for what we are led to believe were her lurid origins, however, are both works of artifice: a picture and a novel.

The most significant secondary source for Polgreen is visual rather than textual, which is unusual for the late eighteenth-century Caribbean. In 1796 the caricaturist Thomas Rowlandson drew what has become the iconic illustration of the woman.[35] It was not done from life. While the artist may have encountered her on the one and only time he visited the Caribbean, he copied his print in London from a draft created by another, unknown artist. Whether she really did look like the woman in the picture is open for conjecture. On one level Rowlandson positioned his drawing within a tradition that reached back into the early eighteenth century of plucky, underclass women making their way in a difficult world. Throughout the century, stories like Defoe's *Moll Flanders* and Cleland's *Fanny Hill* were enormously popular. Rowlandson's caricature played to the powerful clichés that had enveloped Caribbean women by the end of the eighteenth century.

Rowlandson presents a commanding black woman, whose massive girth is clothed in a dress that barely covers her voluminous breasts. She is sitting in front of a house on a chair she completely obscures, in a confident pose, legs apart, with one arm impatiently on her knee, her eyes fixed squarely on the viewer, suggesting that nothing could get past her commanding gaze. It may be a caricature of this free colored businesswoman, but Rowlandson leaves the viewer in no doubt as to her dominance. The background of the scene also leaves little doubt that she is seated in front of a brothel: the sign posted behind her reads: "Pawpaw Sweetmeats & Pickles of all Sorts." While it was the case that Rachael Pringle Polgreen did retail such popular items at the Royal Naval Hotel, Rowlandson is making a sly reference to the sexual activities available within, thoroughly reinforced by the three background characters, who are easily read as a young prostitute and her male clients.

A bad Victorian novel, written by a former resident of Barbados and local newspaper editor, J. W. Orderson, is the other significant secondary source. *Creoleana* was published in 1842 and is a turgid Caribbean love story, verbose even by nineteenth-century standards, that has only passing interest for modern readers and historians. Written from the distance of his London home some fifty years after the time in which the novel is set, when he was old, tired, and broke, its value lies in the glimpses of middling white society in Barbados at the end of the eighteenth century, but the book includes a four-page digression about Rachael Pringle Polgreen.[36] Orderson's work must be treated with great caution, packed as it is with factual errors and a hazy conflation of events. Nevertheless, this novel, together with Rowlandson's caricature, has provided a cliché around which historians have woven the scant archival evidence.

In Orderson's telling, Polgreen was born Rachael Lauder around 1753, the daughter of a dissolute Scottish teacher, William Lauder, and an unnamed slave woman in his employ. Certainly Lauder was a real person. He was a Scottish writer who attempted to claim that John Milton had plagiarized his *Paradise Lost* from hitherto "unknown" poems that Lauder had previously forged. When contemporaries discovered his forgeries and ostracized him, Lauder left Europe in disgrace and settled in Barbados, where he either started his own school or was employed at Harrison's Free School.[37]

After only a short while, to the shock of the governors, it was discovered that he had matriculated no students and taught relatively little. He was sacked from this position and set himself up as a storekeeper. Rachael was said to be the daughter of Lauder's slave, and she remained a slave: at once both daughter and chattel to her father.

Eventually, as Orderson's novel has it, this "remarkably well made" girl "awakened the libidinous desires of her disgraceful and sinful parent," who tried repeatedly to rape her. To her "eternal honour" these "attempts on her chastity" were unsuccessful. Angered by his continued failure, Lauder, the "vulgar, unnatural and wretched brute," ordered her to be whipped by the "jumper," the man charged with public floggings. Lauder's conduct toward his offspring, Orderson remarks, "is a damning proof how debasing to the human mind is the power given us over our fellow creatures by holding them in bondage!"[38]

Orderson's melodrama then introduces "divine mercy" in the form of a gallant seaman who steps forward and rescues the poor girl from the lash amid the "cheers of the thronging multitude." Incensed, Lauder threatens the interloper with the courts for stealing his property and orders restitution. The sailor is a youthful captain named Thomas Pringle, who takes pity on the poor girl and offers to buy her from the worthless Scot. Settling out of court for "an exorbitant sum," he takes possession of Rachael. According to the novel, Pringle then obtained Rachael's manumission and "established her in a small house at the lower end of town which by her industry was afterwards enlarged and ultimately became the celebrated hotel." Rachael dropped the name of Lauder to become Rachael Pringle and, presumably when he was in port, the sexual partner of the good captain.[39]

According to the novel, the relationship did not last long. Realizing the waning nature of their love, Rachael fabricated the birth of a child in order to retain the affections of the sailor. But the plan went awry when the true mother of the child Rachael had borrowed to effect this plan demanded the return of her baby. Angered, the captain left Rachael for good. Unperturbed she quickly found another suitor, a man named Polgreen, whose name she eventually took as her own to become Rachael Pringle Polgreen.[40]

Orderson was not writing history; he was writing fiction, so everything could be made up. Nevertheless some of this short biographical vignette may well be true. We know that she was once known as Rachael Lauder, though we do not know who her father was. Since William Lauder was notorious in England, he was a perfect man for Orderson to drop into the frame. From the will, it is apparent that Rachael did have a relationship of some kind with Thomas Pringle, but there is no reason to assume it was sexual. Indeed, Captain Pringle, who rose to become a vice admiral in the navy, was not in Barbados for very long. Furthermore, he may not have had any sexual interest in women, since he was known to lament the habit of officers taking wives. He would later remark that Lord Nelson's marriage had lost Britain "its greatest ornament."[41] So it is possible there is an entirely different interpretation of their relationship than the salacious story offered by Orderson and others.

For reasons that are not quite clear, there was a manumission strategy in operation in Barbados throughout the eighteenth century, which became much more common after 1801, when manumission fees rose sharply. This involved supposedly selling a slave to a trusted third party, who would then apply for manumission in England. This was the strategy adopted by Robert Collymore for the manumission of his wife and children.[42] If that is what happened, it certainly could explain why Rachael would leave a bequest to Pringle in her will when he did not need the money, and why she might take his surname. The second part of her surname doubtless came from a man named Polgreen, but it does not automatically follow that this man was white nor that she was his mistress. It is quite feasible that she was for a time married to Edward Polgreen, a free man of color in Bridgetown, Barbados, who was born into slavery in 1743 and who later appeared in the St. Michael's parish records as a free man in 1764 and again in 1783.[43]

In his presentation of Rachael Pringle Polgreen, Orderson was conforming to a well-worn trope. His transgressive Rachael represents all that was licentious, malevolent, and untrustworthy about independent, free colored women. She did what white audiences expected her to do; she was aggressive, confident, assertive, manipulative, and ultimately dishonest.[44] It was she who drove her benefactor away, rather than the more likely scenario of a transient sailor deserting her when he grew tired of her. Of course for the novelist, and for large sections of his audience, her color would have barred her from propriety; free women of color could never have a legitimate baby because they themselves were without legitimacy. Women such as Rachael Pringle Polgreen were permanent concubines, who could only imitate white society by contorting the bounds of marriage and motherhood and acting through subterfuge. To white conservatives the events described only underscored the innate inferiority of black women to white women, who by implication would never do such a thing as steal another's child. And by tempting her father into incestuous behavior, Orderson's creation became a symbol of all that was wrong with slavery, a system that could corrupt so totally. The debasement caused by slavery was represented in the body of Rachael Pringle Polgreen.

The most well-known story told by Orderson, and the one most often repeated, is of Rachael Pringle Polgreen's brief and extraordinary encounter with royalty.[45] In 1789 Prince William Henry (the future William IV) visited Bridgetown for about ten days aboard his vessel the *Arathusa*. As a prince, he naturally attracted a great deal of attention from locals and was fêted around the island. Having been there before briefly, for a week in 1786, the prince was familiar with Bridgetown and its nightlife. After dining with the Forty-Ninth Regiment on the last evening of his stay, he and a party of officers moved off for a late night frolic at "Miss Rachael's." Things quickly got out of hand, though, at the Royal Naval Hotel. Within the space of a few hours, with the prince leading the affair, the officers smashed the whole place up, broke the furniture, threw valuables out of windows, and cut up down bedding in imitation of a snowstorm. In Orderson's novel, Rachael sat through the whole drama on her chair near the doorway, and when her slaves ran to her in fright, she calmed them with the words "let he lone! Lay he muse himself—da no Kings son! Bless he heart!" At the end of the night and to "crown their sport," the prince unseated the ungainly Miss Rachael and sent her sprawling on the floor, all of this much to the amusement of his fellow officers. The next day, anxious that the prince might leave without paying the bill, she sent a servant to his ship with an itemized invoice for £700. The prince, struck by the audacity of the woman, duly paid his bill via the local firm of Adwin and Firebrace.[46]

It is an extraordinary story, and was referred to by others who wrote about Bridgetown and its dubious entertainments. It certainly fits the character of the prince, who managed on his two voyages to cause disgust to some with his obnoxious and uncouth ways, "quite unbefitting of a prince of the royal blood."[47] The *Barbadian* in 1842, reviewing Orderson's book, singled out the prince's visit and alluded to the escapade at the Royal Naval Hotel, adding the detail of Rachael Pringle Polgreen promenading with the "high spirited" prince and "leaning on the royal arm."[48]

This part of Orderson's fiction appears to have been freely borrowed from Richard Madden, who visited Barbados just six years before Orderson's book was published. Madden described a similar scene at the hotel of the free colored proprietress Hannah Lewis, and his description is almost the same as that which Orderson used for Rachael Pringle Polgreen. According to Madden, Lewis was "a sedate, sensible woman" who weighed some two hundred pounds, whose constant post was sitting in the capacious doorway of the passage at the foot of the staircase "in all the luxury of her native indolence.... It was all the same to her if the admiral of the station or the smallest of midshipmen were her guest, they were greeted with the same indefatigable indolence of this fat brown lady."[49]

By the time Orderson published his story, William IV had been dead five years, his life one of embarrassing scandal, gluttony, and foolishness, having spent most of his middle years living with his actress mistress and their numerous illegitimate children.[50] Still, fiction or not, the story of Rachael Pringle Polgreen taking titillating liberties with a dissolute prince and her plucky bravado in asking for inflated damages, sits squarely within the trope of an aggressive madam. Yet a notice in the *Barbados Gazette* indicates that, rather than being a submissive plaything of the prince, or a trickster who pretended coy submission in order to gain inflated compensation, she cared deeply about her losses and her possessions. "Lost by the subscriber," she wrote in the paper the day after the prince left, "a small filigree waiter, scalloped round the edge. Seven silver spoons marked S. B. in a cipher and two dessert spoons marked R. P. in cipher. Who ever finds them shall receive four Moidores reward." Desperate to have her possessions returned, she also asked local silversmiths "and others" to "stop the above articles if offered for sale."[51] This notice has very different implications than the image presented by Orderson of a woman only too happy to dupe a prince. The future king possibly paid out of remorse but more likely because he feared the story of yet another night of debauchery would reach the ears of his stern father. In later years the prince's behavior was so outrageous that George III refused to let his son go to sea for fear of more scandals.[52]

Orderson's vignette, just like Rowlandson's earlier print, conformed to Caribbean stereotypes, and both came with the perceived authenticity of personal experience. Yet these sources are not authentic; they are make-believe and reinforced the dominant and degrading trope about free colored women. Each lends credence to a story about Rachael Pringle Polgreen told by a British army officer named Captain Cook, who was asked to give evidence to a House of Commons inquiry into the state of slavery in the Caribbean in 1791. When asked about his time in the Caribbean in 1781, which included a stay in Barbados, he described a scene in which Rachael Lauder, unhappy with the money that one of her slave prostitutes brought back from a ship in port, beat her half to death with the heel of her shoe, till her head was "almost all of jelly." Pushing the girl's head down a toilet, "she would have murdered her had she not been prevented by the interposition of two officers," who happened to be with him at her house at the time.[53] Captain Cook never elaborated on what the three soldiers were doing there in the first place.

A black mistress beating her black slave half to death was just the kind of negative image that white men needed to feel morally superior. Read in conjunction with Orderson's novel and Rowlandson's print, the highly sexualized image of Rachael Pringle Polgreen is conjoined with sadistic anger to make her appear aberrant—in a society marked by shocking violence and sexual exploitation perpetrated by white men. The veracity of this report is rarely questioned, any more than the veracity of the novel or the picture is questioned. Each of these sources is suspect, yet they have assumed huge importance in the construction of the biography of Polgreen because the documentary evidence for her life is so scant.

As one scholar has argued, Rachael Pringle Polgreen's "troubled" archive points to something quite nefarious in the woman's character. In this critique, the well-known businesswoman who operated a large boardinghouse has become a class betrayer who emulated and supported the white patriarchal colonial society. Relying on the crude caricature presented in Rowlandson's print and on stories like the escapade with the prince and the beating of the slave, the enterprising businesswoman has been replaced with the old racist trope of the manipulative free colored madam.[54] By privileging her apparent complicity in the colonial slave project and her supposed abuse of her own chattel, this critique colludes with Rowlandson to present Polgreen as a morally debased black woman who not only controlled the bodies of her black slaves, but forced them to be repeatedly raped for her own profit, as vile a subject as any nineteenth-century author could conjure.

For a free colored woman, pimping has been rendered as a great moral sin, and when joined with the exploitation of slavery it is tantamount to being an accessory to rape.[55] Rachael Pringle Polgreen's provision of sexual services is assumed to be complicity in white abuse and exploitation, and yet wealthy colored men must have also used such services. What has been lost in this interpretation is the wider significance of the sex industry throughout the eighteenth and nineteenth centuries, which was not racially determined. Casually turning tricks was part and parcel of the work in a hotel, and prostitution was a genuine occupational option for up to a fifth of London's working-class females in the late eighteenth century.[56] What was commonplace in the imperial center was no less true for its colonial peripheries.[57]

Rachael Pringle Polgreen was the proprietor of a large, popular hotel that catered to a military and civilian elite, and her role was to provide food, lodging, and other services for Bridgetown's many transients. That she provided sexual services is highly likely, but there is no evidence that she was primarily the madam of a brothel, nor that all of her slaves were forced into prostitution. Indeed most of her slaves were not women in the prime of life. The everyday activities of running a large boardinghouse (with lots of competition from other establishments) have been largely ignored, while sexual activities (that almost certainly went on in every hotel in a major port) have been overemphasized.[58] Still, many of the European sources that discussed the Royal Naval Hotel, and establishments similar to it, placed their emphasis on things other than sex. For writers like Pinckard, Madden, Lloyd, and Bayley the primary focus was the varying standards of their accommodations or the quality of the food on offer. As any traveler might, all four commented on the exorbitant prices for lodging, on their preference for one hotel over another, on how well appointed the rooms were, and on how kind their hostess was or was not.[59]

Rachael Pringle Polgreen's biography, as it has been constructed, unsettles the notion that African heritage necessarily bound enslaved and free people of color into a community of common purpose within the slave society of the southern Caribbean. Castigating Polgreen takes her business out of its context and makes her commercial activity exceptional in much the same way that late eighteenth- and early nineteenth-century writers sought to demean free women of color as dangerous, manipulative, and parasitical. These accounts were created by white men to reproduce the view that women of color were morally corrupt perpetrators of violence and violations, utterly degraded and permanently subaltern.

How likely is it that Polgreen was such a woman? The scant official documentation, which is all we have to reliably go on, does little to corroborate the picture we have been presented. There is no birth record for her and no manumission record. She was universally described as mulatto, which implies a white father, and at some stage she was known as Rachael Lauder, and there were several men named Lauder in Bridgetown at the time. If she were both slave and daughter to William Lauder, as suggested, she would have been no more than eighteen when he died in 1771 and, if she were his daughter, it is highly likely that he freed her upon his death, as was common practice. We have no archival evidence, however, that this is what happened. The story about her abuse and rescue by a sailor is pure fiction, despite her connection to Thomas Pringle. If, as we speculate, she was not manumitted by William Lauder, but by Pringle, she must have been purchased when Captain Thomas Pringle of the HMS *Ariadne* was active in the southern Caribbean, which was for about a year between 1777 and 1778.[60] If Pringle did purchase Rachael, it was from someone other than William Lauder, however, since the latter had been dead for six years.

As a lifelong bachelor given to caustic remarks about females, Pringle may not have been interested in women. The story that Pringle freed her and gave her a house might be true, but there are no deeds for her manumission nor for the transfer of the house. The surname by which she was formally recorded in the official records was neither Lauder nor Pringle, but Polgreen, which strongly implies she had a legitimate connection to a man of that name. Polgreen was the name of an old Barbados family of white descent, but there was also a free colored family of that name in Bridgetown. Perhaps she married Edward Polgreen, a free man of color who is listed as living in Bridgetown in 1783.[61]

The name Rachael Polgreen first appears in the rate, or taxation, books in 1779 in the parish of St. Michael, the division of Barbados that contained Bridgetown. These rate books are a well-preserved archive and list all of the property then taxed in the capital. Organized by streets, they tell us a large amount of detail about who lived where and who purchased what and when. All of Polgreen's free colored contemporaries are listed in this source, buying and selling property between 1780 and 1815. Her property is listed in fits and starts beginning in 1779 with a small house at the end of Canary Street, a smart address just back from the wharves and a stone's throw from Bridgetown's finest area of Cheapside; she was taxed at only £10 per year. This must have been the house visited by Captain Cook in 1781. By 1785 her tax assessment had risen to £50 for what was now a very large house, which became her Royal Naval Hotel.⁶² The changes in tax assessments for the ensuing years show the building's footprint enlarging all the time. In addition, by the middle years of the 1780s she owned several more properties in different parts of Bridgetown. Some were tenements taxed at £5, others were single dwellings evaluated at £10. None of them look appropriate for a brothel. This was the property portfolio of someone who did more than supply white men with sex. Rachael Pringle Polgreen consciously and ostentatiously engaged in the business life of the community. The tax assessments of other free colored women also show multiple property portfolios.⁶³

When Polgreen's known social and business connections are investigated, the narrative about her becomes even more problematic. William Firebrace, the merchant who supplied the prince with the money to pay for his damage to the Royal Naval Hotel, was one of the richest men in town, the agent for the Royal Navy in a colony that was the main naval base, and the owner of some of Bridgetown's finest property on the wealthiest street.⁶⁴ More important, he was also one of the executors of her will and the same William Firebrace to whom she chose to leave much of her estate. Most of the rest of her estate she gave to his female relatives, a clear indication that this woman kept company not only with successful white men, but also with their wives and families, which does not sound like a notorious madam. It can be argued that with the inclusion of his female family members, her friendship with the Firebraces was as domestic as it was commercial. She also left a small legacy to Pringle, who not only came from a wealthy Scottish family but was also a vice admiral in an age of prize money, so he hardly needed it.⁶⁵ Rachael Pringle Polgreen left no real debts, and her solvency is underscored by her largesse at the time of her death. Her will shows the agency of a woman whose enterprising success brought her not subservience but choice, not debased notoriety but moneyed respectability.

WHILE THE STORY OF POLGREEN HAS BEEN misconstrued by historians, another woman who lived nearby came to prominence briefly in the midst of a colonial scandal and has subsequently been ignored almost completely. While Barbadian governor George Ricketts and his mistress Betsey Goodwin roused the indignation of John Poyer, by 1798 Ricketts was joined by other British Caribbean governors with free colored mistresses. And the most notorious governor was in Trinidad.

As part of Britain's counterrevolutionary sweep through French and

Spanish territory in the southern Caribbean, it conquered Trinidad in 1797. The invasion force was so large that on seeing it, the Spanish put up no resistance. The Spanish admiral then in port, the only man with any real firepower at his disposal, burned his squadron of ships to the waterline rather than put up a fight.[66] Coming ashore with the army of occupation was a middle-aged Welsh colonel fresh from the fighting on Grenada and St. Lucia, a man who later would die a hero at Waterloo. In 1797 though, Thomas Picton was just another officer waiting for a post. With the invasion of Trinidad he got the post he wanted. As an acolyte of the conquering general, Ralph Abercromby, he was made the temporary military governor of the new acquisition.[67]

Thomas Picton's administration of Trinidad between 1797 and 1803 was rife with controversy and scandal. Claimed by many to be a heavy-handed tyrant in the negative thrall of some disreputable foreign planters, Picton's descent into colonial notoriety was fast. Extrajudicial executions, the shocking treatment of slaves, and an obsession with his own fortune were just part of his tenure. He surrounded himself with cronies and friends who lorded over the island, and his government was at the very least a colonial embarrassment, at worst a dangerous liability. His term climaxed with the torture of a fourteen-year-old mulatto girl, Louisa Calderon, for complicity in a robbery that probably did not take place.[68]

When Picton's replacement as governor, the liberal-leaning William Fullarton, arrived on the island from Scotland in 1802, Fullarton was shocked by the state of the island's government and by the stories he heard from concerned locals. Almost from the start he set about trying to ruin the former governor and bring, in all its gory detail, his repressive reign to the attention of the British public. In this he was ably assisted by the well-known writer P. F. McCallum, a man with a sharp wit and even sharper pen who, unfortunately for Picton, happened to be traveling through the Caribbean at this time. Both men wasted no time in producing books and pamphlets that laid bare the full ferocity of Picton's government.[69] The embarrassing affair ended up being one of the biggest scandals of the new century and embroiled Picton in a court case that would fatally damage his reputation and take years to resolve.[70]

One of the targets that both Fullarton and McCallum dwelt upon in their invective against the former governor was a woman known as Rosetta Smith. Within months of his arrival, Picton had taken up with this young woman of color from the French community, and the two became lovers. To Picton's enemies she was not just an example of his failings as a governor but was in part responsible for them. She was cast as a malevolent mistress, a sinister "Medea" who used her relationship with the new governor to feather her own nest with perquisites that her lover lavished on her.[71] She was a woman of color who committed outrages against white women and led the governor into the shady world of slave-catching and smuggling, which was not just unbecoming of the island's chief administrator but illegal. Their invective against Smith was a key strategy in turning Picton's governorship into a general scandal of imperial rule.[72]

The *aspera et horrenda virago*—that "acerbic and horrible woman"— was how Pierre Franc McCallum remembered her: "black and livid," her pushy presence leading her half-witted paramour into tyranny and disgrace. In McCallum's telling she became another "sly and insidious female" of Poyer's imagination. It was a common view. Even the free colored mother of Louisa Calderon, the girl Picton had had tortured, talked about Smith dismissively as being just "that girl he lived with."[73] The role of concubine was too important for such a woman in Fullarton's eyes; he reduced her to a "housekeeper."[74] Thanks to the notorious reputation of Picton, no one at the time was prepared to see her in anything but the most negative light, and she has received no coverage by contemporary scholars.

But is any of this negative picture a fair one? It is hard to say since the factual record reveals no more about Smith than it does about Rachael Pringle Polgreen. It is striking that despite being a central figure in the scandals that engulfed Picton's administration and being mentioned often by his critics, and despite being the mother of his four children, Rosetta Smith goes unnoticed in modern Trinidadian scholarship.[75] As a mistress she has been seen as unimportant to the history of Trinidad, and so well did commentators on Picton's administration do their demolition job on Rosetta Smith that not even Picton's three biographers have thought her worthy of real mention.[76] Like Rachael Pringle Polgreen being viewed as a madam, Rosetta Smith is a victim of stereotyping; in this case, the trope of the conniving mistress has accentuated some aspects of her character and left her subsequent biography shrouded in silence.

Examining the deed books from Port of Spain and the slave registers from the nineteenth century and deconstructing the information given to us by Picton's critics, Rosetta Smith emerges as more than a concubine and much more than a housekeeper.[77] She was clever and resourceful, someone whose success relied upon a network of women that she maintained over her whole life. Clearly an astute businesswoman, Smith not only managed a slave-catching enterprise with Picton but also managed a large government contract, jobs that required considerable skill to negotiate. By the time of her death she had thirty-four slaves, and the slave registers show her buying, selling, and manumitting slaves repeatedly in her later life, long after Picton had left the colony and his influence had waned. None of this detail was of concern to her detractors, whose only interest was hitching her to Picton's calumny.

Within a year of Picton's arrival, according to McCallum, Rosetta Smith had left her husband and children to be his mistress. "Allured by ambition she abandoned everything dear to the imagination of a female," he wrote, "to share the pillow and the power of the greatest man in the colony." Besotted with his concubine, a lovestruck Picton then presented her with the fuel contract for the garrison, saying "accept of this bagatelle my darling, the profits of it will enable you to buy trinkets."[78] The writer was merciless in his lampooning of the witless governor. Smith, however, bought more than trinkets with the profits, as McCallum suggested, and was able to "bribe almost all the kept ladies in the colony to reveal the secrets of their paramours." It was due to her influence over other free colored women, McCallum suggested, that the governor was able to know the secrets of the colony's elites.[79]

Rosetta Smith was perhaps in her early twenties at the time of the takeover, although she is often spoken of dismissively as a girl. There can be no doubt that she took up with Picton, but whether she did in fact leave a husband and children to do so is unverified. This was just the kind of detail that would add to the assassination of her character and play to the domestic British audience's preconceived ideas about free women of color and their "ambition." She was painted from the start as the transgressor and the antithesis of everything "dear to the imagination of a female." It was ironic that McCallum tried to appeal to a high moral female sensibility, given that he spent large periods of his life writing pornography for money.[80] Fullarton, on the other hand, saw her as just a low domestic who got ahead of her station thanks to Picton's patronage. Nevertheless, she figures in several of the charges he leveled at the former governor. He claimed that she used the guard to evict two white women from their house so that she could take possession of it; she drew Picton into the world of catching slaves that at her suggestion were sold back to the planters for an outrageous sum; she had a leading hand in determining the guilt of slaves in an outbreak of alleged poisoning; and, if she wanted some item from a merchant, she would hound him with threats till he parted with the goods at a knocked-down price.[81] Like McCallum, Fullarton also remarked on her "weekly levee" at Government House with "all the kept ladies of the colony," and both men decried the infuriating imperiousness with which she conducted herself on the island while her partner was governor. "Who ever breaks with her," McCallum warned, "provokes the revenge of hell."[82]

Like Poyer had done with Betsey Goodwin on Barbados, McCallum and Fullarton used Rosetta Smith as a foil to demonstrate the deep corruption in the British empire. They came from different perspectives, but they found a common use for her. McCallum was a radical; much of his early work attacked conservatives like Picton, writing as he did in reaction to the conservative crackdown after the French Revolution. For his part, Fullarton had been instrumental in the trial and impeachment of Warren Hastings for corruption. To both these men, the empire was sick and needed a palliative. In their eyes, free women of color who gained influence over white senior administrators were the fountainhead of avarice and moral corruption and a symbol of all that was wrong with the empire.

Examining the record for Rosetta Smith allows us to add nuance to this one-sided image. To begin with, there is no evidence, either in the deeds for Trinidad and its capital, Port of Spain, or in the later slave registers, for her having any children prior to Picton's arrival. There is definite evidence for the four children she had with the governor, and this suggests she was far from being an uncaring parent. Her children—Thomas, Richard, Augusta, and Frederick Picton—are listed in the 1810 deeds as being granted "a special sum of money" in perpetuity. Moreover, Picton left £1,000 to each of them in his 1815 will, which was administered by Rosetta Smith.[83] The two eldest children, Thomas and Richard, went to school in Britain, a process of education that Smith must have managed, and Thomas eventually became a doctor in the colonial service.[84] Thomas and Frederick died early, but Smith kept a relationship with her surviving children, and in the 1820s her last transactions record her passing slaves to both Augusta and Richard.[85]

Rather than the plaything of the governor, Rosetta Smith emerges from the archive as a considerable entrepreneur in and around the capital.

Though not as ostentatious in her success as Rachael Pringle Polgreen, the deeds and registers place her within the middling sort among free people of color. Her status was far removed from the wealth of the Barbadian planter Amaryllis Collymore or her Trinidadian equivalent, Madame Congnet, but nevertheless it was a significant stake in the society.[86] But just as Rachael Pringle Polgreen's wealth was systematically increased over her lifetime, so was Rosetta Smith's property, as she expanded her portfolio beyond houses and land plots in the town to large plantations. In 1810 she is recorded conducting business on Grenada; references exist as well to her conducting business even in Venezuela.[87] By 1813 she is recorded as owning a 350-acre estate in the district of Santa Cruz that she called "La Belle Fille." She owned this with a free colored man, Bartholomew Dwyer, who may or may not have been romantically connected to his business partner, but as the slave registers show he was definitely her attorney, as well as being the estate attorney for a number of other properties. He was also influential enough to have his name mentioned in the local paper when he left the colony.[88]

The estate "La Belle Fille" is listed several times in the registers from 1813, when the records begin, to the time Rosetta Smith disappears from the archive around 1825. The registers show it to be a very large provision estate, and the size indicates that after her thirty-three slaves had been fed there would have been a considerable surplus, which she must have sold at market for a substantial profit. It would have been far removed from merely a plot of land kept for her and her slaves' sustenance; rather, it was a major operation that would have involved the labor of scores of slaves, many of whom she would have rented.[89]

In much the same way that Polgreen lived within the confines of Bridgetown and was involved in the hotel trade, Smith seems to have been an urban facilitator and provider of services. Her own slaves were urban slaves, whose job descriptions indicate a life spent in towns and not on plantations. Her workforce was predominately female, and few were classed as laborers. Most had urban skills, such as being cooks or seamstresses. With the demands of the town, no doubt Smith hired them out as the need arose.[90] Ultimately, towns in the southern Caribbean, from Bridgetown to Port of Spain, functioned on the labor of a flexible slave and free workforce of hired hands, hucksters and other street sellers, cleaners, cooks, washerwomen, seamstresses, and storekeepers, people living in poverty doing mundane jobs.[91]

Rosetta Smith knew how to make and maintain contacts through a network of other free colored women with whom she bought and sold slaves throughout her life. We know next to nothing of Rachael Pringle Polgreen's associations or her friendships, but the evidence for Smith is revealing about how successful free women of color operated. Making contacts and maintaining friendships were clearly important to the way Rosetta Smith did business. Rather than her business relying on the largesse of white men, she made repeated transactions with women, often some of the wealthiest free women of color on the island. Most of her entries were for the sale of slaves and occasionally plots of land in and around the capital. Other female slave owners, such as the richest free colored woman in Trinidad, Madame Congnet, as well as Hannah Perpignon and Jane Dellor Rolland, make repeat appearances buying and selling slaves with Rosetta Smith.[92] In the light of this evidence, the receptions she held for the "kept ladies in the colony" at Government House become less occasions for malicious gossip, as insinuated by Picton's critics, and more likely occasions for doing business and networking.

Although the majority of her recorded transactions were between her and other women, it is also significant that Rosetta Smith did business with white men. The first transaction for her in 1799 lists her selling a townhouse to Andrew Benjamin.[93] Later she sold slaves to two white businessmen from Scotland who had been in the region for years.[94] Even more significant was her sale of slaves to William Lushington, who was an enormously successful planter's agent for the Windward Islands and a major landowner, particularly on Grenada.[95] Her transactions with him in 1809 and 1810 indicate that long after Picton's demise, Rosetta Smith conducted business confidently in her own right and continued to operate in circles where this kind of transaction was open to her.

That she had confidence and authority independent of Picton can be seen in the way she used the law to register litigation and "protests" against certain individuals and to defend her interests. When two white women, Rebecca Griffiths and Grace Lilburne, reneged on a deal that they had made with her regarding the sale of a house they lived in, they feigned being aggrieved parties. They argued that the house that they had agreed to sell to Rosetta Smith was actually worth more than they had originally bargained for. She had the guards evict the women and used the law to force them to accept the price as originally agreed. The two women were shocked and incensed that Smith could be such a tenacious and cool-headed businesswoman. It was clearly not what they expected of a free woman of color.

Sometime later, when Picton was in disgrace, Griffiths and Lilburne wrote a joint letter to the Colonial Office complaining of the way they had been treated. In their letter they played the part of chaste and delicate white ladies, trying to elicit sympathy with references to their "sensibilities."[96] But as Rosetta Smith would have known, Griffiths and Lilburne were far from delicate. The house on Queen Street that they had occupied was well known to the officers of the Royal Navy. From the evidence of the curious letter the two women sent to the Colonial Office, as well as *A History of Trinidad* written by E. L. Joseph in 1838, it might be surmised that the property on Queen Street was a brothel.[97] Despite being white women, their complaints to the secretary fell on deaf ears.

Rosetta Smith conducted the business of buying and selling property right up till the deeds archive finishes in 1816, and there is every reason to believe that she continued in much the same way after this date. The slave registers show her workforce to be dynamic, with new slaves brought in and others sold. Certain family groups remained with her throughout the period 1816–25, while others were more transient. This is evidence of someone who had an engaged and ongoing commitment as an entrepreneur, not an opportunist who had some early fortune as a result of taking up with a governor and who then "retired" from a notorious public life when he left the colony.

In different ways, Rachael Pringle Polgreen and Rosetta Smith have been used and abused by white commentators as exemplars of powerful negative stereotypes of free women of color that have been centuries in the making: one as a madam, the other as a mistress. The hold of these stereotypes on the historical imagination has not diminished in modern scholarship, where enterprising free women of color continue to be viewed as notorious. Despite this, a deconstruction of the evidence for their lives points to their place within a broader community of women that was as dynamic as it was tenacious. While both women engaged with white men, their presence in history is quite independent of men and their "libidinous desires."

CHAPTER THREE

By Labors and Fidelity
JUDITH PHILIP AND HER FAMILY

JUDITH PHILIP KNEW a thing or two about slaves; slavery had been part of her life since birth. For most of her adult life she personally had owned well over two hundred people. By 1833 she was one of the most successful planters in Grenada and the matriarch of an extended family that possessed many acres and hundreds of slaves spread throughout the region.[1] Indeed, Judith Philip was one of the most successful slaveholders in the Caribbean.[2] Her largest plantation was 250 acres overlooking Tyrrel Bay on the outlying island of Carriacou, a place that she had inherited from her mother that she called "Grand Anse." It was there that she and her managers oversaw her extensive businesses and where she built "the big house." Her other estate, "Petite Anse," was just 'round the coast, while the third, "Susannah," was a cocoa plantation a little bit farther inland.[3] The three plantations formed a neat triangle, and the slaves were used to being moved around, depending on the season and the need.[4] On Carriacou Philip's siblings also owned property and slaves. In separate but adjoining lots, they owned nearly all the land on the smaller island of Petite Martinique and sizable properties in Grenada's capital, St. George's. In addition, Judith's elder brother J. B. Louis and her sister Susannah invested heavily in Trinidad, owning hundreds of acres there.[5] Judith Philip's family was one to be reckoned with.

Across the three plantations Philip's slaves toiled for their mistress producing cotton, coffee, cocoa, and provisions. As far as can be known, they were hard-working and rarely afforded any trouble. According to the slave registers, there were fewer deaths on her plantations than on those held by many of the other owners in the colony, and her slaves were less "marked by the whip."[6] While not necessarily a sign of good treatment, it was a sure sign of good management. Her slaves also enjoyed considerable freedoms. When their working day was done they could move about, tend to their provision grounds, and visit friends. But in this Judith Philip was no exception. Like many in Grenada, the Philip family came from the French community, and they tended to live closer to their place of work and closer to their slaves.[7]

Judith Philip knew the ways and habits of slaves, where they came from, and who was friends with whom. Living as she did in the heart of her operation this knowledge was both unavoidable and necessary. So it must have come as a surprise when, in June 1834, one of her most trusted slaves, a thirty-year-old creole called Jose who had been in Philip's employ for most of his life, was arrested and charged with malicious wounding.[8] Well known and popular, Jose had certainly never been in any real trouble before. The incident happened on March 18 at around 7 PM when Jose went to visit his girlfriend on the nearby "Debels" plantation. As Jose approached his lover's quarters, the light was fading but he could just make out the shape of another man standing in the doorway. He could also clearly hear the man's raised voice, arguing with her. According to the transcript of his trial, Jose knew the angry man to be a thirty-eight-year-old slave called John Charles from the estate "Cocoa Nut Vale," which bordered "Debels." The two men had had words before, on many occasions.[9]

John Charles was challenging Jose's woman over money. There was also a child that she had borne, who now resided on the mainland, and Charles could well have been the father. Enraged at the intrusion, Jose tried to defend his partner and confronted John Charles. Charles stood in the doorway of the hut and would not let Jose past. Both men squared off and loudly cursed, while others began to crowd around the fence that divided the different huts. Then the fracas began. Jose was first to act, unsheathing a sharpened metal bar that he had been using that day in the workshop. With both hands he struck Charles violently in the stomach and moved past the wounded man to defend the woman.

At the trial, the wound Jose inflicted was described as being between "three and four fingers deep on the right side of the witnesses belly," yet despite the severity of the injury, John Charles was not down and out.[10] He grabbed the bar from the hands of his assailant and went to attack Jose, who quickly shut the door. The two men then continued to curse each other loudly with the door between them, until Jose grabbed a knife from inside, opened the door, and lunged at his partner's assailant. John Charles parried the blow but frightened by this escalation he made a hasty exit with

Jose's metal "ramrod" still in hand. Back on his estate, Charles immediately reported the incident to his owner, a French planter named Marinette Charbonne. She quickly sent for the local doctor, who happened to also moonlight as the estate manager at the Philip plantation.[11] Three weeks later the doctor informed Judith Philip that John Charles had made a reasonable recovery. That could have been the end of it.

On the surface the incident was just a domestic dispute: Jose, whether in a pique of jealous rage or not, had wounded John Charles in a fight in which John Charles was unarmed. This was a commonplace act of violence that would have been subject to rudimentary plantation justice, except that on this occasion Marinette Charbonne decided to rely on official colonial justice rather than be intimidated by her far more wealthy neighbor. Charbonne's father, Pierre, had been a friend of Judith's father. The two families had done business together, and in 1803 Judith Philip had even made Pierre Charbonne one of her attorneys.[12] Since that time, however, and with Pierre's death, the fortunes of the Charbonne family had worsened while those of the Philips had soared.[13] Marinette Charbonne was Pierre's mixed-race daughter and, as far as it can be known, his only child. Insecure, she reported the incident to the English magistrate on the island, who quickly determined that the case should go to trial. Jose was arrested, shipped to the mainland, and placed in Young Street jail in the capital, St. George's.[14] The expectation of his owner was that he might be charged with assault, or at best the lesser charge of affray, or disturbing the peace, but the prosecution brought graver charges to bear. Jose was charged with "feloniously, willfully, maliciously and unlawfully attempting to kill, with malice aforethought, the said John Charles."[15]

Jose's situation did not look good, but Judith Philip was a powerful woman who could pull strings, even in the British community. She insisted that her slave be given a trial on the mainland, and she sent a white planter, James Steele, to vouch for his character.[16] She even went to the trouble of hiring a defense lawyer, an Englishman with the wonderfully Dickensian name of Mr. Snagg. "It is a very severe law," Snagg argued to the jury, "that condemns a man for an offence which does not produce deprivation of life; that all the witnesses are not present and where the medical officer describes it as a very trifling injury." The judge did not agree. "The question," Justice Hayes instructed the jury, "is not what the wound is but the intention." Clearly alarmed, Jose begged the pardon of the court, saying that he "did not know the consequences of his actions." It was no good. The jury found Jose "guilty of the intent to do grievous bodily harm," but they recommended mercy. In his summing up the judge said that "the public law of this colony has awarded the punishment of death to your crime: It is the same punishment inflicted upon our subjects in England. However given the plea by the jury to mercy, I will await more senior advice." He then remanded the prisoner in custody to wait for the governor's deliberation.[17]

George Middlemore had been the lieutenant governor of Grenada for a little over six months when the trial transcript of Jose's case landed on his desk on June 24, 1834. Sorting through the piles of unfinished paperwork left over by his disinterested predecessor, his sharp military eye was caught by the arrival of this odd series of letters and petitions in a tight bundle of papers sent by the attorney general.[18] As both the jury and the judge had recommended mercy, it was beholden upon the lieutenant governor to intervene. Middlemore was a mild-mannered and experienced administrator, who was not about to create contention with severity.[19] His caution was wise. Judith Philip had taken matters into her own hands when the sentence of death was passed. In an impressive display of personal influence, she had organized a petition for clemency for her slave and persuaded most of the major planters on the island to sign it. Her petition also contained the signatures of four justices of the peace and two surgeons.[20] In the face of such a weighty petition, Middlemore thought it prudent to pass the case on to his direct superior, and he sent the details to the governor of Barbados, carefully highlighting in his delicate hand the "letter from Judith Philip."[21]

On Barbados Sir Lionel Smith knew that this woman was important, fully enmeshed in the plantocracy, and among the wealthiest people in the southern Caribbean. He also knew that during the difficult change from a slave economy to emancipation, it was his job to keep planters such as Philip happy. Part of this transition, instigated by the reforming Whig government, was to bring about a system of apprenticeship and to compensate the planters for the loss of their slaves. As part of this process of reorganizing the colonies for a post-slavery world, the territories of the Windward Islands in the southern Caribbean were also to be organized as one colony: the British Windward Islands.[22] This was a grand title for what the British authorities knew to be in reality a vast frontier, most of it the result of fifty years of fighting. Having planters like Philip on one's side was crucial to the management of this territory.[23]

Governor Smith understood that this petition required a careful response so, like Justice Hayes and Middlemore before him, he too thought it was prudent to have a more senior official make the decision. The file was duly again sent on, this time to London, where it was the secretary of state for war and the colonies, no less, who would decide the fate of Judith Philip's slave. After due consideration the colonial secretary, Thomas Spring Rice, recommended a short period of hard labor for Jose, with a period taken off the sentence because of the time Jose had already spent in prison.[24]

That Judith Philip could compel the attention of the colonial secretary in the matter of her slave was impressive on several levels. Not only was she a single woman from the despised francophone Catholic community on Grenada but she was not even a European woman; rather, she was a "free mulatto" whose mother had once been a slave. This is the story of Judith Philip and her family, a story that begins with a French baker and his African wife and ends with their wealthy descendants in the heart of London.

JUST AS JUDITH PHILIP WAS AN impressive woman, so was her mother, a free black woman named Jeanette, who had married a French settler in Grenada sometime in the 1750s. Jeanette's husband, Honore Philip, was a provincial baker whose family had decided to pack up business in France to seek their fortunes in the Caribbean. Coming with him were his two brothers, François and Jean-Pierre, and at least one parent, his mother, Catherine.[25] In the 1750s this was not a choice encouraged by the French government. Good men with trades were in high demand to support the French military, easily Europe's single largest expense in the first half of the eighteenth century.[26] As a result, and with few exceptions, emigration beyond Europe was discouraged. Colonists were needed for unruly border provinces on the German frontier or in the Austrian Netherlands, not for colonies in the Caribbean. Only in the Caribbean colony of St. Domingue were there sizable numbers of French settlers, but even there, beyond the immediate surroundings of Le Cap, Les Cayes, and Port au Prince, settlement was small and patchy. Before the Seven Years' War, settlers from France were few in the Caribbean, and their empire suffered because of it.[27]

At first glance, it is not easy to see why a French baker and his family seeking to emigrate from Europe would choose the nascent colony of La Grenade, on the edge of the French world, over the well-established colony of New France in North America or St. Domingue. This was a colony with less than a thousand whites and no more than five thousand slaves, a place so marginal that it had been designated "neutral" by the British and French in the 1748 treaty that had ended the War of the Austrian Succession. Distracted by the European balance of power, the French signatories had hardly cared what happened to it. Neither had Louis XIV's successor, his great-grandson, Louis XV, who preferred Madame de Pompadour and his pubescent "Stag Park" in the grounds of Versailles to negotiating French imperial power with his foreign ministers.[28] La Grenade was neglected and out of the way, a definite attraction for a family with aspirations and weary of France. It was perhaps the much-lampooned failings of the royal court, the unsettled disputes between branches of the Catholic Church, the corruption of venal ministers, and the high taxes brought on by endless warfare that finally pushed the Philips to emigrate.

Honore, his brothers, and their mother probably left for the Caribbean via Lorient, Bordeaux, or La Rochelle, the principal ports for the French Caribbean; and they probably traveled via Martinique, the French gateway to the Windward Islands. Later one of the brothers would own land in St. Lucia so perhaps they went there also. In midcentury, over two hundred merchantmen a year plied the trade to Martinique and the other islands, and more got involved as the century progressed.[29] Getting passage was easy, and migrants could pick and choose where they wanted to settle, raise a family, and make their fortune. Just a few years after they left France, all three brothers were listed as principal proprietors: Honore and Jean-Pierre on the small outlying Grenadian island of Petite Martinique, where they owned estates producing cotton and indigo, and François on the mainland of Grenada, growing sugar.[30]

By 1760 Honore had married "Jeanette, a free negro woman." It is highly likely that he formed an intimate relationship with Jeanette when she was an enslaved woman, and later manumitted and married her. Together they had eight children, including Judith, who would all inherit from the labor of their parents, their uncles, and their parents' friends. By 1770, Honore was clearly the preeminent sibling; perhaps he was the eldest. In addition to substantial landholdings on Petite Martinique he and his wife now owned plantations on the nearby island of Carriacou and well over eighty slaves.[31]

It was article 9 of the Code Noir that made possible a marriage between a French planter and an African woman. The Code Noir positively encouraged slave masters to take up with an enslaved concubine, then to free the woman with their children, and eventually to marry her. The church sanctioned this miscegenation, at least initially.[32] Although aspects of the comparatively liberal Code Noir, such as the proper treatment of slaves, were capriciously and inconsistently enforced, some articles in the code meant more than others. On marginal islands with very few white women, the tolerance of interracial marriage made a lot of sense. There was considerable opportunity for the first or second generation of ex-slave women to become respectable wives. The rigidity of the racist forms that dominated the last years of the eighteenth century were only just coalescing when Honore Philip married Jeanette. Around the time of his arrival there were no white women on the island of Petite Martinique and only fifteen on Carriacou.[33]

Honore Philip was as astute as he was lucky. He was lucky to have left France before the rush that came in the wake of the Seven Years' War, and to have chosen land on a tiny island well under the radar of controlling imperial interests. (In 1750, according to the census, Carriacou could boast just 199 people on it, including slaves.)[34] It was good sense and made for good fortune. To be sure, the soils on Petite Martinique were not as good as those on the mainland of Grenada, but therein lay the couple's second piece of good fortune. The staple of Grenada and its dependencies up to that point had been tobacco. By the first half of the eighteenth century this trade was in steep decline.[35] The poorer soils found on Petite Martinique forced them to try their hand at what turned out to be more lucrative crops that grew well on the hard slopes. Cotton was easier to grow than tobacco and a lot easier than sugar. Within a few years they had extended their landholdings and acquired several more estates on Carriacou, where there was plenty of room and few people.

Honore Philip had also been astute in his choice of a wife who shared his intelligence and work ethic. After his death in the 1770s, it was Jeanette Philip who managed and enlarged the family's fortunes and kept a tight rein on her children and their inheritance. Not content to remain passive, throughout the decade she is recorded as putting her mark on a number of business transactions along with her eldest son, Honore.[36] This confidence is made all the more remarkable by the presence of the senior Honore's mother, Catherine, who seemed to have no qualms about her African daughter-in-law taking over from her son.[37] In 1785 Jeanette Philip was listed with her children as being the sole proprietors of the estates she had shared with her husband. The document attested to her "labours and fidelity" that had assisted the couple in making the fortune the government clerk put down as being almost 400,000 livres.[38] How much influence Jeanette had in making this fortune we cannot know, but the government scribe thought her efforts worthy of special mention. In his *Description of the Grenadines* in 1778, the traveling British surveyor S. V. Morse wrote that Petite Martinique was an island where all the land—some 477 acres—was jointly owned by "Jeanette Philip and a number of her mixed race children."[39] By 1784 more land was listed as being owned by this family, especially on the larger island of Carriacou. Aside from lots of land in the main town of Hillsborough, a map of Carriacou from that year shows Jeanette Philip owning a 160-acre estate called "Grand Anse" on the hill behind Tyrrel Bay.[40]

It would be easy to dismiss the planter Jeanette Philip as an elite woman, an anomaly in a subaltern world of slaves and free colored people. But Jeanette was an African ex-slave and her white husband was once a lowly baker; they did not count themselves among the elite. Indeed, from an early age all the male members of the family were taught trades, like carpentry or stone working, in case the precarious fortunes of the slave plantation were lost.[41] Only people who have an acute sense of their humble roots have this level of insecurity. Nor was Jeanette Philip sui generis. There were several other free women of color listed in the records for Carriacou and Petite Martinique in the early 1770s; they owned and operated property in their own right, just as any white landowner might have. Marinette Charbonne, the neighbor whose slave was wounded by Jose, was one such; she owned a plantation and twelve slaves. So too was the "Widow St. Louis," who owned twenty-eight slaves on eighty-eight acres, while Henrietta Veseprey, a "free mulatto," had twenty-five chattel working forty acres of cotton. A neighbor to Veseprey was Piero, a "free negro woman," who owned thirty-eight acres worked by just three slaves.[42] But while all of these women were independent, none of them could rival Jeanette Philip's economic power.

She was undoubtedly a savvy businesswoman. On her husband's death in 1779 her eight children—Honore (Jr.), Nicholas Regis, Jean Baptiste-Louis, Joachim, Judith, Susannah, Michel, and Magdalen—along with the senior Honore's two brothers, François and Jean-Pierre, were named as the joint heirs to the Philip estates, although nearly all of the children were underage. There was also some property given to a family friend, Louis Mongre, and what was then the enormous sum of £6,000 was given to Honore Philip's mother, Catherine.[43] Very attentive to the matter of legacy, Jeanette encouraged the tradition among her children of keeping property firmly within the family circle.

Since she was a substantial landowner, the widow Philip would have been an attractive marriage prospect for any of Grenada's free colored planters seeking to consolidate their landholdings in a new British colony. This was especially so in light of their increasing marginalization at the hands of their new imperial masters. Yet instead of remarrying and forming an alliance with another francophone planter, Jeanette Philip relied on the legitimacy provided by her white brothers-in-law and on her own skills. She turned naturally then to her older children to help secure and grow the family's property portfolio. The sheer numbers of carefully worded and witnessed property transactions between siblings, the attention to the details of financial affairs throughout the late eighteenth century, and the insistence on transparency were hallmarks of Honore but were maintained by his wife. Almost all the transactions by the family in the Grenada records are carefully worded and comparatively very lengthy.[44]

By the time of Jeanette Philip's death the property holdings had expanded impressively. Petite Martinique was almost entirely cultivated by her family, which owned several estates with a workforce of well over one hundred slaves; managers, who included white men; doctors; and overseers. The large piece of land on Carriacou called "Grand Anse," managed first by J. B. Louis Philip and then by Jeanette's eldest daughter, Judith, was worked by well over two hundred slaves. There were also several smaller parcels of land elsewhere on Carriacou and on the mainland of Grenada. The family owned townhouses in the Carriacouan settlement of Hillsborough; in the colony's capital, St. George's; and in Grenada's second town of Gouyave. One uncle, Jean-Pierre, owned plantations in the parish of St. Mark and on Petite Martinique, while the other, François, along with his wife, Marie-Magdalaine Vigi, and their children, owned plantation property in the parish of St. John and several properties in St. Lucia.[45]

As an independent black woman controlling several hundred slaves, Jeanette Philip was little different from the white planters in the management of her chattel, employing the same insidious methods that made up the planter's arsenal of control. It was effective to institute a regime of divide and rule, which complemented the hideous litany of punishments that were a staple of plantation management. Slaves were tempted with rewards to report on their fellow workers. This manipulative policy of the Philips came to fruition in 1786, just before Jeanette died, when a conspiracy was discovered among her slaves on "Grand Anse." The plan was for a "great number of valuable slaves to escape to the Spanish settlements," the nearest of which was Trinidad.[46] At that time Spain had declared that all escaped slaves would be free if they made it to Spanish territory, a policy that caused havoc in the colonies of Spain's European rivals and trouble for the Spanish governors tasked with implementing it.[47] This largesse was eagerly seized by the slaves of Grenada, who listened avidly to stories of the unfolding events in Europe and information brought in from other colonies.[48] Trinidad was two days' sailing away, and a slave could make the journey to freedom in a canoe if they were lucky. Pauline, a slave on the "Grand Anse" estate, discovered the conspirators at the moment of their escape and informed her owners. As a reward, the council in Grenada ordered Pauline to be freed in order to "offer every possible encouragement to those who shall be instrumental in preventing the same." Jeanette was compensated for the loss of her property, paid out of the public purse. The council recognized that "the inhabitants of these islands have been very considerable sufferers from the elopement of their slaves." Despite the "treachery" of slaves like Pauline against her fellow slaves, though, these acts of slave defiance were ongoing. It was, the government's legal scribe wearily wrote, "an evil to which they [the planters] are still greatly exposed."[49]

THE BRITISH WERE FIRMLY IN control of Grenada by 1786 and, as the story of Pauline reveals, the Philips understood that their economic interest was intimately linked with Britain. For all that, Jeanette Philip and her family remained staunchly Catholic, and their close-knit interconnectedness allowed them to prosper while keeping a low profile, even within their own familial community. Family loyalty was paramount; it was by sticking together that this mixed-race family could avoid the depredations of the British overlords.

When Jeanette Philip died in 1788, her land and houses were divided among her children to add to the parcels they each owned from Honore's original will.[50] The overall inheritance was large, but when divided among so many children the plots were relatively small and unevenly placed. On Carriacou, Judith took full possession of "Grand Anse," the estate that she had been managing for her mother, while her sister Susannah remained on her neighboring cotton plantation. Nearby were the lands owned by J. B. Louis, who also owned land on Petite Martinique near the estates of Honore, Michel, and Nicholas Regis. Jeanne-Rose, a child of Magdalen, was given a small estate called "North Point" on Petite Martinique that bordered those of her uncles.[51] All of the children were given further property in the form of townhouses, lots of land, and warehouse space on the mainland in St. George's. And when the family friend Louis Mongre died childless in 1784, his wealth also passed to the Philip children as the heirs of his friend Honore.[52]

Within ten years of Jeanette's death this diffuse arrangement of property began to change, as Judith accumulated more land to add to her estate. The Philip siblings interacted with each other almost exclusively, buying and selling property to one another despite the estates being spread across several islands, but it was Judith and her brother J. B. Louis who demonstrated the true entrepreneurial spirit of their parents. An indenture from 1792 lists Honore selling land on Carriacou to Judith; and again, in 1793, Honore sold his share of Petite Martinique, including his house, to Judith along with two more properties, one in the town of Hillsborough and the other in St. George's.[53] A short time later, J. B. Louis Philip moved to Trinidad to take advantage of free plots of land being given away by the Spanish government, and he also sold his land to Judith.[54] When their brother Nicholas Regis passed away suddenly on the night of December 23, 1789, more land passed into Judith's possession.[55] By the mid-1790s she controlled large properties on Carriacou and Petite Martinique, as well as houses and lots in the capital from which she gained rents. Judith had so much spare property that she even allowed one of her houses on Petite Martinique to be used by the local Catholic priest when he needed to visit the outer island.[56] Religiously devout throughout her life, in her will Judith would not forget the Catholic Church, making sure to leave sums of money for the "customary prayers" for her soul.[57]

Yet for all their staunch adherence to the Catholic Church, Judith Philip and her sisters Magdalen and Susannah did not marry into the French community. As young free colored women of considerable property, each of them would have made a highly desirable marriage prospect for a francophone Catholic planter; however, each set her sights in a different direction. While Susannah Philip appears to have remained single at least until sometime after 1796, when she left Grenada to follow her brother to Trinidad, Magdalen Philip had been in a relationship with a prominent English attorney and merchant, Patrick Fotheringham, a man who had worked closely with her uncle François as the protector of slaves. They had two children together—Jean-Jacques and Jeanne-Rose Fotheringham—and they remained a couple until Fotheringham's death in 1794.[58] Jeanne-Rose would later be named as her mother's attorney and representative on Grenada when Magdalen left Grenada after the death of her partner.[59] Judith Philip began a relationship with another Englishman, Edmund Thornton, when she was still very young. This would prove to be a most successful union. The couple was together for several decades and had five children: Ann Rachel, Magdalen, Judith, Louis Edmund, and Philip. While no birth records are extant, there are a number of transactions that involve the children, especially later in life.[60]

Edmund Thornton was the younger son of a prominent merchant from Lancaster. In the 1770s Thornton was listed as a merchant in the Grenadine Islands, but throughout the 1780s he was the manager of two large estates on Carriacou owned by the Urquhart family of Aberdeen.[61] Throughout 1790 and 1791 he is recorded as buying extensive commercial property in the town as part of the merchant house of Baillie, Campbell, and Thornton.[62] In addition, he leased and owned several handsome plantations on Grenada in 1792, and by the time of the Fedon Rebellion in 1795 he had extensive property in and around the capital, with business dealings across the Windward Islands.[63] It was common for British men like Edmund Thornton to take a free colored partner in the Caribbean colonies until they had amassed the financial capital to allow them to return home and make an advantageous marriage. It is assumed that for British settlers this was the norm; however, for white creoles this was often not the case.[64] But the norm was certainly Thornton's career trajectory: in 1794, when he was forty-seven, he returned to England after more than two decades in the colony. In December 1796 he married into the Lancashire gentry.[65]

It would seem that Judith Philip became involved with Edmund Thornton on Carriacou during the period of French reoccupation. At that time there was no reason to presume that the island would revert to British control, so his being English could not have counted as an advantage to Philip, but it is easy to see the benefits of the relationship from Thornton's point of view. Not only did the young woman provide him with intimate companionship, but her French connections gave him a measure of protection and access to useful francophone networks. An intimate connection with this well-placed francophone planter would have been invaluable to Thornton as he negotiated business across the Grenadine Islands in the fraught years that Great Britain was at war with France.

The advantage of the relationship to Judith Philip is not easy to discern. Arguably, she was the wealthier partner, at least during the time that Thornton was on Carriacou. Even though Judith Philip was a young woman, she was the joint owner of and heir to a major estate on Carriacou, with a stake in a number of other properties on other islands. Thornton, then in his mid-thirties, was still an aspiring merchant and plantation manager. Moreover he was an Anglican from a well-born English family, so marriage to a Catholic mulatto woman, however wealthy she may have been, was out of the question. Even assuming this was an affair of the heart, the question arises as to why Judith Philip would choose to become this man's mistress. The answer may simply be that she did not. It could well be the case that she and Thornton did enter into a form of marriage that would accommodate both their needs. At the time, they were living on a Catholic French island forcibly retaken from the British in 1779. It is entirely possible that they were married in a Catholic ceremony. Later, when the British retook the island, this union would have been regarded as a "clandestine marriage" with no legal status in England.[66] On Grenada the British certainly promulgated laws to that effect, as the Fedons had found to their cost.[67] In the French Caribbean community, though, it would still have provided Judith and her children with a measure of respectability. She was a devout Catholic, and in her view she was properly married in the eyes of God even if the marriage had no legal status in England.

It is unclear how long these two remained a couple. Judith and her children seem to have relocated to the capital, St. George's, with Thornton after the Treaty of Paris awarded the colony back to Britain. She certainly held property in that town in her own right. More telling is that when Thornton left Grenada to return to England, Judith and their children went also, and she established a home for herself and the Thornton children just a twenty-minute walk from Thornton's London residence.[68] Having married Jane Butler, the daughter of the archdeacon of Chester, Thomas Butler, and his wife, Thornton's main residence was in rural Lancashire at Whittington Hall, near Kirkby Lonsdale. Judith Philip lived in London at 33 Great

Coram Street for at least a decade, returning to Grenada only once during that time, briefly in 1803.[69]

Did Thornton take his concubine and their children to England and install them in a convenient house in London before going off to secure a wealthy white wife? A salacious narrative of a clandestine mistress installed in London under the nose of the unsuspecting new wife certainly fits the stereotype of the free colored concubine. It is more reasonable to presume, however, that as a wealthy businesswoman Judith Philip chose to be with her children in England, quite independent of Thornton. And, of course, Judith Philip may not have regarded herself as a concubine. As a Catholic she could have considered the legitimate wife to be herself and not Jane Butler, who was safely out of sight in Lancashire. Not only did she live in London within walking distance of Thornton for over a decade, they had two more children, Judith and Philip Thornton, together during that time. No doubt, she took this opportunity to see her children educated in the metropole, using the same strategy as other free women of color who saw a British education as the way to respectability for their children and assimilation into the imperial project. From her large house in London her children, as well as at least two of her nephews, would go to school, while she continued to conduct business in the Windward Islands through her lawyers.

ALTHOUGH SHE COULD NOT HAVE predicted it, the relationship with Edmund Thornton proved very helpful to Judith Philip and her family. At the end of the American Revolution there were three thousand free people on Grenada and the vast majority of these were francophone, with over half of them free colored people. These people had an unsteady allegiance to the British administration, and many must have breathed a sigh of relief when the French briefly reoccupied the island in 1779. Only four years later, when the war ended, the political geography of the Caribbean was still too fluid for them to decide with any certainty on whose side they should be: it was very challenging to negotiate the ill-defined boundaries of European politics, with the tit-for-tat island swapping of successive treaties.[70] The British who reoccupied the island in 1784 made it clear that they had no time for the French-speaking Catholics—either free colored people or their white neighbors—and were determined to subordinate them to British interests and the Anglican religion.[71] In this punitive environment Judith Philip overtly chose to be counted among the British. Her relationship with Thornton had taught her how to read and conduct business in English, and provided her with access to important British mercantile and planter interests. It seems that she did not feel the sting of the heavy-handed discrimination against the Catholic francophone settlers on Grenada, and did not share the bad feelings that reached a crisis point only six years later.

When the revolutionary Victor Hughes arrived in the southern Caribbean in 1794, aggrieved francophone settlers on Grenada were openly supporting the republican cause. Years of abuse and disenfranchisement by the British had caused the free society to become completely polarized: the British and their supporters occupied St. George's, where Judith and Edmund Thornton lived, while most of the French had moved up the coast to the town of Gouyave or quietly avoided conflict in the parishes in the interior and on Carriacou and Petite Martinique. Many had simply given up and left. Coupled with a resentful population of thirty thousand slaves, this profound division among slaveholders meant that by 1795 Grenada was a ghastly nightmare in waiting. Contemporary sources all speak of the dangerous division among the free population on the eve of the conflict.[72] Luckily for Judith Philip, she, Thornton, and their children left for England just before that nightmare began.[73]

Wealthy free people of color like the Philip family were at the heart of the Fedon Rebellion: they had planned the revolution, they had led it, and it was their slaves who were the first to be cajoled into action. In neighboring colonies it was their relatives who supported the revolution and gave them succor. In the transient, mobile world of the southern Caribbean, the familial connections of the free colored community were widespread.[74] Behind the free colored republicans was Victor Hughes, the French revolutionary recently arrived on Guadeloupe.[75] He had been quick to commission the Grenadian planter Julien Fedon as a general in the republican service and make captains of his friends: Stanislaus Besson, a silversmith, and Etienne Ventour, a tailor, both from Gouyave; and Charles Nogues, a landowner from Valera. These men were tasked with bringing the revolution to Grenada and then exporting it to the rest of the Windward Islands. The revolt was supported by Fedon's brother-in-law Michel Belleran, who lived in Trinidad, along with a sizable number of other free colored people on the Spanish island, many of whom either came from Grenada or had close contacts there.[76] On his mother's side, Fedon was possibly even related to Henri Christophe, the general who was second only to Toussaint L'Ouverture in St. Domingue.[77] This was the free colored people's moment, and they were ready to seize it.

FROM HIS BASE ON GUADELOUPE, Hughes had provided Fedon and his compatriots with a large cache of weapons, ammunition, republican flags, caps of liberty, uniforms for the officers, and his well wishes.[78] It was much the same package he had sent to St. Vincent for the black Caribs and to the republican insurgents fighting the British and their royalist French allies on Martinique and St. Lucia.[79] Hughes also tried to give Fedon advice, but he held little sway over the hot-headed general, who had plans of his own. When the rebellion spiraled out of control and Fedon began to summarily execute his high-level British prisoners, Hughes withdrew his support, leaving Fedon and his captains to an awful fate for the most part at the hands of the vengeful British.[80]

Not all free colored people were so alienated from the British that they would choose the republican cause. "Captain" Louis La Grenade was a French free colored man who had thrown in his lot with the British and who flaunted his authority by ostentatiously commanding the prestigious militia regiment that guarded the capital. To many of the free people of color he appeared to be a self-interested turncoat, and certainly his allegiance would pay him and his descendants handsome profits throughout the nineteenth century and beyond.[81] But there were people with genuinely divided loyalties for whom the tenets of the French Revolution gave pause. Religion was central to the conflict between the British and the French on Grenada, and most of the francophone free colored people were devotedly Catholic. The anticlerical republican ideology was a challenge to their loyalty, while the republic's dubious position on abolishing slavery threatened the basis of their prosperity. The rebellion split families and broke up relationships, forcing some into hard choices. Despite any ambivalence, however, when the rebellion broke out in March 1795, many of the free colored people who might have been expected to remain neutral, or loyal to the British, cleaved to Fedon's side.

One individual who felt the pull from his free colored neighbors was Joachim Philip, Judith's younger brother. Until 1794 he was a property owner in Petite Martinique, and through his sisters Judith and Magdalen and his uncle François, he had close personal and economic ties to the British community.[82] Like Louis La Grenade, Joachim Philip may once have taken an oath of loyalty to the British, but by 1795 he had turned against them. No doubt he had his ideological reasons for siding with Julien Fedon, whom he certainly knew prior to the conflict, but another compelling reason was economic. Joachim was deeply in debt. In November 1794 his several creditors finally caught up with him after a prolonged period of pursuit. In a punitive judgment for the recovery of £820 he owed, the Court of Common Pleas awarded several English attorneys costs amounting to nearly £1,500, with interest set at the hefty rate of £6 per hundred per annum.[83] With his debt now at £2,260, Joachim was forced to sell all of his property on Petite Martinique—land, chattel, and houses—and retreat to the family property in Gouyave. Barely six months after the forced sale, he made the choice to side with Fedon's revolution.

Julien Fedon clearly trusted Joachim Philip and made him a captain, issuing him a uniform of a bright blue frock coat with trim, a tricolor sash, and a brass helmet. This was the uniform Philip was wearing when he and Charles Nogues arrived in St. George's on March 4, acting as republican emissaries to the executive council.[84] They had traveled to St. George's carrying an ultimatum from Fedon that ordered the government to surrender the island without delay. But what once may have seemed an exciting prospect of retribution to Philip became a great deal more worrisome as he climbed the hill that led up to Fort George and the audience with the council. It was perhaps his first real intimation that the choice to side with Fedon came with serious consequences.

Blindfolded, but still in their fancy uniforms, Philip and Nogues were led to the council chambers while frightened loyalist residents hurled abuse at them. Some people had to be physically prevented by the St. George's militia from lynching the men on the spot.[85] If the eyewitness testimony is to be believed, the most acute anger directed at Joachim Philip came, unsurprisingly, from his own family. His sister Susannah was furious. She flew at him in a rage and would have "torn him to pieces" had the militia not prevented her. How could he do this to himself, to her, to the family? For her younger brother to throw in his lot with Fedon may have been a matter of personal ideology, but for the rest of the family it was a shocking betrayal. The Philip family had done well with the plantation complex, and Joachim's rash commitment to Fedon's revolt had the potential to ruin them all. Susannah Philip had every reason to be distraught with anger.[86] Like her sister, she had close ties to the British and understood just how powerful they were. She feared that despite some initial success by the revolutionaries it was only a matter of time before the British would send reinforcements and take back what had been taken from them.[87] She seemed to know better than her brother did that this rebellion would bring nothing but chaos and disaster for all of them.

The Philip family had no inducement to support Fedon's republican revolution, which pitted slaves against their masters. In casting his lot with a republican anti-slavery rebellion, Joachim had turned his back on his family whose fortunes were locked into the cycles of slavery and slave owning. The family had little interest in the Rights of Man or a redistribution of wealth. Every member of the family owned slave plantations, except Joachim, who had lost his land and chattel to debt. He could afford to play at liberating the slaves since he had nothing to lose.[88] If Fedon's rebellion were successful, the family might expect no quarter from his slave army. In fact, the family was so involved in protecting its interests from republican threats that in the months leading up to the revolt Michel Philip had requested some guns to help defend Petite Martinique from threats within and without, a request that the nervous Governor Ninian Home felt should not be "complied with."[89] As free people of color they were always distrusted, no matter how rich they were. What they dreaded most was that Joachim's involvement would expose the family to savage British retribution; as wealthy free colored people, all British eyes were on them.

As Susannah Philip had feared, the rebellion did bring chaos and disaster for the free colored community. It was finally put down by massive reinforcements from Ireland in July 1796, by which time at least seven thousand slaves lay dead, while the island and its economy lay in smoking ruins.[90] Julien Fedon, his brothers, and his deputies either disappeared to neighboring islands or were caught and executed in the marketplace along with forty-five other "ring-leaders."[91] An untold number—possibly hundreds—were simply killed during the fighting. Joachim Philip managed to elude capture for nine years, hidden on Petite Martinique, the island owned by his family. Who was harboring him was not recorded in the Grenadian council minutes, but it seems unlikely to have been a member of his family, given that the authorities would have had them under scrutiny, and many of them, including Susannah, had already decamped to Trinidad. Perhaps he found refuge with William Scott, the Englishman who bought

Joachim's estate for debt and who was also a close ally of the Philip family, or perhaps with the Grant family, who were both neighbors and friends. The minutes merely record that in March 1803 "the fugitive Joachim Philip was caught," and a sentence of death was passed "unanimously." He was hanged in the market square of St. George's within days of his capture.[92]

In the awful aftermath of the rebellion, the free people of color who were caught between the two sides had to deftly navigate an environment of vicious retribution. Even King George III was shocked at the level of post-rebellion repression in Grenada. Concern about heavy-handed reprisals was acknowledged by the Colonial Office when it censured the new governor, Charles Green, for being overly influenced by white animosity and for allowing the courts an "unprecedented level of severity" in trying people whose involvement in the revolt was doubtful.[93] A hypersensitive British population perceived conspiracy wherever free colored people gathered, and the net of suspicion spread across the whole francophone and free colored community. How was guilt to be determined among a population caught in the middle? Ringleaders were easy enough to identify, but what of brothers? Sisters?

Free women of color, particularly the wives and family members of the revolutionaries, became a specific target for the governor and his council, who believed, correctly, that women of color had been complicit in the organizing of the rebellion. Marie Rose Fedon had actively taken part, and so had some other women. In September 1796 Governor Green organized a committee to "examine into the character and conduct of certain free women of color" who "were under strong suspicion of taking part [in the rebellion]."[94] After the committee returned with its findings, a large number of women were banished from the colony. Some went to Barbados and Demerara, but most moved to Trinidad. Later that year the Spanish governor of Trinidad complained to the Colonial Office that large numbers of free colored people with "dangerous politics" had swamped his colony. There were, he complained, "too many armed republicans" on his island already.[95] In 1797 many of these expelled women, including some wives and partners of executed rebels, tried to get back to Grenada. With the memory of Fedon so fresh, and the colony so damaged by rebellion, outraged residents refused permission for the women to land.[96]

Yet the siblings of Joachim Philip who chose to remain in the colony were exempt from this reprisal. Why was their land not confiscated when so much land was taken from others?⁹⁷ Certainly, the Philip family had been largely confined to the islands of Petite Martinique and Carriacou, where the rebellion had no impact, and were far enough away to escape close surveillance. There was also, perhaps, a lingering respect for the memory of Honore Philip and his two brothers. Despite being French, they had participated fully in the life of the colony, and François had become a justice of the peace and a protector of slaves. Most important, though, Judith Philip had built strategic alliances with well-placed white men in the British community. The authorities well remembered Susannah Philip's impressive display of outrage at her brother's actions, by which she clearly signaled that Joachim was a family aberration. It was nevertheless remarkable that the family of Julien Fedon's trusted lieutenant could survive the post-revolutionary repression, and that Joachim's sister Judith was able to return from England in 1808 to establish herself as one of the most powerful planters in the colony.

APART FROM A BRIEF VISIT TO Grenada in 1803 Judith Philip had stayed in London, but she continued to interact with her family. In 1807 she arranged to buy from her sister the small cotton plantation with its sixty-eight slaves that bordered "Grand Anse," which she renamed "Susannah" in her sister's honor.⁹⁸ Susannah Philip, having moved to the Trinidadian capital of Port of Spain, managed her wealthy older sister's interest in that colony. The Trinidad slave registers show that Judith Philip kept slaves on Trinidad, probably to serve her sister.⁹⁹ Also on Trinidad was their brother J. B. Louis Philip, his wife, and their two sons, Jean-Baptiste and St. Luce, who lived on his two massive estates: the four-hundred-acre "Philippine" plantation and the slightly smaller "Concorde" estate, both of which were stocked with hundreds of slaves.¹⁰⁰ By 1817 J. B. Louis Philip was one of the wealthiest planters in Trinidad, and his sons inherited a vast fortune.¹⁰¹ The boys lived for a time with their aunt Judith in London, and both of them would eventually go on to study medicine at Edinburgh University before returning to run their father's estates around 1818.

Judith Philip returned from London to Grenada about 1808. The records show that at least in legal transactions she used the surname Philip. She was the eldest female Philip and much of the "labors and fidelity" that her mother had exhibited were part of her inheritance. As well as managing her own affairs she managed much of her siblings' businesses, controlling the land, the slaves, and the title deeds. Along with her brother Michel, she signed the deeds and kept the official records. On Grenada she would be the only one to acquire great wealth commensurate to that of her father or her uncle François. Of her siblings only J. B. Louis in Trinidad could rival Judith's success.

Right up until her death Judith Philip bought property for her children. Although the children took Thornton as their last name, it was Judith who monitored their finances. Perhaps she was hopeful that they, like she had done, might learn the family business. But at least in one case it was not to be. In 1828 she is recorded as purchasing, for almost £1,000, a large lot of land in St. George's from her daughter Ann Rachel Thornton.[102] This was a generous settlement that may have been her way of avoiding the public disgrace of her daughter's poor financial management. As early as 1801, while her mother was still in England, a merchant in St. George's had sued Ann Rachel for debt, and she was forced by the court to relinquish ownership of several slaves to pay it. The property Ann Rachel Thornton was forced to sell in 1828 was recorded as being formerly the property of her "late uncle Nicholas Regis." It was located right on the harbor and was almost ten acres in size. As such it would have been one of the largest single properties in the town and, at £1,000, one of the most valuable. Clearly, Judith's eldest daughter did not have her mother's or grandmother's business acumen.[103]

Judith also had considerable transactions with white men, particularly William Scott, the man who bought all of Joachim Philip's land when he fell into strife in 1794. It is telling that subsequent sales of Philip properties were either to Judith herself or to William Scott. He may have maintained oversight of her estates while she was in England in the early nineteenth century, although she did employ two white men, Duncan Blair and George Abercrombie Mitchell, as estate managers; both would remain loyal to her for over twenty years.[104]

Her connection to Edmund Thornton and his circle remained strong. In London, the magnate James Baillie, a business partner of Thornton, handled her financial affairs, and in Grenada her attorney was another of Thornton's partners, Thomas Campbell. Her wealth spread as far as the metropole, with all of her children having large sums of money invested in the city of London.[105] She was also an active participant in the affairs of the region. In 1831 the *Grenada Free Press* recorded the £8 she had donated to the Barbados Relief Fund for the repair of hurricane damage.[106]

Judith Philip owned a great deal of human property. By the 1820s she owned a total of 276 slaves, making her one of the wealthiest slaveholders in Grenada. When the planters were compensated for the loss of their slaves beginning in 1836, Philip received £3,058 for the workers on her two smaller estates.[107] The compensation she received for her largest plantation, "Grand Anse," added up to £3,546. A payout in excess of £6,500 places her in the top tier of resident slave owners.[108]

Most of these slaves were estate workers, like her slave Jose, with whom this chapter began. There were relatively few domestic slaves, and there were certainly no entries in the slave registers for personal slaves to indicate a domestic retinue such as one might expect for a woman with this kind of wealth. She can be read as a woman whose main occupation in life was business, but she must have lived relatively simply, even frugally. Today there is no sign of the estate houses nor even, despite the property's size, a foundation for the main house at "Grand Anse."

Judith Philip passed away in December 1848, aged around ninety. Three years before, in July 1845, she wrote her will. There was a confident energy written into the testament. "Should I die at Carriacou," she wrote, not the language of someone who was quietly going about retirement and preparing for the end. On the contrary, it speaks of a woman whose sense of place had been flexible for her whole life. The will was written by a woman who was used to traveling and who kept an abode in several places. These were also the words of someone who was dynamic and active, with a keen mind well into old age. Until her last days she was involved not only in the education of poor free colored children, but also in overseeing baptisms in that community. In this she was no different from many other women of color who keenly involved themselves in charitable works and the arts, but hers appears to be a quiet dispensation of patronage. Likewise she wanted no fuss to be made at her funeral, which she demanded be "conducted with as little pomp as possible," while her body was to be interred only in the public cemetery. If she did eventually die at Carriacou, then her gravestone is so nondescript that, just like her house, it can no longer be located.[109]

Judith Philip's will is the last documentary evidence for the astute management of her life and assets. She left everything to be divided up among her three surviving daughters and the four children of her deceased son Louis Edmund, since her son Philip Thornton died childless. Her three daughters were joint executors of the will and were assisted by her "worthy friend" Matthew Davies. For his help, Davies received a gold watch worth the enormous sum of fifty guineas, a telling insight into the size of the estate. The daughters were assisted further by two contacts in London, close to the moneyed center of British life.

Of all the women in this book, Judith Philip is the most contentious. There is nothing to suggest that she endeavored to ameliorate the condition of free colored people, save supporting the education of some, nor did she fight for equal rights, as her brother Joachim had done and her nephews would later do on Trinidad. She moved in white circles, kept white friends, and did not fraternize beneath her social position. She owned people on a large scale almost all of her life. Her wealth was built from plantation slavery, and when the horror of slavery was over, her powerful attorneys made sure she was substantially compensated for her loss. But should we only see women like Judith Philip through the prism of slavery? The British Atlantic was a cruelly capricious place for the descendants of enslaved Africans, and Judith Philip's achievement—astutely enhancing the legacy of her black mother and passing on a significant inheritance to her daughters—is not insignificant. Her singular success marks her as a remarkably enterprising woman, worthy of our attention in a world so profoundly shaped by white men.

CHAPTER FOUR

A Lasting Testament of Gratitude
SUSANNAH OSTREHAN AND HER NIECES

IN 1809 SUSANNAH OSTREHAN WAS DYING. Just months before she had listed all the things she owned in her will. It was a lavish inventory, carefully recorded, with bequests to many people. There were many slaves in her inventory but of all the people she owned, the most important must have been her own mother. Her parent's future welfare was her most pressing concern. She wanted to make sure that her mother was not just nominally a free person, but that she would be properly free. The meticulous wording of her testament reflects a daughter anxious about the future. She knew Barbados was a difficult place for a free woman of color, but it was far harder for an enslaved woman.[1]

Susannah Ostrehan's last wish was that her parent would live her last days as a free woman. However, this manumission was not so easy to effect in the Barbados of the early nineteenth century; Ostrehan had to rely on a bevy of people to make it happen. In an empire of private property, dispensing with houses, furniture, and personal possessions was simple, but in Barbados freeing people was a different matter altogether. At the turn of the nineteenth century the colonial governor had become worried by the large number of manumissions in the colony, in particular the manumissions of women, so in 1801 he had raised the cost of obtaining locally produced freedom certificates from £50 to £300 for women and to £200 for men. Aside from paying the exorbitant fee, anyone wishing to manumit a slave had to show good cause to the capricious Barbadian vestries, offices not disposed to giving freedom to slaves.[2]

In this world, benevolent owners often had to invent various stratagems and ruses to effect the freedom of their enslaved property. This was especially the case for free colored women, whose vulnerability was often exploited and who could expect few concessions from a legal system weighted against them.[3] One strategy, used time and time again, was to claim that the money for the purchase of a slave was the slave's own money, or that they had repaid the amount in full, allowing them to be thus declared free, even though there may not have been any such monetary transaction. Owners like Susannah Ostrehan often claimed that slaves had bought their freedom with their own savings—with the payment of the manumission fee somehow not being recorded. Another strategy was that the owner would will an enslaved person to a poor individual under the proviso that the new owner would undertake to free the slave. The manumission fee could then be waived because the new owner was technically insolvent and unable to pay, but was still beholden to the dictates of the deceased's will. Sometimes owners would simply state that someone else had paid the price of the manumission in a different colony. Grenada and Dominica were sometimes used in this way, since the price for manumission in those colonies was only £10.[4]

By the early nineteenth century the Barbadian society to which Susannah Ostrehan belonged was filled with confusion as to the legal status of many informally emancipated people whose putative owners had avoided, misrepresented, or otherwise obfuscated the situation in attempts to get around the poorly resourced parish councils tasked with policing and controlling freed persons.[5] This situation was made more confusing by the poor state of much of the recordings of manumission, which involved no clear system or "certificate" as such. Church receipts from wardens, deeds of manumission from England, wills, or other evidence and testimony were often offered as proof. Papers, of course, could be easily lost, damaged, or destroyed in bad weather and hard times. The possibility of forgery was obvious. There was much debate in the early nineteenth century about providing a formal registry of free people of color to help differentiate between those who were free and those who were enslaved, but nothing came of it.[6] In 1823 a registry was again recommended by the colonial secretary in his general comments about the amelioration of slavery. But it was not until the 1826 Slave Consolidation Act that a formal procedure was introduced that established the status of freed persons. Various measures were introduced to clamp down on the loose system, from fines for owners whose slaves were found "at large," to the re-enslavement of suspected individuals found without the proper evidence.[7] Untrusting of white Barbadian society, Susannah Ostrehan did not want to leave her mother's freedom and safety to the vagaries of this fluid system. Her mother, Priscilla, needed a formal manumission.

By 1810 the most common way to avoid the prohibitive cost of local manumission was to seek liberty in England. At only £50 it was far cheaper and far easier to gain freedom in the metropole. There were many people in London who had genuine sympathy for the plight of slaves. Slave owners could do it all by proxy, and there were usually no questions asked. Female slave owners, like Susannah Ostrehan, often relied on their contacts in the seafaring world to take the papers to London. Once in London, the sympathetic sea captains and mariners would pay the price of freedom at the lord mayor's office on behalf of the owner, obtain the certificate, and return with it.[8] This was one way the colonial authorities in London could overrule their truculent and independent colony.[9] This loophole was used by hundreds of owners to dispense their freedom patronage, to be rid of unwanted chattel, or to free family members. In this, Susannah Ostrehan was no different.

Ostrehan's poor state of health must have come quickly; she was still a relatively young woman.[10] There was simply not enough time to organize things properly. She arranged for a Captain Welch to organize the manumission of her mother in London, but that would take months, leaving Priscilla in a precarious position. By the time Susannah Ostrehan had written her will, Welch had not returned, and it looked as though her mother's freedom might be at risk. The only thing to do was will her mother to a sympathetic friend, trusting that when Welch returned on the *Berwick* all would be well. In desperation Susannah turned to her friend Christian Blackman to take care of Priscilla and see that the manumission she had ordered from London went ahead smoothly. For this purpose she willed £200 for the purchase of a house and £100 for her parent's continuing welfare. Blackman, a wealthy free colored woman in similar circumstances, was also enriched by the gift of a slave woman, Nancy, with her "issue and increase" for "the use of my mother."[11] This gift was further enhanced by Nancy's potential to produce even more offspring and therefore more slaves. Should those manumission papers not arrive, Priscilla would, in theory, remain Blackman's property "to hold" in perpetuity.[12]

By March 1810 Susannah Ostrehan was dead, and soon Priscilla had written a will of her own in which she admonished Blackman for her failure to pass on the £300 left to Blackman for Priscilla's maintenance and to buy a house for her.[13] It was not an entirely fair accusation, since Priscilla probably remained a resident in her deceased daughter's home while Blackman was waiting for Welch to return in order to settle the probate in its entirety.

In her will Priscilla asked that the balance of the monies owed to her—some £290—go to her great-granddaughter Mary Ostrehan Brett, who was also made the executor of Priscilla's will. By the time Priscilla died later that year, Mary Ostrehan Brett had organized matters satisfactorily, and Blackman had obtained the transfer of freedom that had been finally brought by Welch from London. On November 3, 1810, Susannah Ostrehan's last wish was realized and her mother, Priscilla, died "a free woman of color."[14]

How was it that a wealthy slave owner was in possession of her own mother whom she could will to a friend? And why did Susannah Ostrehan have to jump through so many hoops to effect a simple inheritance? This apparent conundrum was not that unusual in the bizarre world of the early nineteenth-century slave society. And the situation speaks volumes about the precarious world in which free women of color lived, and the ways they navigated a dangerous racial order that favored white male power above all else. Priscilla Ostrehan's misfortune was to be a slave woman who, unlike Jeanette Philip, was not freed by her white lover. However, her several children, Susannah included, must have been granted manumission, although by whom and under what circumstances is unknown. Susannah Ostrehan—like many free women of color—clearly felt that personal ownership of her family members was the safest option in a society ruled by private property. Owning one's own parents, siblings, or children could be protecting them; somehow, Susannah had purchased her parent and she may also have purchased her sisters.

Up until her death in 1810, Susannah Ostrehan was the linchpin of a large, mostly female family that would eventually incorporate five generations of women, who would all profit from owning hotels and property in this contested region. The difficulties in ensuring the freedom of one's own mother necessitated the stratagems these enterprising women used to successfully navigate this precarious world. In each of the wills the Ostrehan women produced over a forty-year period, female family members inherited the lion's share of the wealth.[15] An ongoing matrilineal inheritance is a key component in the success of these free women of color, and was one of the ways they protected each other and their entrepreneurial activities in at least four colonies across the southern Caribbean. Eventually, Priscilla's descendants would own, among other things, the largest hotel in the colony of Demerara and one of the largest buildings in neighboring Berbice. More important than the money, though, was the network of free colored women to which Priscilla's family belonged throughout the first half of the nineteenth century. This then is the story of a matrifocal family and of the power of matrilineality and friendship.

THE VARIOUS PLOYS AND RUSES EMPLOYED to emancipate slaves reveal that Barbados was a capricious place in the early nineteenth century. Britain's second-largest slave colony was highly unstable. The vast majority of the population consisted of human chattel: around sixty-five thousand people were enslaved by the turn of the century. Slavery was the ugly bedrock of this society and permeated every aspect of life. On Barbados slavery was as foul for its banality as it was for its open displays of repression. To own people was the raison d'être of any free person on the island, and the labor that enslaved people performed overwhelmingly dominated the economy. The rest of the population was made up of around sixteen thousand white people and an increasing number of free people of color. Barbados was also unusual in that the ratio of white people to black people was much higher there than elsewhere: about one to four, as opposed to Jamaica where the ratio was more like one to ten.[16] In this oldest colony in the British Caribbean, many of the white families could trace their ancestry back well into the seventeenth century, and planters from Barbados were some of the grandest and most established of all planter families. As a result, the racial hierarchy was highly pronounced, especially among the elite. Because of its age Barbados also had the most settled white families in the Caribbean, and absenteeism was less of a factor than in other colonies. Perhaps because of its racial balance, the size of its militia, and its importance to the British military, Barbados was less marked by slave unrest than were other colonies in the eighteenth century.[17]

But this world was changing. In 1816 a slave revolt tore through the southern portion of the island, resulting in the deaths of hundreds and widespread destruction. A senior officer lamented, "Under the irritation of the moment and exasperated by the atrocity of the insurgents, some of the militia . . . were induced to use their arms rather too indiscriminately," while a naval admiral noted, "The Militia, who could not be restrained . . . put many men, women and children to death, I fear without discrimination."[18] While the initial spark had been political, the rebellion had been years in the making, with economic and social forces building to a crisis point. The Napoleonic wars made the situation much worse, as merchants went broke or stalled on their debt repayments, and hundreds of ships and thousands of pounds' worth of cargo were lost to French privateers. The destabilization of the entire Atlantic economy, not to mention the very real threat of revolts like those seen on Grenada and St. Domingue, added to the tension. So too did the increasing desperation of planters trying to recoup losses. Indeed, many planters and merchants crumpled under mountains of unpayable debt. The awful reality of chattel slavery and the plight of the newly bankrupt contrasted sharply with the status of the few whites who had managed to maintain their elevated positions while living in tremendous opulence.[19]

It was not just the increasing disparity between rich and poor that was unsettling; the increasing number of free people of color also destabilized the island. This population had grown remarkably, from a total of just over five hundred in 1773 to over two thousand just thirty years later.[20] Most noticeable were entrepreneurial free women like Susannah Ostrehan and her friend Christian Blackman, whose success invited envy and spite. Among the few businesses to boom during wartime were hotels, bars, and brothels, which were likely to have been exactly the lines of work Susannah Ostrehan had made her own. Like Rachael Pringle Polgreen in an earlier time, Barbadian women hoteliers profited enormously from the traffic that conflict with France engendered. Their keen opportunism and ability to capitalize on the fortunes of war were more remarkable when contrasted with the poor state of many others. They lived in a colony where racial tensions vied daily with bitter jealousies, and wealthy women such as these brought into sharp focus the long-standing poverty of much of the urban population. In 1783 a law instigated by the Society for the Encouragement of Arts, Manufacture and Commerce in Barbados concluded, "Many Thousands [of whites were] sunk with despair and consequent indolence into a state of profligate and vagrant beggary."[21]

Poverty had always marked the island, but because of the war it had grown much worse. In the early years, indentured laborers who survived their terms had often been unable to capitalize on the small gifts of land they were given for their service and had quickly sunk into destitution. As the society became more fluid, poor white women who had previously been employed as nursemaids, cooks, and seamstresses were pushed out in favor of skilled slave women.[22] These poor white people and their precarious descendants had become, by the end of the century, a tragedy on the streetscapes of the towns. With the depredations of war, and the growth in free colored people competing with them for jobs, the number of poor white people was increasing. By 1829 it was reckoned that 60 percent of white people were living in desperation, their worn clothes and pallid expressions an excruciating sign that all was not well with the colonies.[23]

Travelers particularly remarked on the ragged, dirty-looking white women who had fallen into colonial ineptitude and wanton disgrace. The specter of fallen white women naturally fed into stereotypes based on white race anxiety.[24] It took just a few weeks, remarked one soldier, before an Englishwoman "looked ten years older" than she really was. Noting that many whites had come to Barbados from other islands for their health, he wrote: "Good God, what wretched objects must the inhabitants of these other islands be?"[25] Indeed, so poor were many of Barbados's white population that even as late as 1830 only twelve hundred white people made the ten-acre voting qualification. An 1824 report concluded that out of 5,206 slave owners on the island, 3,671 owned no land at all. Less than half the white population owned slaves and usually then only a couple.[26]

To be sure, the heartbreaking stories of black people dying on the streets thrown into holes "like dogs," or emaciated slaves in rags desperately begging to be bought by kind-looking strangers were part of the grim picture, but what struck many visitors the most was the liveliness of the free colored people in contrast with the poor whites.[27] Richard Wyvill visited Barbados with his regiment in 1805. He had last been to the island in 1796, and he noticed a marked difference in the society. "I have been quite shocked," he wrote in his diary, "at seeing the numbers of white people begging about the streets here"; even the black people, he concluded, "relieved them." The soldier also observed the "miserable ... emaciated countenances and sallow expressions" among the Europeans. By contrast, he observed free women of color "with handsome umbrellas over their heads, walking in a most stately manner up and down—some even with their waiting women."[28]

Like Wyvill, other visitors spoke of the ebullience of the free colored class. They wrote of such people dominating business in the towns and fleecing white customers mercilessly at the shops; of colored workmen who drove their carts at breakneck speed through Bridgetown without any regard for their social superiors; and of the negligent night watchmen who only looked after themselves. Yet, underscoring the tut-tutting about disrespectful "negroes" and swarthy expressions was a sense of the success of this community, juxtaposed as it was against the failure of so many white people. Colored freed women were, John Poyer contended, "often seen very expensively dressed after the European Fashion, parading the streets, attended by their slaves, with no small dignity."[29]

SO WHO WAS THIS WEALTHY WOMAN navigating this unpredictable world who could bequeath her own mother? Where did she come from? One popular story in Barbados is that Susannah Ostrehan came from Suriname, was born around 1770, and was the illegitimate daughter of a Dutch planter and an unknown woman.[30] But this is incorrect. The Susannah Ostrehan listed as a hotelier in the 1811 census for Suriname was a foreigner in Suriname at the time, and she could not possibly be the woman who died in Barbados in 1809.[31] More likely, that was the Susannah Ostrehan who also ran a hotel in Barbados in 1814 and a hotel in Berbice, who was listed as a slaveholder in the Berbice records in 1817. That individual was almost certainly Susannah's niece, who shared the same name and to whom she bequeathed a slave and £200 in her will.[32] One of the complex issues in untangling the web of Susannah Ostrehan's family is their attachment to the name Ostrehan and to the name Susan/Susannah.

The unusual name of Ostrehan is one of the oldest in Barbadian history with a lineage that stretches back into the seventeenth century. This white family derived their money from planting and from the professions, and throughout the eighteenth century they remained prominent in the Barbadian plantocracy.[33] Given the persistent use of the name Ostrehan among her descendants it is quite likely that Susannah was the daughter of one of the white Ostrehan men, who was likely the owner of her mother, Priscilla. Circumstantial evidence points to Priscilla's original enslavement with the family of Thomas Ostrehan, and Susannah probably purchased her mother from that family. Priscilla also had other children, since Susannah Ostrehan's will indicates two nieces, who were both free women by the time of her death. There are no records to indicate when and how Priscilla's children, including Susannah, were manumitted.

Though it is not known how Susannah Ostrehan came be a free woman, she begins to appear in the records for Barbados toward the end of the 1770s. In the Bridgetown tax assessment for 1779 she was the owner of a house on Back Church Street, taxed at the modest rate of £6 per year. It may not be a coincidence that nearby on the same street were several properties owned by Thomas Ostrehan and his son. "Susey" Ostrehan was also recorded as possessing another, larger house on Reed Street, taxed at £7, 10 shillings.[34] The following year that same property came with a tax assessment of £25, while the Back Church Street property had risen to £10. Such a jump in value would indicate that both properties were extended and enlarged considerably by their enterprising owner. Gradually, throughout the 1780s and 1790s, there were further properties bought and sold. Among the files of indentures and transactions for Grenada in 1799 was one for "Susan" Ostrehan, said to be "formerly of the island of Grenada but now of the island of Barbados," who was conducting business through her attorney. The transaction was for the sale of two lots of land she owned in the capital, St. George's, that had formerly been rented.[35] The buyer was the prominent merchant Alexander Fraser, who was busy buying up land across the Windward Islands.[36] Two prime lots on the seafront at St. George's were a not-to-be-missed opportunity. Whether this transaction was for Susannah Ostrehan or her namesake niece is not clear. Either way, it demonstrates the intercolonial connections.

Fragmentary records from Barbados suggest that Susannah Ostrehan may have progressively bought and manumitted the other members of her family, as she did her mother. A free mulatto woman named Lydia Ostrehan, who was probably a sister, first appears in the baptismal record of the parish of St. Michael in Bridgetown in 1785. On that occasion Lydia Ostrehan was baptizing her two daughters, Susannah and Elizabeth, and five years later, a son William was baptized.[37] While Lydia Ostrehan was a free woman, the children must have remained enslaved, since Elizabeth was manumitted by the elder Susannah Ostrehan on August 19, 1806, and William was manumitted according to a provision of her 1809 will.[38] There is no record of manumission for the child named Susannah, but she is almost certainly the namesake niece who was a beneficiary of the will and the same Susannah Ostrehan who was baptized with a sister named Elizabeth and who later went to Berbice.

Mary (Molly or Polly) Ostrehan was the other niece named in the will; her mother is unknown. She was first listed in the parish of St. Michael at the baptism of her son Henry, said to be the property of Mrs. Penny, who was a daughter of Thomas Ostrehan. She was married to Thomas Woodin Penny, and their firstborn child was called Thomas Ostrehan Penny.[39] In 1792 Mary Ostrehan was a free mulatto who baptized her slaves in St. Michael, and in 1794 she baptized her daughter Susan in the same parish. In addition, in 1793 she was recorded as the joint owner of a slave manumitted through proxies in Grenada, where she was named as "Mary Ostrehan alias Mary Warner." Warner was the married name of Margaret Ostrehan, a sister of Thomas Ostrehan.[40] Mary's son Henry was manumitted by Susannah Ostrehan on August 19, 1806, together with his sister (also named Mary) and his cousin Elizabeth.[41]

Susannah Ostrehan remains perhaps the most enigmatic entrepreneur from this period of Barbadian history.[42] Despite popular opinion, there is only circumstantial evidence that she was a hotelier. Although there are many transactions for slaves that Susannah Ostrehan made in the record, just one reference is said to allude directly to her business. In 1814 Matthew King, a wealthy merchant from Guadeloupe, sold a property in Barbados that he described as being on a street that led "to Susanna [sic] Ostrehan's hotel." But that mention was written five years after she died,[43] and it is most likely that this reference was not to the elder Susannah Ostrehan but to her niece with the same name. There exist only the inventory of her estate and the occasional sales of slaves in the rate books to give any clues to her main occupation.

Susannah Ostrehan owned two very large houses. There had been other houses, such as the large property she owned on Cheapside and several others on Back Church Street, but by the time of her death there were only two named in the will. The largest, which could well have been a hotel, was situated on lively Cumberland Street and valued at £1,750. The other, its exact location unknown, was probably her home and was appraised at £1,100. There were also several smaller properties. She also owned thirteen slaves valued at varying rates, including three highly skilled people priced at over £80 each.[44]

While Susannah Ostrehan's inventory contained much the same things as Rachael Pringle Polgreen's, such as valuable china, mahogany furniture, silver, and the like, there was much more of it. The whole estate ran to several pages and was valued just shy of £4,000. Unlike Rachael Pringle Polgreen, who seems largely to have invested heavily in her main operation, the Royal Naval Hotel, Susannah Ostrehan's inventory suggests that she lived in style, removed from her establishment. If this second property was a hotel it was arguably even more richly appointed, perhaps because there was a greater degree of material wealth in Bridgetown twenty years later or because her establishment was designed for a higher level of client.[45]

Ostrehan's will also contained large bequests to white male friends, including William Willoughby, a local merchant; her doctor, Gibson Beresford; and her executor, Lionel Parks, who each received £100. She also gave £100 to Susannah Collymore, the young daughter of Robert Collymore, a very wealthy white planter, and his free colored wife, Amaryllis. Her close association with this elite family was underscored by the fact that Robert Collymore, like Lionel Parks, was also an executor of her will.[46]

Susannah Ostrehan died childless. In fact there is no evidence that she was ever intimately involved with any man. A lack of direct descendants meant that she bestowed her largesse on her extended family and her friends. Similarly, her mother, Priscilla, who died a year later, bestowed legacies on some of the same people. The real story of Susannah Ostrehan's will, and indeed her mother's will, is what the names of those mentioned can tell us about the women's wider family and their social networks.

Since Susannah had no children, Priscilla's family was carried on through her other children. According to the birth records for Barbados, Lydia Ostrehan had at least three children: Susannah Ostrehan, who left for Berbice and is recorded as owning slaves in that colony after 1816; Elizabeth Ostrehan; and William Ostrehan.[47] Since the Susannah in Berbice seems to also have died childless, and since there are few further records for Elizabeth and William, it is through Mary Ostrehan that Priscilla's line continued. Mary Ostrehan had four children by the time of her aunt Susannah's and her grandmother Priscilla's deaths in 1809 and 1810, respectively. All these children are mentioned in their great-grandmother's and great-aunt's wills. Their surnames indicate that three different men fathered them while their mother was still enslaved, but no concrete records can be found to indicate exactly who these men were. The children were Henry Magee, Mary Ostrehan Brett, Susan Woolsey, and John Woolsey.[48] In both wills, Mary Ostrehan and her children, in particular Mary Ostrehan Brett, are singled out. Both Mary Ostrehan and her daughter would continue to expand the family's economic fortunes, and it was through Mary Ostrehan Brett that the matrilineal legacy of the free colored Ostrehans was carried well into the nineteenth century.

Mary Ostrehan was given £100, a share of the estate, and four slaves in her aunt's will, while her daughter Mary Ostrehan Brett was given £200, three slaves, a share of the estate, jewelry, a gold watch, and other "trinkets." Mary Ostrehan Brett was not only given an equal share of her great-grandmother's will but also named as an executor. Moreover, her daughter Susan Ostrehan Haynes was also mentioned specifically and given a slave called Nancy.[49]

The world of Caribbean female hoteliers is often portrayed as highly competitive: a dog-eat-dog environment ruled by the profit principle in all its unbridled ferocity. An early nineteenth-century Barbadian poem said that "if you go to Nancy Clarke, she'll take you in the dark and give you Aqua Fortes." This refers to a story around the free colored hotelkeeper Nancy Clarke, who was apparently jealous at the good looks of a rival and threw acid in her face, disfiguring her for life. Wyvill, the soldier-visitor, made mention of the attack when he encountered the victim of Nancy Clarke's rage in 1806. A "shocking object," he called her, "extremely handsome, now dreadfully disfigured."[50] This was just the kind of story that he loved. And yet elsewhere, in more thoughtful accounts of hotelkeepers, a different story emerges, much less colorful and dramatic, which points to a mutually supportive world of women. That is the environment reflected in the Ostrehans' wills, which can be further glimpsed in the careful ways that vulnerable women were provided for by the preceding generation.

George Pinckard saw this other side when he visited Barbados around the same time as Wyvill. He remembered the mistress of his hotel, Mary-Bella Green, and recalled the way she treated one of her female slaves, Betsy Lemon, who was described as being "very superior to her degraded station ... of respectable and interesting demeanor and in point of intellect far above her colleagues." Together with "a gentleness of manner and pleasant address," Pinckard thought she possessed "an understanding and ability worthy of respect." He noticed that she was a great support to the house "[as] a barmaid and the leading manager of the family," and was surprised to learn that Mary-Bella Green would not part with Betsy even when offered one hundred guineas for her.[51] Green simply could not countenance her best employee being sold off to a white man. Yet Pinckard toasted her freedom just two months later. "You will recollect the name Betsy Lemon, that respectable mulatto I formerly mentioned," he recalled, "you will [be] pleased to learn that she is released from the toils of slavery and placed in a more independent situation. She has opened a new tavern in Bridgetown where we have taken a party of encouragement and drink to the success of the hostess."[52] Mary-Bella Green not only had offered protection to Betsy Lemon, but she emancipated the woman and possibly helped her get a start in her new "situation." While there is no manumission document for Betsy Lemon, it is possible that Green used the common strategy of giving slaves their freedom by claiming they had provided the money for their own purchase. Indeed, Lemon may have saved the money to buy herself out of slavery, but the collusion of Mary-Bella Green was essential in her becoming an independent woman.

Survival strategies like those witnessed by Pinckard are found also in Susannah Ostrehan's transactions. In 1801 she purchased a mulatto woman named Mary Ann from a merchant in Bridgetown and then promptly signed another deed to declare that the money used for the purchase "was the proper money of the said mulatto woman named Mary Ann." In this way Mary Ann became a free agent, avoiding the hefty manumission fee.[53] Perhaps this was the mechanism used to secure the freedom of her niece Mary Ostrehan, who appears in the St. Michael's baptismal records as a free mulatto in 1792. Between 1801 and 1805 Susannah Ostrehan was recorded in several transactions outside the colony where slave purchases were immediately followed by manumission. Two of these manumissions were secured by selling slaves to residents in Dominica and Berbice, respectively, where the manumission costs were much lower than in Barbados.[54] In an earlier transaction, her niece Mary Ostrehan manumitted Jenny Mingo, a slave whom she owned jointly with two other women, Ann Cook and Mary Best, using the good offices of a local clergyman and a lawyer in Grenada.[55] In 1806 Susannah Ostrehan sought manumission for a woman called Elizabeth Swain Bannister, enlisting the help of a prominent merchant, Captain James White, to whom she had "sold" this woman, who was in fact her niece, in order to secure Elizabeth's manumission in England. This strategy, which involved a high degree of trust between the two parties, was also employed to secure the manumission of her mother, Priscilla, and her nephew William.[56] In 1814 her niece and namesake would make a similar agreement to sell "a mulatto girl slave named Polly" to the merchant Thomas Best, who then secured her manumission in London. It was a common practice. Research has identified forty-seven mariners who were involved in the manumission of some four hundred slaves in the period 1795–1830.[57]

In all the Ostrehan wills, the main beneficiaries were female friends and relatives. Aside from her daughters, granddaughters, great-granddaughters, and Christian Blackman, Priscilla's will gave a legacy to her friend Sabina

Brade. Brade also ran a hotel, like Susannah Ostrehan may well have done.[58] Both women owned large properties on Cumberland Street, and they were neighbors. Sabina Brade was a woman in middle age at the time of Priscilla's death. She is not recorded in the rate books in the eighteenth century. The legacy left to her by the older woman amounted to some furniture and personal items, but Brade certainly needed no money. She already owned property not just on Cumberland but on several other streets, and was well on the way to becoming a hotelier of note.[59] In an 1833 memoir, Sabina Brade was described as "an old fat woman well stricken in years," who provided "great consideration" for her guests.[60] The items bequeathed by her elderly friend point to a world that while violent and capricious—as the story of Nancy Clarke lays bare—was also one of mutual support, a kind of sorority of free colored women who looked out for one another.

Susannah and her mother died in rapid succession, but the family tradition of running hotels continued through Susannah's namesake and through her niece Mary Ostrehan. Inheriting from their forebears, these women were poised to take advantage of the opportunities arising in the British empire after decades of colonial upheaval. The timing was fortuitous.

A NEW WORLD OF OPPORTUNITY OPENED in 1796, when the British took Demerara and its neighbors Essequibo and Berbice from the Dutch. The opportunity was seized upon not just by British speculators but also by savvy free women of color. It was a chance not missed by Susannah Ostrehan's nieces. Leaving for Demerara sometime in the early nineteenth century, Mary Ostrehan was among the first women to take advantage of this wind of change, and she would profit enormously. Mary stayed in Demerara for over twenty years before returning to Barbados shortly before her death. Sometime after 1814, her cousin Susannah Ostrehan would brave the wilds of Berbice and build a profitable business there.[61]

After 1796 Demerara and its tiny neighbors changed. What had been a dangerous backwater filled with squabbling planters, isolated companies of soldiers, and shocking rates of mortality had very rapidly become the going concern for the British in the southern Caribbean.[62] There they found boundless opportunities, kept in check only by the endless tropical jungle and endless tropical diseases. Within ten years of the occupation, British slave traders had dragged fifty thousand slaves to the place, adding to the numbers already there. By the 1820s the slave population would peak at almost ninety thousand.⁶³ All of them worked with little respite in the most appalling conditions the Atlantic world ever produced. The place was venturesome, violent, and wild. In the dying years of the British slave trade the rapid expansion of Demerara and Trinidad (captured from the Spanish in 1797) became a major concern for abolitionists who feared, quite rightly, yet more slave colonies being added to the grim tally.⁶⁴

Demerara and its tiny neighbors sat on the edge of the great South American rainforest. The atmosphere was fetid, frightening, and unforgiving. Over the course of the eighteenth century a thin coastal strip had been cleared which, around the main towns, had been subdivided into fifty- or hundred-acre lots, mostly planted in sugar cane, coffee, and cotton. The rain fell hard and tropical there. Everywhere, water abounded, gathered in mosquito-ridden stagnant pools crawling with malaria or in execrable drainage ditches beside the mud roads. Planters worked desperately to control the water. Sluice gates, dams, dykes, channels, and canals were all built in complex, adjoining systems to try and make the land workable. But it was a thankless and unrelenting task, one that demanded continual construction and maintenance and took many slaves' lives. While hurricanes never came to those shores, the tropical rain and overflowing rivers swept away whole settlements and entire livelihoods. During the eighteenth century many estates were entirely destroyed, leaving the hapless planters and their pitiable slaves nothing to do but start again.⁶⁵

The British allowed the continuance of the local Dutch government and the maintenance of Roman-Dutch law, but in every other respect they quickly came to dominate. By the end of the eighteenth century there was already a sizable proportion—perhaps two-thirds of Demerara's three thousand white residents—that were British. Many of these people had arrived in the colony when the British first tried to occupy the place in 1783 and had stayed. In 1815 they would formally take these colonies over. Aside from the British, there was (even by Caribbean standards) an astonishing array of opportunists and adventurers from other countries, each of them making a living from mercantilism in the capital, Stabroek, or running estates. Recalling the time he lived in Demerara between 1799 and 1806, Henry Bolingbroke wrote, "Destiny . . . heaped together Dutch, Germans, Prussians, Russians, Swedes, Danes, Spaniards, French and Americans" in a strange concoction. But he also remembered the uncompromisingly aggressive and ambitious character of the region. "All national enmity seems to be forgotten," Bolingbroke wrote, "while the pursuits of this motley group are directed unanimously to climbing the ladder of fortune."[66]

Indeed, by the end of the century Demerara and its two neighbors had grown rapidly. Huge merchant companies moved their offices there, and legions of factors, agents, bookkeepers, and managers came with them. Major planting interests included those representing the Douglas family, the Gladstones, the Frasers, and a host of others. But the infrastructure could not keep pace with the explosion, and Demerara groaned under the weight of commerce. New wharves and warehouses were built by Robertson, Sandbach and Parker and other companies that made this frontier their home.[67] Throughout the settlements, produce, stock, and supplies lay in abundance all over the place "as if every road were a wharf,'" while on the banks of the rivers hastily built wooden sidings and piers were constructed in a desperate attempt to keep up with demand. By 1805, up to four hundred ships a year plied the trade to Demerara.[68]

By the time of Mary Ostrehan's arrival, Stabroek had swelled considerably. Within a few years the British would rename it Georgetown after the prince regent. It was a settlement made almost entirely of wood, in varying states of decay, made worse by the foul, unrelenting climate. What once had been the outlying settlements of Newtown or Werk en Rust were absorbed into a town that rapidly spread down the east banks of the Demerara River. There were government offices, a tax office, a customs house, a building for the courts, and a mansion (of sorts) for the governor. There was also a small room attached to the law courts that the Dutch Reformed Church had made into a place of worship. The Dutch shared this space with the Anglicans in alternating and poorly attended services.[69] At the mouth of the river lay Fort William Frederick, which was supposed to protect it all but which was poorly constructed and built so low that at high tide "a frigate might fire directly into it," as one military officer put it, a fact that rendered it virtually useless.[70] Indeed almost the totality of Stabroek was poorly constructed, and not helped by the fact that the shingles and the clapboards rotted easily in the sodden atmosphere. Mahogany and other tropical woods were good for furniture, but jungle wood was not suitable for building, and the residents often had to wait weeks for American timber to arrive. This was especially problematic during the war with France, which at best made merchants nervous, at worst brought total ruin. The main streets were bounded on either side by tidal ditches that frequently overflowed, filling the town with sewage and "filthy drainings."[71] In the wet, tropical conditions the bricks that served to stabilize the main roads were useless at controlling the disease-carrying effluence that ran through the place. Thousands died, of everything from yellow fever to yaws. Unsurprisingly, visitors to Demerara at this time all spoke of rampant alcoholism; it was a place awash with empty bottles, which were so ubiquitous they were "natural to the soil."[72]

As one visitor observed there were no public inns or places to socialize in late eighteenth-century Demerara. The town boasted no taverns, theaters, hotels, or accommodations. Instead visitors who had no official post relied on letters of introduction and hoped to be put up by sympathetic planters. Many of the residents kept hammocks and spare beds for just such a purpose, while others made a small amount of money on the side by providing more formal, if temporary, lodgings.[73] As makeshift as it sounds these were still better circumstances than the military situation: officers were alarmed to discover that the forts that defended the place were rife with malaria and other sickness. One visiting officer managed just three months before he was clutching at life and invalided out of the colony.[74]

The state of entertainment was such that in his six years in the colony, which completely lacked in refinement, Bolingbroke only saw one group of actors—touring players from America. They were, he remarked "in a rude state." Lacking in numbers, they were forced to reproduce only key scenes from Shakespeare in an open-air makeshift theater, which they built themselves from materials they brought with them.[75] The only break in this colonial monotony in the 1790s was a small coffeehouse populated by weary locals and lonely young merchants desperate for conviviality.[76]

Women were in high demand in this society, free women especially. Just ten years before the British occupation there had been only eighty-eight houses in Stabroek, populated by 809 people, but by 1807 there would be 8,500 people in the capital, with more arriving all the time.[77] In all Caribbean societies free women of color made desirable housekeepers for men who could afford them. The men destined to spend years wrestling with the South American frontier were no different. What they wanted was the companionship of women with a level of sophistication beyond that of their slaves, women who might help them find some comfort in that miserable, godforsaken place. Through his English gentleman's eye, Bolingbroke saw intimacy in Demerara as nothing more than a crude commercial transaction. "In these colonies where the population of females is so small and the demand for them so great," he wrote, "the common method of supplying the deficiency is to send orders to Barbados and other fully populated islands for ladies who are always to be procured either by purchase or by inducing those that are free to come and settle."[78] In his misogynistic vision, £100 could buy a white man a woman for life.

The first place for procurement was Barbados, the colony that was more sophisticated than any other in the region. Regarded as the "London of the West Indies," Bridgetown was a known world where many British settlers and merchants had contacts and business already, and they were thus familiar with its enviable abundance of free women of color.[79] Many more, especially soldiers and sailors, would have passed through there, and Bridgetown's charms, not to mention its seedy nightlife, were legendary. But this was no crude trafficking in women's bodies. There were plenty of women who had their own economic strategies in play, and were willing to brave the frontier to find new opportunities on the continent far away from the competition of Barbados. If these women were happy, or at least willing, to provide intimate companionship and facilitate the wheels of domesticity that was well, but it was not their sole or even primary aim. Mary Ostrehan was such a woman—and what better place to build a hotel than in a place without one?

Alongside Mary Ostrehan came a raft of colored women, who appeared at the beginning of the nineteenth century and who needed no procuring. Ann Cook, who had been in business with Mary Ostrehan in 1793, followed her friend down to Demerara, and by 1808 she was listed in the capital as the owner of seven slaves.[80] Rebecca Ritchie also arrived from Barbados and became a very wealthy woman, owning thirty-seven slaves in Demerara and at least one large property. Rebecca Ritchie's daughter Mary Ann was for some years the common-law wife of John Douglas, and Ritchie's well-placed grandson James Douglas would go on to become governor of British Columbia. Also among this first group of women who arrived in South America was Christian Blackman, who had been charged with taking care of Priscilla Ostrehan.[81] And Dorothy Thomas, the wealthiest of them all, arrived from Barbados similarly to set up in the hotel business sometime before 1807.[82]

These were the sort of women Bolingbroke observed at the start of the nineteenth century. Although he could not miss their keen entrepreneurialism, Bolingbroke's take on these new arrivals fell into well-worn and arguably spurious tropes, fostered in Georgian England, about free colored women selling off their daughters and younger compatriots to the highest bidder, a kind of blackface version of the bon ton culture of Regency England.[83] "There are colored women residing in Stabroek," he recollected, "who have of late years made a traffic in feminine importation and [who] receive a premium for whatever ladies they introduce."[84] Such male visitors' accounts need to be read with caution.[85] Perhaps there was a trade of sorts, but all these women knew each other, and "feminine importation" could just as well have been a network of persuasion. Women like Mary Ostrehan would have been quick to tell their friends about the opportunities that Demerara held. The presence of many free women of color and the longevity of their relationships with white men indicate that these relationships could be mutually beneficial and successful. While Demerara and Berbice were transient societies that favored the owners of hotels, they could also be places where people could live on the frontier as husband and wife, and raise children who could go to school and inherit wealth.

So many women came to Demerara from Barbados that an area of Georgetown (known under the Dutch as Albinus) became known as Bridgetown because of the large number of Barbadian women who lived there.[86] While many were poor, some women did very well. The Georgetown tax assessment from 1808 lists 275 free people of color in the town who owned slaves; 197 of these people were women.[87] Enterprising from the start, the wealthier women looked for opportunities: hiring out slaves, managing hotels, and running the hucksters who supplied the outlying plantations with much needed goods. The slave ownership of free people of color, as reflected in the slave registers in 1817, shows that they dominated the service industry. Many owned large and complex workforces of slaves who were employed to do a wide range of tasks: these included male carpenters, stevedores, and blacksmiths, not just young women.[88]

With little development in the colony, free colored women had to start from scratch. The money they brought from Barbados and elsewhere must have gone straight into property, buying workers, obtaining wood from American sawmills, and stocking their kitchens. In the first years Mary Ostrehan must have worked hard to turn a profit, investing capital in her operations to a degree that would have carried considerable risk in these contrary, nervous places. While land was cheap, sometimes even free, everything else was not, and residents and visitors alike complained bitterly of the prices.[89] At the same time, Mary Ostrehan's daughter Mary Ostrehan Brett was relied upon in Barbados to manage the family's property there. When her work in Barbados was done, she too followed her mother to Demerara. Meanwhile, the younger Susannah Ostrehan moved from Barbados to Berbice, where she started one of that colony's only two hotels.[90] In 1817 she was listed with ten slaves in the slave register there. She was known to have manumitted several slaves, and she was awarded compensation for eight slaves in 1836.[91]

Berbice was older than Demerara, smaller, and even more isolated and underresourced, which gave even more opportunities to free people of color than its neighbor did. By 1800 free colored people owned a higher proportion of land in that colony than they did in Demerara, and they dominated the militia.[92] That said, it was a wretched place, feared for its high mortality and arguably even more notorious for its violence than Demerara was. In 1762 a terrible slave revolt had rocked the colony, and order was not reestablished for eleven months. Many people were killed, and the memory remained on the minds of residents. When the first British invaders waded through the mud in 1796 to reach the principal hamlet—ambitiously called New Amsterdam by the Dutch—the garrison was so relieved they roasted some beef and hoisted a makeshift Union Jack on the flagstaff, grateful for the reprieve.[93] Just over one hundred properties straddled the Berbice River in the 1790s.[94] The association that ran the place till 1831 would have been pleased at the arrival of the sophisticated women from Barbados.[95]

The younger Susannah Ostrehan staked her future in Berbice, and so too did her sister, Elizabeth Swain Bannister. Bannister arrived with William Fraser, a prominent planter and the owner of the sizable "Goldstone Hall" plantation and several others.[96] She had her own business interests, however, and was independently wealthy, holding a large number of slaves in her own right. By 1822 she was the owner of sixty-six slaves and significant property in her name, even though she continued to live with Fraser. Until her death in 1828 Bannister was also listed prominently in the slave registers for Berbice. Her children, like many other children of free women of color, were sent to Scotland for their education, and when she died she left substantial legacies, including £3,000 to her daughter Jane in Scotland for "her maintenance, education and support."[97]

Within just a few years the social life of both Demerara and Berbice began to change, in some part as the fruit of the endeavors of the free colored frontierswomen. Beginning in the early nineteenth century "subscription" balls were held, and each ticket allowed the man to bring two women. Balls were also held for the garrison, especially for the officers, and for the local militia. When free colored people were allowed into the officer ranks of the militia after 1823, they were then included in the balls. Such events were common throughout the Caribbean and would have benefited both single men and the enterprising colored women who participated in them and organized them. Then there were celebrations: for the feast of St. Andrew, for St. Patrick's Day or St. David's, and even the feast of the nativity was celebrated, although the vast majority of the residents were Protestants. The king's birthday and other royal events were also notable and well-publicized occasions. Even as late as the 1850s visitors were still talking about the drinking that went on and how their time in the colony was marked by it.[98]

Subscription balls were held all over the Atlantic world, and most notoriously in Louisiana. Traditionally thought of as a kind of sexual market perpetrated by mothers and madams, the foundation for this pervasive story has been shown to be a collective narrative based on the reminiscences of white, predominately male travelers, which makes it highly suspect.[99] Balls, dances, feasts, and theater were part of a broad array of entertainments on offer in colonial towns in the Caribbean; the larger the town, the more elaborate and diverse the distractions. Demerara was no exception. By the 1820s not only had hotels been built but Georgetown could also boast of Mary Ostrehan's assembly rooms, a Masonic hall, a library, a proper theater—a far cry from the makeshift stage brought by the Americans twenty years before—and the sizable ballroom at Government House.[100]

As in Barbados, free women of color, women like Mary Ostrehan and her daughter Mary Ostrehan Brett, were a prominent feature of the colony's life and dominated the busy social calendar. The events listed for St. George's Day on April 23, 1823, seemed to have been celebrated with more enthusiasm than normal, according to one old resident. "There was a dinner by the governor at Camp House, a subscription ball at Mrs. Dolly Thomas's in Cumingsburg, a dinner at Miss Rebecca Ritchie's, a subscription Ball at the Royal Hotel Vlissingen and several other parties," he wrote, "but the event of the day was the Ball and supper at Miss Ostrehan's Assembly Rooms given by the Sons of St. George."[101]

Mary Ostrehan's assembly rooms were the toast of the town, and as one resident recalled, they were in "the largest public building in the colony ... in an enviable position."[102] The rooms shone "above them all," another resident remembered, "with a gallery convertible to an orchestra. The room was dedicated to public meetings, national festivities, convivial parties, concerts and exhibitions, [and there was a] ... billiard room in the yard. Here then under one roof the whole concerns of the colony either of business or of pleasure may be carried on with the greatest of convenience." Ostrehan's rooms also served as a post office where business or tenders could be offered, and as a meeting place for ships' captains or the assembling of super cargos back to Britain. "Here, in short, a public life may be led as privately as may be desired," the resident recalled fondly, "and a private one maintained even in the center of publicity."[103]

After two decades in Demerara, Mary Ostrehan made plans to return to Barbados in 1824, selling her large residence in the capital in the process. Described earlier as being in "an airy and pleasant part of Cumingsburg," it was situated in Georgetown's wealthiest neighborhood. While the entry in the *Demerara Gazette* does not give the value, the house was "very commodious and in complete repair, [containing] many rooms and comfortable apartments ... the whole forming an eligible establishment worthy of the notice and attention of a genteel family."[104] She died in Barbados in 1829.[105] Her daughter Mary Ostrehan Brett, who assumed the family business in Demerara, was the main beneficiary of her will, including her largest house and the assembly rooms. Also in the will were sizable amounts of silver and gold in the form of cutlery, jewelry, watches, and trinkets. Mary Ostrehan did not forget her women friends; one beneficiary was her goddaughter Mary Jane, the daughter of the Barbadian hotelier Betsy Lemon, while another was Mary Fullerton, the granddaughter of Dorothy Thomas.[106]

The *Demerara Gazette* has many references to the business dealings of free women of color, which attest to the increasing confidence of this group in public affairs. The women who ran the social calendar kept a tight circle and well remembered each other, and not just in each other's wills. Following the end of the Demerara slave rebellion in 1823, the government of Benjamin d'Urban initiated a clampdown on the good times. Especially targeted were successful free women of color who, like Mary Ostrehan and her daughter, had grown wealthy by providing accommodations, entertainment, and other services in the colony. A tax was to be levied specifically on free women of color, a kind of sumptuary law designed to instill discipline among the population and to reassert authority, which had been sorely tested in the revolt. Many believed that the rebellion that had begun in the east and spread rapidly had been caused not just by proselytizing missionaries but also by a lack of vigilance among the rest of the population.[107] Free women of color, as the organizers of entertainment, were the ones to be targeted. But the women had worked too hard and come too far to let this unjust law stand; they were not going to let a new governor single them out for discrimination. Pooling their ideas, it was decided that the wealthiest free woman of color among them, Dorothy Thomas, who regularly went to England, should go and get the act overturned by the British government. Six months later, she was back and the law was repealed.

The last act of Mary Ostrehan's public life before she passed on her great wealth to her daughter and her granddaughters was to sign her name to a memorial of gratitude to her friend Dorothy Thomas. As reported in the *Demerara Gazette* on October 9, 1824, the memorial read:

> Madam, a few coloured ladies of Georgetown are desirous of presenting you with a pledge of their respect and their esteem and to express the high sense they entertain of your services rendered them in removing an oppressive tax, request your acceptance of a silver cup and waiter valued at fifty guineas as a lasting testament of their gratitude.[108]

Mary Ostrehan, Mary Ostrehan Brett, Rebecca Ritchie, and Christian Blackman signed the notice. Next to their names were those of Elizabeth A. Ross, E. Richards, and Sarah Ann Delph, all wealthy free women, as well as Dorothy E. Coxall, Dorothy Thomas's granddaughter. In her uncharacteristically genteel reply, Dorothy Thomas acknowledged the sorority these women had formed through many decades of working together. She was deeply touched by the response to her "humble exertions," she said, and even "though a memorial were unnecessary for those friends in whose society I have spent the greater and most agreeable part of my life" it was a gesture which was "most gratifying to me, and which I shall always remember with great satisfaction."[109]

CHAPTER FIVE

The Queen of Demerara

MRS. DOROTHY THOMAS

IN THE SPRING OF 1824 Lord Bathurst was surprised to receive a deputation from Demerara, an undistinguished colony on the northern edge of South America. Unannounced, a coach with six iron-gray horses drew up to the modest buildings that served as the office for the secretary of state for war and the colonies, and two liveried footmen jumped down to assist their sole passenger to step into the cool London air. In 1824 the secretary of state for the colonies was busy organizing the affairs of a sizable section of the world, yet this woman was neither awestruck nor trepidatious. She had no appointment to see the colonial secretary, but that was no matter. Dorothy Thomas knew how to make an entrance.

Thomas was an enormous, old woman with an almost totally black complexion, and she wore a colorful turban adorned with ostrich feathers and diamonds, and a heavy necklace of gold Spanish doubloons, while her considerable girth was clothed in a dress made from five-pound notes issued by the Colonial Bank of the West Indies, "ingeniously sewn together."[1] People from all corners of the empire regularly called at the Colonial Office, so the attachés who rushed to meet her were well used to greeting Indian princes, South Sea islanders, Chinese mandarins, and all manner of people. Perhaps they assumed this visitor was an African princess, come to pay her respects. When she confidently asked to speak with the colonial secretary, they found space for her in his schedule. Ushered into his office, the purpose of her visit, Thomas explained, was to lay before Lord Bathurst the unjust action of the Demeraran governor, who had levied a discriminatory tax of ten guilders on free women of color such as herself.

The governor of Demerara was new to the job in 1824, and he was understandably anxious in the role, especially since his predecessor had been undone by a violent and costly slave rebellion the previous year that was only put down with immense brutality.² Worried about the economic damage the rebellion had wrought, the new governor had imposed this tax to raise additional revenue from those who were still prospering in the wake of the revolt. Even before the rebellion the colonial administration had tried to get additional taxes from the free colored cohort by imposing huckster licenses.³ The latest tax had been levied solely on women because free colored men (it was argued) were required to serve in the militia. It was grossly unfair, however, given that the majority of free colored people in Demerara were women, and many had personally lost slaves and other property in the slave rebellion. Dorothy Thomas was one woman who had lost substantial property. Emboldened, she demanded of the colonial secretary that he repeal this unreasonable tax—and he did.

The story of Dorothy Thomas's formidable entrance at the Colonial Office, as later recounted by the U.S. consul to Demerara, is probably apocryphal. There is no record of such a meeting in the Colonial Office archives, and Thomas kept no records because she was illiterate. However, other commentators remembered the visit of Dorothy Thomas to the Colonial Office and remarked upon it. Sometimes these accounts had a slightly different date, or added some nuance to the story of the meeting, but the narrative thrust remained much the same. All the accounts concurred on one thing: Lord Bathurst was so impressed by Dorothy Thomas that he had the noxious law repealed. The most reliable evidence comes from the *Demerara Gazette*, which reported her triumphant return to the colony, where she was fêted and thanked publicly by a number of wealthy free colored women, including Mary Ostrehan Brett and Christian Blackman, who commissioned a silver plate and ewer "in lasting memorial to her efforts."⁴

As this curious vignette suggests, Dorothy Thomas was a woman to be reckoned with: wealthy, imperious, and bold. By the 1830s she was reputed to be one of the richest, if not *the* richest, resident in the colony of Demerara. Visitors to the colony invariably recorded their encounter with "the celebrated Mrs. Thomas" with varying degrees of awe or amusement. She was handsomely compensated following the abolition of slavery in the colony in 1836, and when she died ten years later, aged nearly ninety, she left a considerable estate to be split among her many children and grandchildren. Sadly, the story of Dorothy Thomas had been almost completely lost in the history of Guyana, and this remarkable woman had faded back into the total obscurity from which she sprang.

DOROTHY THOMAS (NÉE KIRWAN) WAS BORN a slave in the Leeward Islands around 1756. She first came to the attention of colonial record keepers in the colony of Dominica in the spring of 1784. The American Revolutionary War had finally ended, and Dominica was booming, with more merchant vessels in the port of Roseau than had visited the island over the previous five years of French occupation.[5] Before the war, Roseau had operated as an entrepôt for a lucrative re-exporting slave trade to Guadeloupe, South Carolina, Virginia, and parts of South America. Although its free-port status had lapsed during the war, cash-strapped merchants were flocking back to the newly restored colony on the heels of the British victory in order to recoup the fortunes that had been lost to war and trade embargoes. That was the reason Joseph Thomas and Alexander Fraser were at the Roseau offices of the prominent merchants Thomas Brayshaw and Charles Bates on July 10, 1784. Fraser was a kinsman of the Baillie family who later moved to Demerara. Thomas was a minor merchant who had associations with John Garraway. Brayshaw and Bates acted as executors of the estate of the late William Foden, and on that day they were responding to an application from a mulatto woman named Dorothy Kirwan to execute a formal deed of freedom in accordance with the intention of Foden's will. Joseph Thomas and Alexander Fraser were witnesses to the deed of manumission.

William Foden had died some eighteen months earlier. He had been a planter and an estate manager on the plantation of the Lancaster merchant William Barrow, and in his will he bequeathed to Dorothy Kirwan his household goods, one-third of all the stock he owned on the Barrow plantation, and a "full discharge of the amount of what ever debt or debts might therefore appear to be due from her." In a hasty codicil, the dying Foden clarified that the bill of sale for the purchase of Dorothy Kirwan had been made in his name, but it was she who had paid him the money for the sale. On looking into the matter, his executors agreed that "the monies paid by the said William Foden ... was the proper money of the said Dorothy Kirwan," and they agreed to "manumit, enfranchise and make free from slavery the said mulatto woman Dorothy Kirwan with her three mustee children William, Charlotte and Nan ... to enjoy all the freedom privileges and immunities normally enjoyed by people of colour made free in the West Indies."[6]

For an enslaved woman to purchase her own freedom and that of her children and then insist on receiving a formal deed of manumission was impressive, and it was apparent to at least one of the four men who signed the document that Dorothy was both a very canny young woman and highly desirable. The late William Foden had been the father of her children William and Charlotte, but it was Joseph Thomas who fathered her baby daughter, the child named Nan in the document but thereafter known as Ann Thomas. Joseph Thomas would become the most significant man in her eventful life, but in 1784 he was just one of several white men Dorothy enlisted in her project to get freed from the dehumanizing indignity of chattel slavery, along with her children, her mother, and at least one sister.[7]

Dorothy was a recent arrival in Dominica, having been brought by Foden from the nearby colony of Montserrat, where she was born. That tiny island was a somewhat aberrant British colony, settled by Irish Catholics and with a landowning elite largely drawn from twelve prominent merchant families, derisively called "the tribes of Galway" by Oliver Cromwell when he deported them to the island in the 1650s.[8] Few of these elite families openly expressed allegiance to the Church of Rome, but they all engaged in the clandestine practice of their Catholic faith. One "tribal" family was the Kirwans, who also had landholdings on Antigua, Nevis, and St. Kitts, with business interests that stretched across the Caribbean.[9] Dorothy was born a slave because her mother was the property of the Kirwan family, and she herself was the property of Andrew Kirwan, who called her "Doll." She was said to be very black in complexion, but was described in official records as mulatto, which tells us she had a white father, who was most likely one of the Kirwan men. A familial relationship is also suggested by the fact she was given the surname Kirwan and was brought up Catholic, a religion to which she adhered for the rest of her life.[10]

By 1780 Dorothy had given birth to at least three children, Elizabeth, Catherina, and Edward, who were, like their mother, Andrew Kirwan's property. In her later life Dorothy was concerned about recording the correct paternal surnames for her children, and those surnames indicate that each of them had a different white father. Elizabeth Kirwan may have been the child of her owner or of another member of the Kirwan family, while circumstantial evidence points to the father of Catherina Cells being a peripatetic planter named John Coesvelt Cells. The father of Edward Iles was Ellis Iles, a planter from a distinguished Montserrat family.[11] At some stage all three children were manumitted, presumably on the payment of their purchase price to Andrew Kirwan. That was the case for "the mestee boy slave called Ned—son of a mulatto slave called Doll Kirwan," who was manumitted by Andrew Kirwan on July 24, 1781, on receipt of forty pounds from Ellis Iles.[12]

Since Edward appears to have stayed with his mother after this transaction, it is a reasonable presumption that Dorothy intervened to have Iles buy the freedom of her youngest child at the same time she arranged for her purchase by William Foden, and that the monies paid by both men actually belonged to her. When she secured the freedom of her two elder daughters is unknown; they were not with her in Dominica. The question remains though: how did she get the money for these purchases, given that she was the property of the Kirwan family and her labor belonged to them? As Andrew Kirwan's kin and possibly the mother of his child, it is unlikely that she was laboring in the fields. Perhaps she was permitted the mobility and independence to sell her person as an enslaved courtesan to the planter class.

The date of the transaction with Ellis Iles is telling. The colony of Montserrat was in desperate straits by the middle of 1781; plantation production was in serious decline because the available arable land had been exhaustively cultivated in the seventeenth century and by the latter half of the eighteenth century the island had entered "the long wind down."[13] But it was the American Revolution that brought the real commercial disaster. Even before the entry of France and Spain into the war, the British embargo on trade with the American colonies had cut off the British Caribbean islands' economic lifeblood, a blow from which they never fully recovered. The planters in the Leeward Islands used all the arable land to grow cash crops with slave labor, while they imported their food provisions from the American colonies, so by 1778 all the islands were facing the specter of famine. On Montserrat about twelve hundred slaves had died from starvation, as had some poorer whites, while the situation on Antigua was even worse. Planters across the islands were terrified of a slave revolt driven by hunger.[14] Compounding this disaster, the most deadly hurricane ever recorded swept through the island chain in mid-October 1780, killing over twenty-five thousand people. On Montserrat as elsewhere it smashed infrastructure and flattened the crops of sugar and coffee, as well as the nutritious plantains on which the people of Montserrat had come to depend. Six months later, waterborne disease and starvation stalked the island, and Montserrat's plantation economy was in total ruin.[15] For those planters and merchants who had the wherewithal, it was time to move.

When Andrew Kirwan entered into the transactions with Ellis Iles and William Foden, he was on the verge of moving to the Dutch possession of Demerara, which had been missed by the force of the hurricane and looked ripe for development. In a place the size of England, there were only a few hundred white settlers, who came from highly diverse backgrounds: Dutch settlers, Sephardic Jews, Huguenot refugees, and Scots and English adventurers. This diversity made Demerara a politically insecure place, poorly defended by the Dutch West India Company and wide open to a British takeover, which occurred in January 1781.[16] This first British occupation was short-lived, ending with the Treaty of Paris in September 1783, but the Kirwans stayed on and were among an increasingly powerful minority of British landowners named by the Dutch authorities in July 1785. Another British planter named in that document was John Coesvelt Cells.[17]

The treaty that ended the American Revolution also restored the imperial balance to the Caribbean, confirming Dominica as a British colony and returning Montserrat and Grenada to the imperial fold. Mercantile activity was frenetic, especially in the re-exporting slave trade out of Dominica (even though Roseau would not regain free-port status for another three years). Between 1784 and 1787 some fifteen thousand slaves, more than half of those imported from Africa, were dispatched on smaller ships that worked the inter-island trade.[18] Doubtless, this inter-island trade was the mercantile activity that engaged Joseph Thomas from Grenada. He owned a quarter of one such trading vessel, the *Mary* out of Lancaster, and the mercantile records list him as resident in Grenada. But, like the merchant Alexander Fraser, he also spent time on St. Kitts, Nevis, and Montserrat, moving between the various islands. He did not enjoy an exclusive relationship with Dorothy. Sometime around 1786, she gave birth to a daughter, whom she later had baptized as Frances Owen(s).[19] The father of this child was most likely Captain John Owens from Barbados, the skipper of the sloop *Nelly*, co-owned by William Barrow, the absentee employer of William Foden. The vessel had been captured by the French on the way to Liverpool in 1781, but it was ransomed and later made several voyages between Liverpool and the Leeward Islands.

By August 1786 Joseph Thomas was again resident in Dominica and had reestablished his intimacy with Dorothy. He was registered as a witness to the manumission of a "negro woman slave Sally" in Dominica on August 28, 1786. The small sum paid to the owner to secure the manumission suggests that this woman was well past her prime, and it is likely that she was a relative of Dorothy, perhaps her grandmother.[20] The manumission was later transcribed into the Grenada deed books, as was the manumission of Dorothy, her three children from Dominica, and Edward Iles in Montserrat.[21] These manumissions were transcribed after Dorothy moved to Grenada in March 1787 in order to clarify their legal status in a new colony. On the first of June that year her daughter Eliza was baptized in the town of St. George's, Grenada, registered in the parish records as the "daughter of Joseph Thomas by Dorothy a free mulattress."[22]

Joseph Thomas was doubtless the reason that Dorothy made the move to Grenada in March 1787. St. George's was declared a free port in that year, and his economic fortunes were definitely on the rise since he and his British partners purchased a second vessel, a sloop called *Jack*, sailing out of Liverpool. To all intents and purposes, he and Dorothy had become husband and wife. It would never have been acceptable for a white man and a recently manumitted free woman of color to publicly exchange vows, but they may well have entered into some kind of marriage contract, such as was prevalent in England before the Marriage Act was introduced in 1753. Grenada did not bring its marriage laws into line with England until the early nineteenth century, and so the Marriage Act did not apply in that colony, but the local House of Assembly did enact an anti-Catholic law in 1789 to legislate that only marriages conducted by the rites of the Church of England were legal. In her later years Dorothy would insist on being called Mrs. Thomas, and she remained focused on the issue of marriage for her children, requiring some kind of marriage contract for her daughters. It makes sense that as a free woman with her own capital she would demand a contractual arrangement that conferred a more respectable status than mere mistress.

The birth of Eliza Thomas was followed by the birth of a son named Joseph in 1789, and in the following year another son, Harry, was born. All three children were properly baptized in the parish church of St. George's with the father named as Joseph Thomas. The baptismal record did not list them as his "natural" children, however, and the mother was recorded as

"Dolly Kirwan, a free mulattress." In writing the document in this way the church scribes recognized that she and Thomas were not married according to the rites of the Church of England. This attitude was not entirely consistent, though, as shown in the belated baptism of Frances Owens in December 1789, where the "infant daughter of Dolly Thomas" was written in the ledger. This suggests that in some circumstances she was accorded the status of wife.

This is not to say that Dorothy was the dependent of Joseph Thomas. They were never married according to English law, so she was free to keep her own surname and, more important, to keep her money and property completely separate from Thomas's. It is unknown which of the couple was the more economically secure at the time she moved to Grenada, but certainly after the resumption of the war with France in 1793 she was doing much better financially than Thomas. It is unclear what the nature of Dorothy's business in Grenada was, but if her later life is any indication, she was involved in huckstering, that is to say she was employing enslaved women to sell merchandise door to door and to outlying plantations. She may have even owned a shop or two in the capital.[23] She owned at least one hotel in St. George's, where her son Edward Iles died in 1792,[24] and presumably she also had an involvement in the provision of housekeeping and sexual services for white men in the colony. In the rare surviving deeds that record her transactions, she signed her name with a cross as Dolly or Dorothy Kirwan, and Joseph Thomas took no role in the transactions. Her economic independence was even more remarkable when one considers her almost continuous state of pregnancy.

Dorothy Thomas was making money after 1793, no doubt about that, whereas Joseph Thomas was losing his. The resumed war with France meant that the inter-island trade in which he was engaged had become an extremely risky business, and in 1794 his ship *Mary* with its cargo was taken as a prize, which would have been a huge economic blow. The Fedon Rebellion of 1795 basically destroyed the plantation economy of Grenada for several years and had a seriously negative impact on Thomas's mercantile activity. Worse came when his other ship, the sloop *Jack*, was sunk off Grenada in 1797.[25] Their last child, Dorothea Christina Thomas, was born on June 26, 1796.[26] After 1797 Joseph Thomas was sporadically recorded as the attorney for various clients, including members of the Philip family, and as selling slaves, which is a sure sign his business had fallen on hard times. Joseph

Thomas disappears from the records after December 1799, and he must have died not long after. In later testimony, Dorothea Christina Thomas said her father died "when she was an infant."[27] There is no evidence of a will, so he probably died intestate.

During the years that Dorothy Thomas was building her business enterprise on Grenada she had not lost sight of her two eldest children, nor her mother and sister. Whether her daughters remained the property of Andrew Kirwan, or where they were located, is unknown, but it is conceivable that they were in Demerara. It can be established that in 1793 her daughter Catherina was living in Demerara as a free woman, married to the planter and long-standing resident D. P. Simon, a Caribbean creole and one of two sons of a planter in Demerara under the Dutch administration. He was possibly of Sephardic Jewish background, and was a neighbor and friend of John Coesvelt Cells, her likely father. Dorothy's daughter Elizabeth Kirwan was also a free woman by 1794, living in Grenada as the common-law wife of John Coxall, the son and heir of the English merchant John Cavalero Coxall. How the manumission of the two daughters was accomplished is a matter for guesswork because there are no extant records for Demerara before 1795, and the Grenada records provide no evidence of the manumission of Elizabeth Kirwan. It is not farfetched to speculate that Dorothy arranged the purchase and subsequent manumission of her elder daughters, because that is what she did for other members of her family.

Over a period of sixteen years, Dorothy Thomas managed to buy freedom for herself, for her children, and for several other members of her family. An insight into her modus operandi can be found in a transaction on December 1, 1794, when she purchased "the mulatto slave Mary Rose" from Benjamin Webster, who was the registrar of the Supreme Court but absent in England, through his lawyer, for the sum of £165. When she sought to manumit Mary Rose, who was said to have "fully repaid" the sum, it was revealed that the lawyer did not have Webster's power of attorney and Mary Rose remained the property of Webster, so another transaction was required where both Webster and Dorothy agreed to the manumission.[28] It is not known who Mary Rose was, but she must have been a close relative, perhaps a sister. Some years later, a free colored woman named Mary Thomas transferred property to Dorothy Thomas's daughter Frances Owens, whom she described in the deed as "her kinswoman."[29]

At some stage Dorothy Thomas purchased her own mother. Like Susannah Ostrehan, she probably felt that having ownership was the best way to ensure her mother's safety. On October 24, 1797, the Grenada deed book recorded that Dorothy Kirwan "in consideration of the faithful services and affection ... by these presents, do enfranchise, manumit and make free my said mother named Betty and she is hereby declared free accordingly."[30] The deed does not indicate when she acquired her mother, and the standard wording of "in consideration of the faithful services" suggests it may have been years earlier. The timing of the manumission was opportunistic: the Grenada House of Assembly was just about to enact legislation to limit manumission by imposing a tax of one hundred pounds, plus an additional annuity of ten pounds a year, for every slave freed.[31]

In 1797 the members of the Grenada Assembly were especially anxious about freed slaves; the colony had just emerged from the brutal and economically catastrophic Fedon Rebellion. On several occasions the governor of Grenada expressed disdain for free women of color, expelling many of them and denying sanctuary to others.[32] A prominent and successful free colored woman, especially one who was the common-law wife of an Englishman, presented a problem for the British community in post-Fedon Grenada. Dorothy Thomas was careful to establish that she was of the English party; she kept her religion to herself and her children were baptized and buried in the Anglican Church. Although her relationship with Joseph Thomas had provided her with immunity from deportation, it may have begun to work against her, since such relationships blurred the racial demarcation now being encouraged.

After Joseph Thomas died, Dorothy found it prudent to leave this maelstrom of heavy-handed, arbitrary reprisal and economic desolation, and to relocate to the more prosperous colony of Barbados and reestablish her business in Bridgetown. But there is no evidence for Dorothy Thomas/Kirwan in Barbados, except the testimony of her daughter Dorothea Christina Thomas that when she was an infant her mother moved the family to that island.[33] Dorothy's eldest daughter, Elizabeth Kirwan, was by that time living comfortably as the common-law wife of John Coxall, while Ann Thomas had become the common-law wife of John Gloster Garraway, arguably even more wealthy than Coxall, and Charlotte Foden had partnered with another merchant, John Fullerton.[34] These couples each had a large number of children, and they stayed together until the death of one or both partners.[35] There is no record of what happened to Dorothy's son William

Foden, but her daughter Frances Owens appears to have stayed on Grenada, where she later transacted business.

Bridgetown was a thriving maritime center, home to the British Caribbean fleet, and an obvious choice for such an entrepreneurial woman now that there was a war with France. Dorothy Thomas had useful connections there, such as Captain John Owens, the likely father of her daughter Frances. Her sister, known as Henrietta Moore, had been living there for over a decade and is listed in the Bridgetown levy books with property on Regent Street. She was described as "a free negro women" in the St. Michael parish registry at the baptism of her daughter Susannah Charlotte on September 10, 1796.[36] Like many free colored entrepreneurs, Dorothy often conducted her business outside the official channels, and her name does not appear in the Barbados records. Almost certainly she was a supplier of accommodations and services to feed the voracious appetite of the British military. But in Bridgetown she was a newcomer in a fiercely competitive environment already dominated by Nancy Clarke, Betsy Lemon, and Suzy Austin.

DOROTHY MUST HAVE BEEN ONE OF the first of the free colored women from Barbados to take advantage of the new frontier that opened in the wake of the British takeover of Demerara. Her daughter Catherina Simon was already established in the colony. By 1802 her daughter Charlotte Foden was also there, living with John Fullerton. Both John and Gavin Fullerton are listed in the *Demerara Gazette* in 1805 as is Gilbert Robertson, who became the partner of Dorothy's daughter Eliza Thomas. Having three daughters and their well-placed partners in the colony provided Dorothy with excellent connections.[37] In 1807 she was listed as running a rooming house or hotel in Werk en Rust on the southern edge of the capital, Georgetown. A notice in the *Demerara Gazette* on October 31 from W. R. Carroll and Son instructed clients to contact them "at the house of Miss Thomas." Her status as the widow of Joseph Thomas was unstable since there were people who knew her from an earlier period in her life. Members of the Kirwan family were still living in Demerara and so was Alexander Fraser, who was a witness to her manumission in Dominica. In another notice placed by one of her guests in the *Demerara Gazette* in 1808, she was named as "Miss D. Kerwan." However, that was the one and only time that name was applied to her. Henceforth she was able to insist on her name being Thomas, and eventually the use of the appellation "Miss" disappeared. There was a sound economic basis to her determination to be known as Mrs. Thomas.

Her son Joseph Thomas Jr. must have been in Demerara for a while, but he died sometime around 1815. He was listed in the *Demerara Gazette* in 1813 as a free colored subscriber to a monument, but then he disappears from the record. His plantation "Kensington" was listed in the *Gazette* in March 1816 as "late the property of Jos. Thomas."[38] The "Kensington" plantation was subsequently known to be the property of Dorothy Thomas and was listed in slave registers for 1820 as being jointly run by Dorothy's daughter Charlotte Fullerton and her son-in-law Gilbert Robertson.[39]

In 1808 Dorothy Thomas paid taxes on sixteen slaves. She also moved to another "dwelling-house" in the new and fashionable area of Cumingsburg on the northern edge of the tiny capital. The move to Cumingsburg indicated she had made a real success in Demerara. This district, recently carved out of the plantation of Thomas Cuming, had become a wealthy area where a number of merchants built grand houses; Dorothy owned several lots there. That she was in the business of supplying accommodations, and much more, was suggested by a runaway notice posted in July 1808 for a "tall, good looking, full breasted Negro girl named Sarah," who took with her "a few articles for sale." Huckstering and the provision of personal services were a key element of Dorothy's business success, as remarked upon in the later recollections of a resident who remembered that Dorothy Thomas had by "huckstering and hiring out negroes, accumulated an immense fortune."[40] Sporadic advertisements in the *Demerara Gazette* draw attention to a range of enterprises: several runaway notices for women, usually described in physical terms such as "yellow-skinned," and notices for the sale of male slave artisans, such as painters and carpenters. There were also notices for the rent of various substantial properties in Georgetown and Cumingsburg and goods for sale at her "dwelling-house." In 1812 she advertised a large three-bedroom house for rent with outbuildings and a "capital store" on the lower ground floor. This may be when she moved into her prestigious house in Robb Street.[41]

Dorothy was certainly well placed to make a successful mercantile business. Through her relationship with Joseph Thomas, she had connections to extensive merchant networks, and she had the three prominent Grenada merchants who were her daughters' husbands. For their part these men would have been very happy that their enterprising "mother-in-law" gave them access to the new South American market. She also appears to have had a familial connection to William King, the son of the prominent London merchant Thomas King. William King's common-law wife, Elizabeth Ashfield, looks to have been a close relative of Dorothy, probably a sister, and their son William was her godson. Dorothy's granddaughter Sarah Fullerton had the middle name King. As well as owning plantations in Demerara, Thomas and William King were slave traders, and they remained Dorothy Thomas's business associates all of her life, named in her 1843 will as the London correspondents who invested her money in "government and other securities" in Britain.[42] Dorothy's mercantile connections in Demerara were given a further boost by the fact that Gilbert Robertson, in a common-law marriage with her daughter Eliza Thomas, was the Demerara agent for the enormously influential company of Robertson, Sandbach and Parker, major players in the trade of the southern Caribbean and well known to Dorothy from her time in Grenada.[43]

Since she was not carrying crippling debt, nor was her enterprise subject to the vagaries of shipping convoys or vulnerable to attack and seizure by French privateers, this free colored woman enjoyed considerable financial advantage over her white sons-in-law. Whereas their mercantile operations were under huge strain during the long war with France and their debt level rose exponentially, her business flourished. Circumstantial evidence points to Dorothy Thomas providing money to support the white men her daughters had married, an ironic reversal of the stereotype of the parasitic free colored concubine. She certainly gave money to her daughters and their families. Her 1843 will, proved in 1846, subtracted the money she had already laid out on Catherina Simon and Eliza Robertson, and neither of them received a further portion.

D. P. Simon was in financial trouble as early as 1794 and by 1804 his plantation "Chance Hall" was sequestered for debt, and his entire estate was sold in 1807.[44] In a long letter to the *Demerara Gazette* he defended himself against a scurrilous attack from another planter, but it lays bare his financial state: "That I have no estate at present is very true; that my estate was sold. . . . I became from that moment the loser of upwards of 20,000. But poverty is no sin."[45] He and Catherina had at least six children to support despite their much-reduced circumstances. Housed in rental accommodations, Simon eked out a living as the official translator for the colony.

Their eldest child, Henrietta, went to private school in England, apparently paid for by her grandmother.[46] Even though Simon was reduced to poverty, Catherina Simon was recorded as dealing in land and slaves in her own right, presumably with the financial backing of her mother, and in 1812 she purchased her own pew in the Anglican church.[47]

D. P. Simon's one-time neighbor Gilbert Robertson, the partner of Catherina's younger half sister Eliza, was another man mired in debt. When he took up with Eliza Thomas, he managed the plantation "Woodlands" for Charles Parker, and he purchased the smaller plantation "L'Amitie en Libertie" nearby. In 1810 Parker expressed deep concern about his kinsman. "I am sorry to say that accounts of Gilbert Robertson . . . are far from flattering," he wrote to his wife. "He is over his head in debt, I see nothing for it but compulsive measures to get what can be got out of his hands." Although Parker was very guarded about the particulars, the subtext of the complaint carries the strong suggestion that Robertson was somehow in financial thrall to a free colored woman.[48] By 1818 Parker had recovered "L'Amitie en Libertie" from his wife's cousin, but it is significant that the deeply indebted Gilbert Robertson came to be listed as a joint owner of the "Kensington" plantation, which adjoined that property, with Dorothy's daughter Charlotte Fullerton, who managed Dorothy's plantation for her. This suggests that Gilbert Robertson and Dorothy Thomas were in business together.[49]

In Grenada Dorothy's sons-in-law fared better for a while because each had inherited a substantial fortune from his father. John Coxall had inherited his father's huge shipyard and mercantile business, so Elizabeth and their six children lived very well. However he and Elizabeth both drowned on a return voyage from Madeira in 1818, and his will bequeathed only a quarter of the business to his "natural children"; the rest of the shipyard and most of the slaves went to his three brothers.[50] While the Coxall orphans drew an income from their quarter share of the profits, they basically became the dependents of their grandmother.

John Gloster Garraway, the partner of Ann Thomas, inherited his father's mercantile empire with his younger brother, Robert Garraway, in 1812. Maybe Robert's dissolute ways brought them undone, or perhaps the business was so debt-encrusted it was not viable. Probably it was a mixture of both, compounded by the damage wrought by years of war. By 1820 John Garraway was in serious financial trouble, and he went to England to fend off his creditors in 1822, to no avail. On December 5, 1824, he lost his entire business and all his Grenada property, signed over to the Bristol and London merchant firms Evan Baillie Sons and Company, Smith Payne and Smith, and Lang Chauncy and Lucas.[51] Garraway returned to his family in Grenada a much-diminished man, reduced to working as an attorney. His massive slave workforce in St. George's was reduced to two or three after 1825. But that was not the end of it. Over the next decade the number of slaves held at the same location grew to around forty, but all of them were listed as the property of his wife, Ann, and were probably paid for by Dorothy.[52] He was able to regain his property on the harbor of St. George's courtesy of his mother-in-law. Dorothy Thomas managed to retrieve Garraway's property by purchasing the indentures from George Smith of London and James Baillie of Bristol.[53]

It was Dorothy, not her white sons-in-law, who paid for the education of their children in Britain. Dorothy fully understood the value of a British education, and by the time she was established in Demerara she had already enrolled her sons at an elite private school, possibly the Inverness Royal Academy, which had by that time several mixed-race students from Demerara.[54] Her youngest daughter, Dorothea Christina Thomas, was at a small Catholic school that was run in Kensington House, then on the outskirts of London, where her eldest granddaughter, Henrietta Simon, was already a pupil.[55]

While Dorothy encouraged her older daughters into successful relationships with prominent merchants who were useful to her business, it was the education she provided for her younger children and her grandchildren that made for her family's most enduring successes. Despite remaining illiterate her whole life, she understood that education was the key to success in the British empire. In sending her children and grandchildren to Britain for an education, she was contributing to a long-established tradition of using education as a route to legitimacy, whether that be social or, as in this case, racial. A good education could be translated into positions of expertise, authority, and legitimacy for her sons and grandsons, while her daughters and granddaughters, once educated to be ladies, made congenial partners for the kind of men with whom Dorothy Thomas sought to do business. She had a clear-eyed understanding that wealth could only take her family so far in a society constructed around white racial supremacy, whereas a good education would secure them a niche in the heart of the empire.

The presence in British schools of mixed-race children, who were then able to use their education to find a place in the geography of polite London society, was the subject of some commentary at the end of the eighteenth century.[56] Edward Long sardonically observed that the many mixed-race children sent to England for their education had given rise to the curious view that "the children born in Jamaica of white parents turn swarthy."[57] Popular novels such as Thackeray's *Vanity Fair* (1847–48) revealed that the English were well aware of the phenomenon of mixed-race children in English schools. Yet it was always assumed that it was their white fathers who had organized and paid the enormous costs required: passage to Britain, school fees, room, and board, all of which were paid from colonial currency converted into the more expensive sterling. No one expected this major financial commitment from the progeny of African slaves.

Dorothy knew plenty of white men who sent their mixed-race children to be educated in Britain, although the process was very discreet and rarely acknowledged, even in private letters. That was the modus operandi for the members of the mercantile company Robertson, Sandbach and Parker.[58] A senior partner, John Robertson of Tobago, paid a Glasgow agent to provide for the board and tutoring of his two mixed-race children, Charles and Daniel Robertson, who were both privately educated in Glasgow.[59] His brother George Robertson had a son (referred to in letters as "Black George") who was educated in London. Charles Parker sired two sons whom he sent home to Scotland in 1791, and Gilbert Robertson sent his firstborn son home to Scotland about 1805. Gilbert Robertson Jr. was educated by his grandfather the Reverend Harry Robertson, the younger son of the chief of clan Robertson of Kindaece, and his great-uncle the Reverend George Rainey.[60]

Discretion was not what Dorothy Thomas cared about in April 1810 when she announced her intention to join a convoy to Britain.[61] Coming along for the ride were some of her Coxall, Garraway, Simon, Robertson, and Fullerton grandchildren, much to the surprise and horror of Charles Parker, who encountered her in Glasgow in August of that year. "Who do you think is in Glasgow but Gilbert Robertson's Mother in Law, Doll Thomas," he wrote to his wife, "with about 19 of her children & grandchildren come home for education."[62] To quietly place one's own mixed-race sons with one's family or a tutor was a tolerable practice in Parker's family, but he did not appreciate Dorothy Thomas's ostentatious flaunting of miscegenation right in his own backyard. There was nothing discreet about her venture to enroll her grandsons at school in Scotland and her granddaughters at Kensington House.[63]

Dorothy Thomas was impressively mobile. Notices for various shipping convoys during the Napoleonic wars indicate that she came and went from Demerara several times, either traveling to Britain to check on her educational investment, or making excursions to Grenada, where she had both family and property. Sometimes she was accompanied by one of her daughters, but always she traveled with enslaved "servants."

By 1816 she was rarely referred to by the diminutive "Doll"; she insisted on being called Dorothy, and on some grander occasions she became Dorothea. The size and status of her hotel in Cumingsburg reflected her enhanced standing. In February 1817 she boasted a restaurant with haute cuisine, having secured the services of "traiteur et Restaurateur" Louis le Plat. A few months later she had an even more exotic offering in the form of a live African lion to amuse her guests. This "strikingly majestic" creature was said to be "perfectly docile and obedient to his keeper, ... will lick his hand and permit him to fondle his paws," and it could be viewed at her establishment, though probably not fondled, for less than a Spanish dollar.[64]

Dorothy Thomas regularly bought and sold property along the waterfront and had interests in plantations in nearby Mahaica and in the colony of Berbice. According to the Demerara slave registers, by 1826 she owned eighty-two slaves, and her daughter Charlotte Fullerton owned another seventeen, most of them coming from her mother.[65] Until the abolition of slavery the number of slaves she owned never fell below eighty, and many of them were urban slaves, including hucksters, housekeepers, seamstresses, nursemaids, boatmen, painters, and carpenters.

Dorothy Thomas was a wealthy woman of no small influence in the colony. Her status was apparent when her slave Sally, who was eight months pregnant, was arrested by four white men of the nightwatch patrol in 1820, supposedly for being out without a pass. When she subsequently died in the stocks at the jail, the men of the nightwatch denied any brutality and the three doctors called to examine the body said they could find no signs of violence. All agreed that Sally had died of a "hysteric fit." But Dorothy Thomas was having none of it; she insisted that she had heard Sally outside her door calling out, "oh my god, you will kill me—I belong Mrs. Thomas, see lookee Missee house," and that the nightwatchers had continued to beat and drag Sally to the jail. It was the word of a free colored woman against that of numerous white men, yet in this matter Thomas prevailed. Other witnesses were found to support her account of a violent assault on Sally, and the four men were convicted at trial and each was given six months' imprisonment.[66]

Thomas was never considered to be an indulgent slave owner; rather, she was known for her firm management of her chattel. There is no evidence that she manumitted any of her slaves, nor did she allow them to buy their freedom. The *Demerara Gazette* regularly featured her runaway notices for hucksters who had absconded, taking her merchandise with them. On February 22, 1823, she offered "a liberal reward" for Princess, who had run away five months earlier, and for Betty Dash, who had run with her infant children two months before. Both women were soon back working for Dorothy as enslaved hucksters, but in 1830 the well-named Betty Dash took off yet again with her children. She had been sent to get payment for dry goods she claimed to have sold, but she did not return, as was her common pattern. She was arrested several weeks later and returned to Dorothy Thomas, who confined her to the stocks she kept in her own house until a purchaser could be found for Betty and the children. Betty was released from the stocks to be sent up to the "Kensington" plantation, but she became "abusive and violent" and was confined once again. This time she managed to break free and run to her white lover, who encouraged her to make a complaint. The protector of slaves wrote up the matter in his report for that year. Betty Dash complained that she had been confined in the stocks for eleven days, which was longer than the period allowed. The protector heard evidence from several slave witnesses, including Princess, that Betty Dash was a persistent runaway who owed a great deal of money. They said they never saw their mistress mistreat her and that she was only confined in the stocks by one leg. Dorothy Thomas wearily explained that since 1823 Betty Dash had repeatedly absconded with large amounts of dry goods and that she now owed her mistress over 1,000 florins for stock she had been issued, to which must be added the cost of her recovery and jail fees. While the protector agreed that Betty Dash's behavior was "reprehensible," Thomas was required to pay a fine of 220 guilders, which she promptly did. What subsequently happened to the costly Betty Dash was not explained.[67]

Betty Dash may have been an expensive investment for Thomas, but in the main Thomas made a lot of money by running slaves as hucksters and by hiring slaves out. She was the richest woman in Demerara; several white women were much richer than she was, but they were absentee owners. When compensation was paid after emancipation, she was granted £3,413, the largest sum of money paid to a free colored person in the colony.[68] There were other women of color in the colony who owned slaves and received large sums of money, like her friend Rebecca Ritchie, but no one received as much as Dorothy Thomas did.[69]

Hers was the most prestigious hotel, although she was rivaled by Mary Ostrehan Brett's assembly rooms and Rebecca Ritchie's Royal Hotel, each establishment vying to give the most elaborate subscription dinners or balls on the annual celebration of the king's birthday.[70] Her flamboyance and prominence caught the eye of nearly every visitor to the colony. A visiting American army officer remembered "the celebrated Mrs. Thomas, the free negress," who "had a water-cistern capable of holding 5000 or 6000 gallons."[71] She fascinated Marianne Pemberton Holmes, a white resident of the colony and the wife of the prominent Demerara barrister Joseph Henry Holmes. She observed that "tho' totally illiterate ... she was a very clever woman; she used to have the management of all the grand entertainments."[72] In particular Holmes recalled how Thomas was put in charge of the reception for the newly appointed governor of Barbados, Lord Combermere, in 1819. She was also in the habit of sending expensive gifts to prominent white men in her acquaintance, and Holmes personally knew of "one gentleman she lent £1,000 to for his wedding." She was convinced of the truth of the story that Dorothy Thomas had beguiled the colonial secretary, and she also recalled that on the same trip to London, Thomas had a private meeting with the king, who remembered her fondly from years earlier when she had "danced with him when he was a Reefer."[73]

Matthew Henry Barker, another visitor, hired his slaves from "the well-known Doll Thomas," and he was also fascinated by this woman for whom he felt a grudging admiration, acknowledging that she "was at this time the richest person in the colony." It was a step too far for the condescending Barker to admit that a free colored woman could have become so rich entirely on her own account, so he attributed her success to her being "well provided for" by the white man who had freed her, and he would not pay the compliment of taking her too seriously. In his narrative she was called "Doll" even though he made the point that "she insisted upon being called Mrs. Thomas." Nevertheless he could not help but be impressed, as Holmes had been, that not only had she petitioned the colonial secretary, but she had been honored with a private interview with George IV, of which she was hugely proud. Whenever she felt slighted, he recounted, she would roundly rebuke the offender by exclaiming loudly, "I hab *sit down* wid King George."[74]

The story of Dorothy Thomas's royal audience is probably fanciful, yet it does have some elements of credibility. Not that she would have met King George IV, but she may have met Prince William Henry, the Duke of Clarence, who would later become King William IV. He was "the sailor king" who was once a midshipman in the Caribbean to whom Holmes must have been referring. Dorothy's granddaughter Henrietta Sala had a close connection to William Henry's illegitimate family, the Fitzclarences.[75] It is quite plausible that Dorothy may have danced, or otherwise cavorted, with the prince when he was cutting up during his tour of duty in the Caribbean, given both the young prince's schedule and his dubious (and proven) reputation for licentiousness.[76] Maybe they did renew their acquaintance when Thomas was in London.

If Dorothy did meet the Duke of Clarence, however, it would have been later than 1824, perhaps on one of her other visits to London. She was definitely there a few years later, possibly late in 1829, when she met the celebrated Victorian journalist George Augustus Sala, who wrote about the encounter many years later. He was only a small boy when he came calling with his mother, the flighty theatrical diva Madame Sala, but the memory of "Mrs. Doll Thomas" remained vivid. It was the oddest thing, he thought, that he would be taken to visit a woman who "was herself very nearly black," and who was referred to with contempt by his nurse as "a mulatto woman." He described Thomas as hugely fat and old, dressed in the latest European fashion, with her enormous bulk covered in gold and jewels. He could remember the strength of her voice and that she was followed everywhere by "her sable handmaidens," whom she routinely chastised. "You Tarn Nigger You," she would bellow at some poor woman, imperious to the end. As Sala recalled, she had no shortage of "niggers" to shout at, and "Tarn" was one of her favorite words. He remembered seeing slaves on the steps of the school "with little coloured handkerchiefs tied round their heads," hunched up and shivering, "crying to be sent back to their own country." He understood though that it was not Africa for which they pined, but an even more exotic place on the edge of South America, from where the formidable old woman brought the jars of preserved ginger, yams, and guava jelly that she pressed upon the wide-eyed boy. Thomas also gave him, as a special birthday gift, "a parcel of Guiana peggalls, calabashes, clubs, tomahawks stained with human gore, and poisoned arrows," but Sala was deemed too young to play with such bloodthirsty implements, and they were later sent by his mother, or so he believed, to the British Museum.[77]

As Sala understood it, the fantastical Mrs. Thomas did not own the red brick mansion that served as the Kensington House academy.[78] She stayed there because she was a major benefactor of the institution. Counted among the school's former and present students were several of her daughters and granddaughters. Sala's beautiful mother, Henrietta Catherina Florentina Sala (née Simon), had been one of them, although he withheld that vital piece of information from his readers.[79] He was at the height of an illustrious career when he wrote this piece about his childhood, and he was not about to acknowledge his blood tie to a vulgar, "very nearly black" ex-slave. He did let it slip that his family had financial expectations of this woman. "Was it to myself, or to my brother, or to my mother, that Mrs. Doll Thomas was to leave all her vast wealth?" he pondered in an unguarded moment.[80] His mother was something of a famous musical talent with royal connections, but the reality of their life was a rather sordid struggle to make ends meet. The reason for their visit to Dorothy Thomas was to curry favor. Perhaps, in order to impress her fabulously wealthy grandmother, Henrietta Sala had engineered a meeting with one of her high society patrons, the Duke of Clarence.

By the time these stories about Dorothy Thomas were in circulation, she was enjoying the final act of her life's drama, playing the role of the "Queen of Demerara," always extravagantly dressed and followed around by a slave carrying a box of gold coins, dispensing advice and patronage on the streets of Georgetown.[81] The American consul to Demerara remembered that Dorothy Thomas was not only very wealthy but also highly respected. Although she was totally uneducated, he found her "affable in her address and intelligent in conversation" when she took it upon herself to represent the interests of the free colored community of Demerara. The consul recalled that it was "her custom to make formal calls on all officials and distinguished strangers arriving in the city.... After passing the compliments of the morning, she introduced, very naturally, topics upon commercial affairs and the political state of the country."[82] Dr. William Lloyd, who traveled through Demerara in 1836, on recommendation stayed briefly at her hotel when he arrived in the colony. He called her the "richest woman" and thought she charged "exorbitant fees" for accommodations. He also noted the wharves and other property she owned, from which she made tidy profits, and the workers she had at her beck and call. At the dinner table she kept for distinguished guests, he had an "engaging conversation" with wealthy planters visiting from Berbice.[83] Her networks spread around the southern Caribbean and even into the heart of the empire, where she also had important friends.

Dorothy Thomas was a great survivor. She lived to a ripe old age, outliving most of her children and surviving the terrible yellow fever epidemic of 1837. This outbreak saw 914 burials in Georgetown alone, which may well have included some of her children.[84] She died a decade later, in 1846. Dorothy Thomas, sharp to the end, considered the disposal of her estate to be a matter of the utmost importance. In the preceding five years she had made an extensive will that she modified with three codicils. The first-named executor to the will was "my daughter Ann married to John Garraway of the Island of Grenada"; the others were George Robertson, the free colored son and heir of the merchant George Robertson; John Errol, a planter from Demerara; and Gavin Fullerton, the brother of John Fullerton, who was now a London merchant. Replacement executors for George Robertson were named in two codicils: John Lurie Smith Jr., a wealthy planter who became the advocate general, was in turn replaced by John Kennedy, the administer general of the colony.[85] The names of the witnesses to the mark of Dorothy Thomas, in her will and the various codicils, read like a roll call of influential white men in the colony.

There can be no doubt that Dorothy Thomas was in full possession of her faculties in directing how her considerable estate was to be disposed; her will was a very carefully considered document. In death, as in life, she called the shots. The will suggested that her only surviving children were Catherina, Ann, Harry, and Dorothea Christina. They were not her automatic beneficiaries, however, since Dorothy was determined to deduct the money she had already invested in them and their families. Her daughter Catherina Simon, whom she called "Dolly Simon," whose late husband had been such a disappointment and whose family had required so much financial support, received only some wearing apparel and table linen. The other two daughters fared better. Ann, always described as "married to John Garraway of the Island of Grenada," was entitled to a sixth share of the estate. Dorothea Christina's sixth share was bequeathed directly to her children, but should she be dissatisfied with that arrangement, Dorothy agreed that she could have a share in her own right "after deducting what I have already advanced and paid her," which would leave very little. The other equal shares in the estate went to her son Harry, who also inherited additional houses and water lots, the Coxall grandchildren and great-grandchildren, and the Fullerton grandchildren.

Thomas's grandson Harry Robertson, son of her deceased daughter Eliza, received a lump sum of money but did not receive a share of the estate, since the amount of money already advanced for his maintenance and education in Britain was deemed to be more than equal to Eliza's portion. The Fullerton grandchildren, who may have been living in Britain, received equal shares in the money that William King had invested for her in government bonds and other securities in Britain.[86] However, the Simon grandchildren did not receive a mention, much to the chagrin of her great-grandson George Augustus Sala, who had big expectations and needed the money sorely. "She never left me a penny," he noted bitterly in his memoir, "going back to Demerara in a fit of pique ... and bequeathing all of her money to some twenty-five uncles and aunts I have the honour to possess in that country."[87]

CHAPTER SIX

By Habit and Repute

THE INTIMATE FRONTIER OF EMPIRE

IN AUGUST 1813, Robert Garraway had expectations. His father, the merchant John Garraway of Cadogan Place, Sloane Street, London, had died a few months before, leaving his estate, which included prime property on the harbor of St. George's, Grenada, to Robert and his older brother. Robert Garraway was now able to persuade the beautiful seventeen-year-old Dorothea Christina Thomas that he had good prospects and she should allow him to take her to his bed. To seal the deal he made a legal agreement, with a bond of £2,000, to marry Dorothea Christina according to the rites of the Church of England. Besotted though he was, Garraway was still a lawyer, however, and he included the escape clause that "if he arrives in England before she is 21 the said obligation shall become null and void." In other words, he was only prepared to marry her in the Caribbean, but such a clause probably had no legal status if tested in the courts.[1]

Dorothea Christina was the youngest of Dorothy Thomas's seven daughters. She had just returned to the Caribbean after spending several years at a school in London, where she had learned to sketch and paint, do needlepoint, play piano, keep accounts, and write letters in an elegant hand. She was on her way home to Demerara, where her mother hoped she could find a suitable husband. But when the convoy reached Caribbean waters, Dorothea Christina went to Grenada instead. Her grandmother Betty was there, and so was her older sister Ann, whose husband was John Gloster Garraway, Robert's older brother. Living with her sister and her brother-in-law, it was not long before Dorothea Christina had rashly fallen into the younger brother's embrace. Her journey to Demerara was not resumed. Dorothy Thomas was furious; she had other plans for her accomplished daughter.

Dorothy Thomas had known Robert Garraway for over twenty-five years and had little time for him. His father had been a business associate of Joseph Thomas, and both Robert and his brother had always been closely associated with her family. John Gloster Garraway was a successful merchant who had been living with her daughter Ann for many years. Robert Garraway was in partnership with his brother, but so far had lived a dissolute life, managing affairs for absentee planters and displaying scant evidence of enterprise. He acted for Dorothy's business in Grenada, but that was of small consequence to her. She had no need of a lawyer in her family, especially a dissolute one, and no need for a man who already had a number of children with at least two other women. Doubtless, Dorothy Thomas knew Elizabeth Nunes, with whom Robert Garraway had a child who was baptized on March 17, 1803, and Margaret Campbell, with whom he had at least three more children.[2] There was no way she would agree to let her youngest and most educated daughter squander her beauty and talent on this wastrel. Unfortunately, the formidable Dorothy Thomas, hampered by the limited communications of wartime, was trapped in distant Demerara so there was not much she could do to stop the liaison.

Dorothea Christina Thomas was under no illusion that her mother would give permission for her to marry Robert Garraway; hence the odd contract to marry when she reached her majority. Apparently she did not consider that it was four years away, which was time enough for him to take advantage of her youth and then beat a hasty exit to England. That this inherent flaw in the contract did not cause the intervention of her more worldly sister is revealing. One possible explanation is that in making a promise to marry followed by cohabitation, Robert Garraway was entering into a form of marriage with Dorothea Christina. Ann had a similar kind of marriage with John Gloster Garraway, as Dorothy Thomas probably had with the sisters' father, Joseph Thomas. A marriage of this kind was not blessed by the church but involved formal promises and obligations, the exchange of a ring or token, and most important, public recognition that they were a stable, monogamous, respectable couple, that they were indeed husband and wife. This was a form of marriage still common among the creole community in Grenada, where the Marriage Act that had been introduced in England in 1753 did not apply.[3]

In England, Lord Hardwicke's Marriage Act had finally restricted legal marriage to the ceremony performed by an authorized clergyman according to the rites laid down in the Book of Common Prayer, for everyone except Quakers and Jews. Prior to 1753 a valid marriage could be created by a verbal contract, an exchange of vows by a man and a woman who were over the age of consent. The gift of a ring, or another significant token such as a bent coin or a keepsake, was taken to mean that the contract had been entered into and that the couple was "married in the sight of God." Such a verbal contract, duly performed in the present tense before witnesses and followed by sexual consummation, was recognized as a legal marriage and considered indissoluble. However, in legal matters of property, this kind of contract had no standing and could not confer the rights of a legally constituted church marriage. Thus the husband could not legally exercise rights over the wife's property, and the wife had no dower; she could exercise no claim to a portion of the husband's estate, while their children had no automatic claim as legitimate heirs to his property. The wife was not restrained in any pecuniary interest and was therefore free to make contracts in her own name and run up debts for which her husband, in turn, could not be held responsible. These old marriage customs were persistent and, even in England, forms of irregular marriage were commonplace for another fifty years or more after Hardwicke's act became law. Couples not wanting a public marriage found ways around this law, especially since it did not apply in Scotland, hence the popularity of irregular marriages just across the border in Gretna Green and other Scottish villages.

There is ample evidence from the experience of Dorothy Thomas and her daughters that free colored women in long-term relationships with white men *did* believe they were respectably married, and they behaved accordingly. The most interesting thing suggested by the evidence is that apart from Dorothea Christina, these women generally preferred not to marry "according to the rites of the Church of England" because they wanted to do business, hold property in their own right, own slaves, and keep their money quite independent of their husbands. Dorothy Thomas had very strong views on that particular matter.

A formal marriage, performed according to the rites of the Book of Common Prayer, was of no consequence to Dorothy Thomas. She was, after all, a staunch Catholic. Equally, a church marriage as required by the law of England was probably no great matter for white creole men such as Joseph Thomas and John Gloster Garraway, who had neither the obligation nor the inclination to live in Britain. Such a marriage required a public announcement in the form of published banns, which could be read in England, and they wished to avoid that. While these men lived in Grenada or other

Caribbean colonies, and as long as they remained in stable unions and were careful to acknowledge, baptize, and make provision for their children, their free colored partners could enjoy a respectable status as their wife within their social sphere, even if not at Government House.

Dorothea Christina Thomas was different. She had spent three years in England being trained in the arts of being an English lady, so she wanted the additional promise of a marriage according to the rites of the Church of England, even if her mother would not give permission. Robert Garraway appeared to be offering that security, and she readily dived headlong into a relationship with the man who for all intents and purposes was now her husband. As it transpired, Dorothy Thomas had good reason to be watchful of her daughter and to be concerned for her welfare. Dorothea Christina made bad choices, and Robert Garraway was one of them. It would not be the last time she did as she pleased and earned her mother's disapproval. Dorothea Christina Thomas's troubled marital arrangements eventually became the subject of a landmark legal case in Scotland, which reads like a subplot from a novel by Jane Austen. The details of this case can be found in the National Archives of Scotland and provide an invaluable window on the management of intimate relationships in the British Caribbean prior to the Victorian era. This case offers a rare insight into the strategies employed in a colonial society where powerful conventions rendered an interracial marriage sanctioned by the church out of the question for a white man who needed to maintain his social standing. Unlike the North American colonies, interracial marriage was not illegal in the British Caribbean. But despite the legality of interracial marriage, it was still rare. As a British traveler warned, "It would be considered an indeniable stain in the character of a white man to enter into a matrimonial bondage with one of them [a woman of color]; he would be despised in the community and excluded from all society on that account."[4]

AS HER MOTHER MIGHT HAVE PREDICTED, Dorothea Christina came to appreciate that she had made a "calamitous" error of judgment that day in Grenada when she accepted the promise of marriage from Robert Garraway. Fifteen years later her lawyer attempted to explain her misstep by arguing that "a disagreement with her mother, attended with peculiarly distressing consequences, induced her for a short time when she was very young to connect herself with a person of the name Garraway with whom she had a child."⁵ The child in question was Ann Garraway, the namesake of Dorothea Christina's sister, baptized in January 1816.

In August 1817, Robert Garraway was just about to depart for England when he wrote a will instructing his executors to use his estate for the maintenance of his four "reputed" children, including his "daughter Ann, aged 18 months."⁶ An obvious reading of this action would be that Robert Garraway was taking advantage of his escape clause to get quit of his naïve free colored mistress before he was obliged to formally marry her. The story is easy enough to imagine: a wily white man dupes a young, impressionable free colored woman into being his "wife," only to leave her in the lurch with a child on the eve of her majority. But that was not how the story played out. Robert Garraway had urgent business with his creditors in London in 1817, and in any case he had left it a bit too late to cut and run. Dorothea Christina had already turned twenty-one.

Robert Garraway was not deserting Dorothea Christina because she had long since deserted him, doubtless with her mother's active encouragement. She was not even in Grenada when their daughter Ann was born, having gone to Barbados, the colony where she had grown up. In Barbados her daughter, Ann Garraway, was baptized in the parish of St. Michael, with no father acknowledged.⁷ Before Robert Garraway had left for England, she was back in Demerara with her mother, who assumed responsibility for the care and maintenance of the child. Robert Garraway came back to Grenada early in 1820, but Dorothea Christina never returned to him. In 1822 he died, possibly a suicide.⁸

Dorothea Christina's decisive break with Garraway encouraged Dorothy Thomas to be reconciled with her daughter, and once again she assumed responsibility for securing an appropriate husband for her youngest. In March 1817 Dorothy Thomas and her daughter left Demerara, taking with them two enslaved servants.⁹ Their destination was unstated, but the excursion must have been related to negotiations with a new suitor for Dorothea Christina, a man who resided in Tobago. He was apparently a free man of color, who must have been wealthy and well connected, given that Dorothy encouraged the relationship by offering to provide him a dowry of £5,000 against her daughter's inheritance. Things did not go well. Early in 1819 Dorothea Christina came back to Demerara, alone. Perhaps, in light of her checkered past, the suitor thought the dowry insufficient, or else, as seems more likely, Dorothea Christina had changed her mind. A relationship with "the coloured man" who refused a dowry of £5,000 to marry Dorothea Christina is referred to several times in her subsequent legal case.[10]

Dorothy Thomas's wayward youngest daughter was certain to have been the subject of lively gossip around the Windward Islands. Major John Gordon, a Scot in the Queen's Royal Regiment of Foot, may have heard something of the scandal around her when he was stationed in Trinidad, which is just a stone's throw from Tobago. He certainly would have heard all about her after his regiment moved to Demerara in 1818.[11] All the officers knew Dorothy Thomas; her hotel in Robb Street was a popular venue for regimental dinners and many other functions in their social calendar. Also, as other visiting soldiers observed, Thomas was the supplier of slaves for their households.[12]

Major Gordon came to Demerara as a widower, having lost his second wife in Trinidad the previous year. According to regimental history, two hundred officers and men, and half the women and children, died of dysentery and yellow fever within three months of being stationed in Trinidad.[13] Gordon was not a man to be without female companionship, and when Dorothea Christina appeared at her mother's establishment he was smitten. Such was his ardor that he was able to overlook the disturbing evidence that this lovely young woman had "ruined two men before."[14] He was determined to have her. According to Dorothea Christina's later court case, Gordon persuaded her to leave her mother and live with him by making a formal promise that they would be married in a church when he left his regiment; he was due to return home in a year or so. But his career prospects would be harmed, he gave her to understand, if their marriage was made in public and if there was a publication of banns. In March 1819 there was a private ceremony, attended perhaps by Dorothea Christina's sisters Eliza and Charlotte and their husbands, all of whom were living in the former Dutch colony. At this occasion, Gordon "put a ring upon her finger," declaring it as "a pledge of their permanent union." This was all that was needed to be legally married in Demerara, as her counsel later pointed out. The ceremony with witnesses and a ring were "facts sufficient in Dutch law to establish marriage in that country."[15] In Demerara, despite the British takeover, Dutch law still mattered.

Gordon may not have wanted his fellow officers to know that he had made a formal matrimonial pledge to Dorothea Christina, but he was not concerned to keep her out of sight. According to her later testimony, she took the name Mrs. Gordon and was seen on his arm on social occasions, while he openly wore the gold watch and chain she had given him. Of an evening he "rode out with her," which, as she pointed out, was hardly the action of a man engaged in a clandestine affair. She managed his household, stocking it with fine pieces of furniture and silver that belonged to her, as well as supplementing his meager salary with an allowance from her mother. All of Gordon's correspondence, "from an invitation card to the most important matters," even his regimental reports, were penned by Dorothea Christina in her exquisite handwriting. When he was posted home in the spring of 1821 there was no question that Dorothea Christina would go too. Gordon sold the household, including her furniture and silver, to provide the money for her passage on a merchant ship to Glasgow, where a family friend was "engaged to secure lodgings for Mrs. Major Gordon." Their son, Huntly Gordon, was born in Glasgow on August 2, 1821.[16]

A few days after his son's birth, Gordon came up to Scotland from England, where he had been stationed, on a leave of absence. The boarding-house keeper and the servants all agreed that he acknowledged Dorothea Christina as his wife, and when his leave expired they returned to England together. Their son was baptized at the Anglican church at Chester, where his regiment was stationed. Not long afterward, in the summer of 1822, Gordon was posted to Ireland. Before leaving he promised Dorothea Christina he would sell his commission and retire from the military, so she and their son returned to Glasgow and waited for Gordon to secure the sale. It proved problematic. "I can't leave the regiment this summer and go to you," he wrote to her in April 1823, warning that he was "going as close to the wind as I can." Gordon had hoped to get a good price by selling his commission on the open market, but unfortunately his commanding officer had a poor opinion of Gordon and forced his resignation, which meant that Gordon had to accept the regulation price of £3,200 for it. This was much less than he needed to support his current family in the manner he expected, not to mention providing for his two older sons from his previous marriages. Along with that bad news, he included a letter to Dorothea Christina from Dorothy Thomas, which had been sent by way of his regiment. Desperate for money, he now fixed his attention on Thomas. A hefty dowry of £10,000 from her, he argued, would make everything all right.

In June 1823 he wrote that being able to spend only a week with Dorothea Christina was enough to "break my poor heart" and added that while he was in Edinburgh he went looking for houses for them "in case your mother should come down handsomely." A few weeks later his tone had changed, and he found it necessary to remind Dorothea Christina that she was not his legal wife and had no claim on him. Having opened one of the letters from her mother, he was appalled to read that Dorothy Thomas was bringing Ann Garraway, referred to as "that girl," to a school in Britain. "It will be all over if she takes her to Glasgow," he warned, making it clear that if it became known that Dorothea Christina had an illegitimate daughter, he could have nothing more to do with her. Instead, she must get Dorothy Thomas to come to Glasgow alone, he hectored, and Dorothea Christina must persuade her mother "to give you £8,000 down, and leave £2,000 till after her death." If Dorothea Christina could extract that promise, he would "see what can be done." Gordon's letter alternates between affection and threat. "Kiss my darling Huntly," he writes, "and tell him if he is so unfortunate as to lose his father he will have settled on him as soon as I can get it £1500."

Bewildered and distraught, Dorothea Christina appealed to her mother, who remained stubbornly pragmatic, agreeing to put up the same dowry that she had offered once before—£5,000 against her daughter's inheritance—but no more. Gordon was outraged. "I will not take one penny less than the sum I mentioned to you," he wrote on October 6. "Your mother need not sell a house or a slave till the price is good. She can get money from any merchant." He was not asking such a lot, he argued; after all, when Dorothea Christina inherited her full share of her mother's estate, she would be "richer than I ever expect to be in this world." A mother who would not give her daughter money when she could so readily afford it was "less than a brute," he insisted. His friends would never hear of him taking less, he told her. He put the position bluntly: "If I was to marry you, we could not live on our money," and he offered an alternative solution that she and Huntly live by themselves in Glasgow with financial support from her "horrid mother." However, he warned, if Dorothea Christina were to leave Glasgow, as her mother wanted, then "I am done with you."

Despite his threats, Gordon was not able to keep away from Dorothea Christina. During October they were living together in a respectable boardinghouse in Glasgow as Major and Mrs. Gordon. Meanwhile her mother had arrived in Britain to place Ann Garraway in school and to check on her other grandchildren who were living there. Gordon insisted that if Dorothy

Thomas came to Glasgow, he would leave; he would not endure the humiliation of being under the same roof with her. Gordon was clearly afraid of Thomas and deeply resented being in her power. "You always tell me about your famous mother," he wrote. "Do you really think I am afraid of her? I would soon have her put in prison where she would get her heels cooled." For all his bullying and bluster, Gordon stayed put for three weeks after Thomas arrived, sitting with her at table every night as she was waited upon by her enslaved servant.

During this time he pressed his offer that for £10,000 he would enter into a formal marriage to make her daughter "respectable." Dorothy Thomas remained unmoved. Her recalcitrance was not about finances, however. As Gordon later bitterly remonstrated, her refusal to meet his demand was not about money; rather, she did not want her daughter in a legitimate marriage: "She said she did not care for your getting married and that you were not better than your other sisters who are living in a different way." The spin that Gordon put on this comment was that Thomas was a disreputable woman who cared nothing for marital respectability. For her part, Dorothy Thomas took the view that in Demerara and Grenada her daughters *were* respectably married, and at the same time they were financially independent, which was what mattered. She saw no good reason to give a large sum of money to Gordon, but she did agree to give Dorothea Christina a generous allowance. If her daughter and grandson would not come back to Demerara as she had proposed, then she would make sure they could live a decent life in Scotland.

In light of her mother's disapproval, Dorothea Christina was reluctant to continue to live with Gordon, but he was able to overcome her doubts by promising, yet again and still without a dowry, "to solemnise with her a regular marriage as soon as he should be able to get his [eldest] son John off his hands." For the next two years Major and Mrs. Gordon and their son, Huntly, lived as a family in nice lodgings in Edinburgh. They kept a servant, who later gave evidence that "they appeared to be much attached to each other and the child." The evidence of the lodging keeper, servants, and shopkeepers was that Mrs. Gordon met most of the household expenses and they behaved in every way as a married couple. John Gordon's three brothers often dined with them, as did other male friends. Thomas Gordon, one of the brothers, called almost daily and dined alone with Dorothea Christina if his brother was away, "treating her as his near relation." It was noted, however, that on the occasions of big parties with Gordon's friends, she stayed out of sight and that she did not accompany him when he went out to dinner or when he went out of town. Gordon dined out frequently, the witnesses said, and was often absent.

The reason for Gordon's absences became apparent after the summer of 1826, when Dorothea Christina spent a few months at the seaside with their son. In September 1826, he wrote to inform her that he had become acquainted with a widow with an income of £300 a year (broadly the equivalent of interest from a capital sum of £10,000) whom he intended to marry. This and subsequent letters indicate that he still loved Dorothea Christina and did not desire this marriage but could see no other course of action to get an adequate income. "Do for godsake forgive and forget a man who loves you and ever shall continue to do so while in life," he begged her, adding, "I know you would not allow me to be destitute if it were in your power." Once again he impressed on her that they were not married and that she had no claim to make on him, even sending a lawyer to reinforce that idea. A legal document was presented to her on November 29, requiring that she acknowledge they were never properly married and that their son was illegitimate. In return for her signature on this document, Gordon would provide an allowance for the education of their son. No allowance was proposed for her. "Pray what allowance have you had from the two you had before me," he shot back in response to her expression of alarm. "I am ready to pay your expense back to Demerara," he wrote, adding that she would not be "worse off" than when he found her there.

Dorothea Christina was dismayed by these "black settlements," as she called them, and Gordon's lawyer was keen to get her signature. He knew something that Dorothea Christina did not: in Scotland the law was different from that in England, and so Gordon was not automatically free to marry the widow with £300 a year, despite the fact that banns had already been published in the newspaper. In Scottish law, being married by habit and repute had legal standing. Gordon and his lawyer were worried that Dorothea Christina would discover this and take the issue further. Getting her signature on the "black settlements" would free Gordon from his contract with her. Dorothea Christina had been educated in England, so she had no reason to know that the marriage law in Scotland was different. However, she had the sense to make some inquiries of a lawyer, who urged her to apply to the court for a "Declarator of Marriage" on her own behalf and a "Declarator of Legitimacy" on behalf of her son, Huntly. Faced with this unwanted turn of events, Gordon was forced to apply on his own behalf for a "Declarator of Freedom" to disprove his marriage.

Dorothea Christina's case rested on being able to prove her marriage to Gordon "by habit and repute." As the lawyer subsequently laid out in her statement of claim:

> the circumstances of the parties living at bed and board as man and wife, of the wife assuming her husband's name in his presence and with his approbation, still more when so styled by himself, of the existence of children acknowledged by both parties, and of the wife with his approbation and concurrence being permitted to discharge the duties of domestic management which usually fall under her department as one of the heads of the family. When parties live together on such a footing for a length of time and when there is no impediment from relationship or prior marriage, such parties are according to all the authorities of the law of Scotland held to be married just as effectually as if [the] marriage had been regularly solemnised.

He relied upon four legal conditions: A promise of marriage constitutes a marriage if cohabitation follows and cannot be affected by any conditions attached to it. A marriage can be lawfully established by habit and repute. No man can plead turpitude for representing a woman as his wife when he meant to ultimately treat their cohabitation as illicit. And a marriage cannot be dissolved by consent, especially when one party is ignorant of their legal rights.

The subsequent case took several years, first in the Sheriff's Court and then in an appeal to the Court of Sessions. Ultimately, it did not go well for Dorothea Christina. The judge resolved the matter in Gordon's favor on July 8, 1829, and the case set the precedent for what was required in order to prove a marriage "by habit and repute." In his final judgment the chief justice expressed his view that the proof Dorothea Christina produced was insufficient to prove the marriage. "The sort of evidence which we are to look to in cases of this kind is that of the friends, relations, and families of the parties," he argued. "The general reputation among these must be looked to; and if we have it not, there is no grounds for establishing the marriage." Gordon's well-placed friends and family members had sworn that they believed him to be a single man, although Thomas Gordon, who had been so assiduous in his attention to his brother's wife, did not. He was perhaps the only friend Dorothea Christina had in Scotland, but he was not going to give evidence against his brother. Bereft of relatives and friends in Scotland, she was only able to produce as her witnesses some keepers of lodgings, servants, and shopkeepers, who uniformly swore she and Gordon were believed to be married. But evidence from people of their sort carried little weight.

GRIPPING AND HEARTRENDING AS THIS NARRATIVE IS, what is of particular interest is the light it sheds on the marital arrangements of Dorothy Thomas and her daughters and, by extension, on the choices of many other free colored women in long-term relationships with white men in the Caribbean colonies. A key point in Dorothea Christina's case, which was openly acknowledged by Gordon's counsel, was that "the law of marriage in Demerara is precisely similar to the law of marriage as it now exists in Scotland." And that was true for Grenada also. This information casts a different light on Dorothy Thomas's insistence on being called "Mrs." Thomas, something a visiting commentator sought to draw to his reader's attention as if it were a presumptuous affectation on her part.[17] Like most English visitors, his expectation was that the role of a woman of color in the Caribbean colonies was that of mistress, and that such a woman could never aspire to the condition of wife. Yet it is quite apparent that the formidable Dorothy Thomas was not merely the mistress of a white man who had freed her and set her up in life, as the visitor suggested. She may have been the mistress of more than one man when she was a young woman, but the relationship she had with Joseph Thomas endured over a period of fifteen years and looked very much like a marriage.

The familiar trope of the free colored woman casually taken as a mistress and just as easily cast off was invoked by Major John Gordon in his defense to the Glasgow courts. A man in his station in life would never have considered Dorothea Christina as his wife, he argued. Responding to various pieces of evidence she provided to prove their sustained cohabitation, he wrote, "the picture which they exhibit is one over which most men so situated would rather have been disposed to throw a veil." Gordon implied that a daughter of Dorothy Thomas was expected to become a concubine, and he pointed to her sisters as evidence. This was firmly rebutted by Dorothea Christina's lawyer, who insisted that his client's sisters, on the contrary, were "both married."

The two sisters in Demerara were Catherina Simon and Eliza Robertson, who were both in lifelong partnerships with white men. It is unlikely that either couple actually exchanged formal marriage vows, but their relationships readily met the requirements of a common-law marriage. D. P. Simon, Catherina's husband, was possibly of Jewish heritage and came out of a Dutch colonial tradition where marriage across racial lines was commonplace. He and Catherina had six children and were together until his death in 1847. His letters to the *Demerara Gazette* show how proud he was of his children.[18] Gilbert Robertson, the husband of Eliza, was a Scot whose domestic arrangements in Demerara earned the opprobrium of his relatives at home. Charles Parker, who had himself fathered two children in the Caribbean, was most indignant about his cousin's public relationship with a free colored woman in Demerara. He was not just being sardonic when he referred to Dorothy Thomas as "Gilbert Robertson's Mother in Law."[19] After Eliza's death Gilbert Robertson returned to Scotland, where he lived alone until his death in 1840.[20]

Only two sisters in Demerara were mentioned in the court documents, which indicates that by that time her sister Charlotte, who lived with the Scots merchant John Fullerton for two decades, had died. Having made provision for his children, who were all in school in Britain, Fullerton returned to Scotland and settled back in Ayrshire, where in 1827 he married a Scottish woman many years his junior. Dorothea Christina's sister Ann in Grenada had been living with John Gloster Garraway for a quarter century, and she continued to live with him for the rest of their long lives. Ann is consistently referred to as "married to John Garraway of the Island of Grenada" in Dorothy Thomas's will, and it may be that Garraway legally married Ann after the Marriage Act became law in Grenada, especially since his putative mother-in-law had recovered significant parts of his forfeited property.[21]

THE VIEW THAT A FREE COLORED WOMAN could only be the mistress of a white man, which continues to permeate the literature, relies on highly subjective travelers' narratives, rather than on any hard archival evidence. Travelers' accounts are appealing because they combine the credibility of primary sources with highly quotable narratives, and they also save the trouble of hunting through obscure archives to find a more accurate view of social mores. The place that most attracted these prurient scribblers was the long-established colony of Barbados, where it became de rigueur to comment on the predilection of dissolute white planters to set up house with free colored women.[22] The writers of these commentaries often arrived in Barbados primed with salacious expectations about the exotic and morally lax slave colonies.

The much-quoted John Waller was in Barbados for a year in 1807 and later published his experience in an 1820 book, where he laid claim to the high moral ground by exposing the turpitude of creole planters. "The natives cohabit with people of color from a very early age," he wrote, seeking "bare testimony" to the fundamental "immorality which prevails in this respect."[23] While he was resident in the colony, he claimed, a free mulatto woman offered to sell him her quadroon daughter on the condition that he manumit the girl when he left the island. The girl apparently had been left to her mother in her white father's will. Waller did not report whether he agreed to be a party to this manumission strategy, and in relating the event he was appealing to titillating narratives about the sexual mores of slave societies.

It is likely that Waller was drawing on notions about planter sexuality that were circulating in Britain. An English traveler, Thomas Ashe, in his book *Travels in America, Performed in 1806* described the louche world of New Orleans, where free women of color "are interdicted, by custom, from intermarrying with the whites; but they are allowed, by the same authority, to become mistresses of the whites." Desirable free colored women were available as casual mistresses for "the married and unmarried, and nearly to all the strangers who resort to the town." The sexual contract was a commercial transaction in which "mothers always regulate the terms and make the bargain," generally charging fifty dollars a month.[24] This titillating narrative, a staple of travelers' accounts, has been accepted almost without question by generations of historians, but it has now been exposed as a collective myth. A rigorous archival excavation of court records, deeds, wills, probate records, and contemporary newspapers related to 330 interracial couples living between 1780 and 1860 in New Orleans found little historical basis for such a custom. Rather, the evidence reveals that contrary to popular anecdotes, these relationships "look[ed] much more like common law marriages than concubinage."[25]

At a superficial glance the trope of the free colored mistress does seem to sit comfortably on the daughters of Dorothy Thomas, while she could be readily typecast as the venal mother trading her daughters' bodies to white men for money. But that was nothing like the reality of their experience. Of Dorothy Thomas's seven daughters, five had long-lasting, stable, and apparently monogamous relationships that looked like proper marriages. Even the discarded Dorothea Christina had a common-law marriage with John Gordon (although the court in Scotland did not agree), and Gordon would have legally married her but for the inadequate dowry. As it was, she went on to make a respectable marriage to an unnamed merchant in Demerara.[26] Thomas's daughter born in Dominica, Frances Owens, appears not to have formed a domestic partnership nor to have any children. As for the stereotype of the venal mother, in Thomas's case the shoe was usually on the other foot, with the partners of her daughters taking money from her, rather than the other way about.

Of all the women in this book, Rosetta Smith in Trinidad provides the most straightforward case of the free colored mistress, but even her short-lived relationship with British governor Thomas Picton was much more of a domestic and business partnership than a sexual transaction. Unlike George Ricketts, the governor of Barbados and Tobago, who also lived openly with a free colored woman, Thomas Picton was not a married man when Rosetta Smith moved into Government House.[27] It can never be known how their relationship might have progressed had Picton not been recalled to Britain in disgrace. Certainly, he never married and he maintained a business and personal connection with Rosetta Picton, as she called herself, long after he left Trinidad. He was also careful to provide for their children and to see them well placed.[28]

Judith Philip was a legitimate and wealthy young French woman when she became the partner of Edmund Thornton, who was managing an estate on the island of Carriacou, where she lived. There was no way that she would have been content to be the mistress of this Englishman and so ruin her reputation as a respectable, moral woman. She was a devout Catholic who allowed the priest to use her house on Carriacou, and she presided over most of the baptisms, so she was unlikely to be a mistress of an Englishman.[29] We think it is very possible that this couple had a Catholic marriage on Carriacou, conducted discreetly by the local priest, that gave the union legitimacy in both French law and the Catholic Church. Edmund Thornton would have been well aware that a Catholic marriage was not legal in England. Even before the Marriage Act, a clandestine marriage had no standing either in church law or common law. After the British reclaimed Grenada in 1783, a Catholic marriage no longer had any legal standing in that colony either, which obliged some French couples, such as Julien and Marie Rose Fedon, to be married by Anglican clergy to ensure the legitimacy of their children.[30]

Edmund Thornton was never going to submit to remarrying according to Anglican rites, which involved the publication of banns and a public ceremony. The great attraction of a clandestine marriage, as many a well-born gentleman, including the prince of Wales, could attest, was that it was a secret, known only to the participants and the "eyes of God." Regardless of his attachment to Judith Philip, which seems to have been genuine and longstanding, Thornton was an Englishman from a well-connected family who was expected to marry well and within his own social group. In Lancaster his family and associates would never have tolerated a mulatto and Catholic wife, no matter how wealthy she was. For her part, Judith Philip would have understood that she was properly married in the Catholic religion to which she was devoted and therefore not engaging in illicit or immoral behavior. She may even have known that Thornton would ultimately seek to marry again in England, but that any such marriage would never be recognized by the Catholic Church. In a curious reversal of the stereotype, Judith Philip may have considered Thornton's subsequent English wife to be the concubine, while she was the legitimate wife in the eyes of her church, if not in English law.

There is no evidence that Rachael Pringle Polgreen was the mistress of any white man, despite the rich trove of salacious anecdotes about her. Thomas Pringle looks to be an unlikely candidate, and the fact that her business transactions were recorded with the surname Polgreen implies that she had at one time a legitimate husband with that name. She had no partner in evidence when she was the target of George Pinckard's observation that "the hostess of a tavern is usually a black or mulatto woman who has been the enamorata of some Bukra man . . . who now indulges in indolence and the good things in life, grows fat and feels herself to be of importance to society."[31] Of course, Pinckard could just as easily have been directing his disdain toward Susannah Ostrehan. In the cases of both these women, exhaustive research in the Barbados archives has not unearthed any evidence of an intimate domestic relationship with a white man, nor any evidence of a white man dispensing his largesse to them.[32] Paradoxically, the evidence of their wills shows that each woman bequeathed money to white men, and not because of any sexual connection. There is nothing to suggest that these women were anything other than self-made entrepreneurs who by their own wits had pulled themselves out of the bondage and penury that was meant to be the lot of people of African descent in Barbados. Yet even a sensible, humane commentator like Pinckard was unable to see beyond the miscegenation that was coded into the complexions of these women. In his eyes, everything about them was illegitimate: their success, their property, even the right to own their own bodies were to him all dispensed by white men as part of disreputable sexual bargains.

The assumption that free women of color got their wealth and standing from the largesse of white men is deeply ingrained in commentary about the slave colonies of the British Caribbean and has been thoroughly absorbed into the historiography. It is so pervasive that it was our assumption, too, when we began researching this book. We had no reason to doubt Matthew Henry Barker's explanation for the immense fortune of Dorothy Thomas: "She had formerly been a slave herself in Montserrat, but having a liaison with her master, she bore him two daughters (as fine girls as ever), and she was not only emancipated, but well provided for."[33] Barker's story made sense, since Dorothy Thomas's will stated that she was born in Montserrat and her surname had been Kirwan. It was our natural assumption that Dorothy Thomas was emancipated by a Kirwan from Montserrat and that this man had also set her up financially.[34] Little by little, however, our research in archives in unlikely places revealed that this received story did not stand up to scrutiny. It was a huge surprise to discover that Thomas had a much more complex narrative of self-emancipation in which her Montserrat owner, Andrew Kirwan, played no conspicuous part. True, she was freed by her next owner, William Foden, who willed her his household goods, plus one-third of all the cattle that he owned on the plantation he managed in Dominica.[35] But while this generosity might have given her a start at a life of freedom, and perhaps allowed her to secure the freedom of her other children, there was no way this modest bequest set her up to become "the richest resident in Demerara."[36] Her long-time partner, Joseph Thomas, left no will, but it is hard to see that she inherited anything from him, since he was reduced to near penury after 1797.[37]

We can find no real evidence that any of the women examined in this book gained their wealth and their property from a white lover. Amaryllis Collymore, who inherited substantial property from Robert Collymore in Barbados, stands out in the archives as much for being an exception to the rule as for the size of her inherited property. Another woman with a substantial inheritance, who also stands out as something of an exception, is Judith Philip in Grenada. As the legitimate daughter of a French planter, she and her other siblings together inherited his estate. Given the number of siblings, it was a modest inheritance, but she vastly increased it and in turn left it to her children. All the available evidence shows that Edmund Thornton had no financial role in the business dealings that made her such a significant property owner in Grenada and that her considerable wealth was held quite independently of him. Her children with Thornton went on to live comfortable, middle-class lives in England, not because they inherited from their father, but because they were the beneficiaries of their wealthy mother. Thornton may have made a financial settlement on his children before his marriage, but we have no evidence of that, nor were they among the heirs in his will.

Elizabeth Swain Bannister, the niece manumitted by Susannah Ostrehan in Barbados, provides an interesting counterpoint to Judith Philip. She was certainly not the beneficiary of a white father, a man we have not been able to identify. She was not manumitted until 1806, yet within two decades she was an independently wealthy woman. Around 1810 she took up with the planter William Fraser, and they moved to Berbice with their baby son and took over the plantation "Goldstone Hall"; they were also the joint owners of several other plantations. The couple had four children: John, George, Jane, and Elizabeth, although the last child did not survive. Elizabeth Swain Bannister kept her own name in business transactions, and she was listed under that name in the slave registers in 1817 as the owner of thirty slaves, and again in 1822, when the number had increased to sixty-seven as a result of her buying slaves from William Fraser, probably to help him out of his financial difficulties.[38] The source of her wealth is not known, but given her close connections to the Ostrehan family it is possible that she was in business with her sister Susannah Ostrehan.[39]

In 1823 Fraser took his family back to Britain, placing George and John in Paisley Grammar School and Jane at school in Liverpool.[40] But in Britain he was forced to confront the hard reality that his relationship with Elizabeth Swain Bannister was not a legal marriage and his children could be considered illegitimate. He took the unusual step of petitioning the secretary of state for the colonies to have his children declared legitimate so that they could inherit his estate. In making this curious application, Fraser explained to the secretary of state that in remote Berbice he was not able to make a "satisfactory marriage."[41] He was only in his mid-thirties when he made this application, so his petition implies that he had no intention of making a proper marriage in order to provide himself with legitimate heirs. He did return to Berbice, and the scant evidence suggests that Elizabeth Swain Bannister was still living with him when she died in 1828.[42] Her will left property in Berbice, including her many slaves, to her children and included a bequest of £3,000 "to be applied to the maintenance, education and support of my daughter Jane Fraser who is at present at school in Glasgow."[43]

Like John Fullerton, William Fraser returned to Scotland after the death of his long-time partner. Before he left, Fraser undertook to buy a plantation in Suriname for his son George.[44] Arriving back in Scotland early in 1830, he married a nineteen-year-old woman from Munlochy, near Inverness. In Scotland at this time were his children John and Jane Fraser, and also Anna Maria Fraser, his first child from a previous relationship in Barbados, who lived with him and his new wife.[45] When he died in August of that year, his estate was divided between his wife, his sister, and his children. The huge irony is that William Fraser was so debt-ridden that his estate in Berbice was sold for debt and his children inherited very little. In 1834 Anna Maria Fraser wrote to the colonial secretary seeking monetary compensation, stating that "the only money I possessed I laid out in the purchase of a negro slave."[46] John and Jane Fraser went on to lead comfortable lives in Scotland and George Fraser secured his plantation in Suriname because they inherited from their mother, the manumitted slave woman Elizabeth Swain Bannister.

Another variation on the received narrative about interracial coupling and inheritance in the Caribbean can be found in the Garraway family of Grenada. Like many Caribbean merchants, John Garraway went home to England for the last years of life, and he was living alone in London when he died in 1813. His will left the majority of his extensive estate to his two "blood sons" in Grenada: John Gloster Garraway, who married Ann Thomas, and Robert Garraway, who did not marry Dorothea Christina Thomas. The will had other beneficiaries, prominent among them a "free mulatto woman" named Frances, who received £2,000 to be paid immediately, plus half of all his furniture, plate, china, and books for "her faithful service and attendance upon me for the forty years past she lived with me." The other half of Garraway's effects went to his and Frances's three daughters, who also received the residue from the sale of his house and lot in St. George's, plus £5,000 to be equally divided among them.

Ten years after his father's will was proved, John Gloster Garraway was ruined and his brother was dead. In 1824 all the property of the Garraway brothers was sold for debt. Anticipating a forced sale of their assets, John Gloster and Robert Garraway had manumitted several of their long-serving slaves.[47] By 1825 John Gloster Garraway had managed to retain only one or two slaves of his once vast slave property. At the same time there was a marked increase in the number of slaves owned by Frances Garraway, the surviving free colored companion of his father. Many of these slaves had the same names as those originally listed with John Gloster Garraway, and it would appear that she bought some of his original chattel. The same pattern can be seen in the increased slave ownership of his wife, Ann Garraway. The number of slaves held by these two free colored Garraway women continued to increase steadily over the next decade, while John Gloster Garraway's chattel never climbed above five.[48] By the 1840s he had clawed back his social standing, becoming the master of the Chancery Court.[49] John Gloster Garraway would have been encouraged by the success of his free colored son, who had the stellar legal career that Robert Garraway never achieved, a success made possible by an excellent education provided by his free colored grandmother.[50]

Dorothy Thomas was clearly proud that her daughter Ann was married to the master of the Chancery Court, but there was no way she was going to surrender any of her money to this white man. True, she bought Garraway's property from his creditors in 1837, but she was far too canny to hand it back to him. Instead, she gifted the property to her grandson Joseph Garraway, permitting Ann to have the use of the property during her lifetime. The will Thomas so carefully crafted insisted that Ann Garraway could only inherit a share of the estate on "the express condition that such a portion is not to be liable for her husband's debt [nor] yet in anywise subject to his control."

So it was not so farfetched for Major John Gordon to believe that Dorothy Thomas deliberately offered him a lesser dowry because she did not want a legal marriage between him and her daughter. Thomas may have been illiterate, but she understood exactly the property implications of a legal marriage, and she was determined to keep her hard-won wealth in her daughter's hands. The restriction she placed on Ann Garraway's inheritance was also applied to Dorothea Christina, who had married on her return to Demerara, and to her granddaughter Ann Garraway should she marry in the future.[51] In each case, the wording of the will was unambiguous, adding for further clarity, "her receipt alone, not withstanding her marriage, shall be valid to my executors."[52]

CHAPTER SEVEN

Uncertain Prospects
MIXED-RACE DESCENDANTS AT THE HEART OF EMPIRE

JUDITH PHILIP WAS BURIED with her eldest daughter on the steep slope of the Hillsborough public cemetery on the island of Carriacou. It was October 1848. Her funeral was a Catholic ceremony, a simple, somber affair, befitting Judith's last wish that her passing be marked "with as little pomp as possible."[1] Whatever carried off Judith Philip must also have taken the life of her daughter Ann Rachel Thornton, who passed away in Carriacou just three days after her mother, on October 23.[2] The graves of mother and daughter would have been marked with headstones, but nothing ostentatious. Neither grave, however, can be located in the overgrown cemetery today.

Ann Rachel was the third child of Judith Philip and Edmund Thornton to die relatively young. The couple's eldest son, Louis Edmund, had died in London almost twenty years before, and their youngest son, Philip, was also gone.[3] Not too much is known about Louis Edmund Thornton, but he was a merchant like his father, working out of London. There is no evidence that he spent any time in Grenada after his childhood. In 1813 he married Elizabeth Charlotte Western, and they had five children.[4] Philip Thornton was the youngest of the children Judith Philip shared with Edmund Thornton, and he must have been born in London. In 1816 Louis Edmund was recorded arranging a position for his younger brother with Stacey Grimaldi, a noted attorney whose office was in the same building as that of Louis Edmund Thornton and the prominent lawyer James Baillie.[5]

Of all the children Judith Philip had with Thornton, only the daughters, Magdalene and Judith, outlived their mother. Magdalene Thornton, as executor of her sister's estate, would have taken charge of matters to do with the funeral. Magdalene was good like that; she oversaw the legalities of the family's probate and later would make sure that both wills were signed by the governor's secretary and subsequently at the archbishop of Canterbury's office in London.[6] With Ann Rachel's death, she was now the eldest. Judith was born in England and was twenty years younger than Magdalene.[7] Despite their age difference the sisters were devoted to one another. The Thornton children always took care of each other and remained a close-knit family. What was true for the children of Jeanette and Honore Philip was no less true for their grandchildren and great-grandchildren.

With the death of Judith Philip there was now little to keep Magdalene and Judith Thornton on the island where the Philip family had become rich. For many years the only real Philip business on Grenada had been that of their mother, and what remained of the large Philip family was scattered about the southern Caribbean. It is highly likely that the children of François Philip left Grenada for their father's property on St. Lucia. The children of J. B. Louis Philip remained on Trinidad. For Magdalene and Judith Thornton, of all their aunts, uncles, and other family only the children of their aunt Magdalene, the children of their great-uncle François, and the grandchildren of J. B. Louis on Trinidad remained. Michel, Susannah, Honore, Nicholas Regis, and Joachim had all died with no known descendants.

Unsurprisingly, within just four months Magdalene and Judith Thornton were at the government office in St. George's announcing their intention to depart for England. They owned real estate in London, and that was where the children of their late brother Louis Edmund Thornton still lived.[8] The two women placed advertisements announcing their desire to sell, at the earliest convenience, most of the property that they now owned jointly with the children of their late brother. To this end they instructed their executors, the long-time family friends Dr. Duncan Blair and George Abercrombie Mitchell, to begin a wholesale survey and inventory of the same. Nothing was to be missed. Clearly, Judith Philip's surviving daughters did not share the loyalty of their mother and grandparents to the land that was the source of their wealth. In just three pages of indenture, the estate that had been founded by Honore Philip, the French baker, and his ex-slave wife, Jeanette, and so judiciously grown by their daughter Judith would be sold off with only the main property, "Grand Anse," kept "for rents."[9]

By the third generation, Honore Philip's descendants found plantation business squalid, perhaps even dirty. The golden age of Caribbean plantations was well over by 1850, and a deep pall of depression was settling permanently over the once-booming world of slave-grown success.[10] While the

Philip plantations were mainly raising cotton, and so were still profitable, the daughters of Edmund Thornton knew that their prospects were better served in London, a place of opportunity and legitimacy. Judith Thornton had been born in London in 1807, and Magdalene Thornton had spent many years in that city so she knew it well. In the Caribbean these women would always be identified as free colored, defined by their race, whereas in London they might have the opportunity to redefine themselves, now that they had their own money. In London they could become someone else.

That Magdalene and Judith should remake their lives in London was exactly what Ann Rachel Thornton had intended when she had given her "dear sisters" the lion's share of her estate in her will, a document in which she referred directly to their "prospects." Since Ann Rachel's will was written some sixteen years before she died, a concern for the future had obviously been a major preoccupation with Judith Philip's female children. Ann Rachel willed only £500 to the children of her late brother Louis Edmund, and then only "when my sisters can do so without inconveniencing their prospects."[11] When Ann Rachel wrote those words, there may have been some expectation that her younger sisters could still make decent marriages, but by the time she died, her sisters were middle-aged spinsters living on the tiny island of Carriacou, managing plantations and organizing produce for shipment for ever-decreasing returns. As such, their "prospects" were dire. Ann Rachel Thornton's concern for her siblings' future points to an anxiety, not about money—they had plenty of that—but about the thorny issue of their legitimacy and whether they could be accepted in white British society.

The quest for legitimacy and acceptance in the heart of empire is the theme that links many of the mixed-race descendants of the women of our study. In exploring the choices made by the children and grandchildren of the enterprising women in this book, we seek to add to a corpus of studies by scholars such as Daniel Livesay and Nick Draper, as well as the remarkable project headed up by Catherine Hall, that have in different ways contributed to our increasingly complex understanding of the many and various legacies of slavery in Britain.[12] The wealthy London socialite Sarah Hunter Taylor Cathcart and Britain's first colored MP, John Stewart, are just two of the many people who have recently been investigated by researchers.[13]

The overwhelming majority of free people of color remained in the West Indies to seek acceptance there, as Jerome Handler, Arnold Sio, Pedro

Welch, and Melanie Newton, among others, have explored.[14] Most people had neither the money nor the inclination to move to the metropole or seek a career of service in the empire. Many sought sanctuary in the anonymity that their skin color provided in the colony that had been their home for most of their lives. With the abolition of slavery and the rolling back of the ignominious apprenticeship scheme, the racial dynamic of the British Caribbean changed. Without slavery, the divisions between free black and free colored were less pronounced. With a less stark division between the groups, free people of color could be more easily absorbed into the black community.

Many free colored people, whether they remained in the Caribbean or not, lobbied for greater civil rights and access to professional and civil employment. Some of the descendants of the women discussed in this book are part and parcel of this reformist trend. Many returned to the Caribbean after being educated, more often than not, in Scotland. The sons of Judith Philip's brother, for example, would follow this path and return to the Caribbean to fight for equality. In the 1860s one of their descendants would become one of the first mixed-race individuals to be elected to a legislative council, and he eventually became the mayor of Port of Spain.[15] A few doubtless joined in the chorus for civil equality in their respective colonies. Many more, though, simply disappeared from the records.

For others, an acceptance of sorts was found in notoriety. They felt that it was far better to be exotic in London than to be a free colored person in the Caribbean, and it was far easier to operate in London as the supposed child of an Indian princess than as the descendant of a slave. Perhaps that was why, writing in the 1840s, Emily Brontë made her Heathcliff a racially ambiguous figure, sometimes called a "gypsy," as a nod to the roles some were forced to adopt when racial lines hardened in the Victorian era.[16] The great-grandson of Dorothy Thomas, the Victorian journalist and novelist George Augustus Sala, chose to describe his mother as the daughter of "a Brazilian lady from Rio de Janeiro ... [with] some Red Indian blood," while he often described himself as a "gypsy" to elide his own racial heritage and get around the problem that he, like his siblings, was "dark, even to swarthiness."[17] His venomous racist diatribes against people with African heritage, together with his addiction to alcohol, gambling, and flagellation, suggest a deep self-loathing fueled by the denial of self involved in "passing"—that easy euphemism of contemporary language that describes those who hoped to live as whites in a society determined by cruel racism.[18]

Judith Philip's children and grandchildren were among those who sought acceptance through prosperity and respectability in the heart of the empire. In a gradual process of integration, generation to generation, they were able to insert themselves into the middle class and gradually pass as white. In focusing principally on the mixed-race descendants, such as the Thornton children, who went to Britain, this chapter seeks to complement work already done on the "children of uncertain fortune" who continued to live in the Caribbean colonies.[19] Whatever choices these mixed-race children made, their trajectory is an imperial story that reaches from the metropolitan heart of the empire to the frozen wastes of northwestern Canada, from the tropical coasts of Africa to the farthest reach of the Antipodes.

ANN RACHEL THORNTON'S HOPEFUL WORDS about her sisters' prospects belie the difficulties that wealthy free colored women could have in finding suitable partners. This was certainly the case on a quiet island like Carriacou that was well off the beaten track and a place where they knew everybody and everybody knew them. The Thornton girls were rich, but that money was no good to them squirreled away in the city of London or locked up on plantations. Much has been written on the desirability of a quadroon mistress for white men, but for respectable, wealthy women of color who could afford to make their own choices finding an appropriate match was a problem.[20] As long as they stayed in Grenada the pool of possible husbands was very small. Despite concerns for their futures, it may be that the Thornton women thought it better to live an independent life without a husband than to choose badly. Times were hard in the Caribbean, and after the abolition of slavery the big money that had attracted talented and ambitious white men, like their father and grandfather, was no longer available.[21] England could have provided better opportunities, as Ann Rachel clearly believed, but until the death of their powerful mother these women had little money in their own right and had been obliged to stay.

So despite the pain of losing both their mother and beloved sister, Magdalene and Judith Thornton welcomed the opportunity to capitalize on their Grenada inheritance and to quit the colony. They were keen to be away and so were content to let the trusted Blair and Mitchell manage "Grand Anse" for them and line up a buyer for the rest of their mother's estate. Wasting little time, they made a public announcement with details of their intention to leave "for England and there to reside" on July 3, 1849, and soon after the two women took passage to their new home in London.[22]

There is no helpful manifest to tell us where or how they traveled or where they landed, but within months the two sisters were listed as living as "visitors," with their servant Sarah Harwood, at an exclusive lodging house at 14 Bedford Place, one of London's finest streets.[23] Very close to this address was the home of their late brother Louis Edmund Thornton, who had lived at another of middle-class London's fine addresses: 8 Montagu Square was an expensive location in the heart of Marylebone, where their nieces still lived. Living there also was Louis Edmund's widow, Elizabeth, and her sister Mary Western along with their three servants.[24] The Montagu Square residence was a fine home spread over five floors that they probably rented from Lord Portland, whose family owned the area,[25] but whether they owned it or not Louis Edmund must have been quite a success in his short lifetime, and he left his children and wife well provided for. The Thorntons were particularly attracted to this district of the capital, and the whole family in succeeding generations lived in the area. Moreover Bedford Place and Montagu Square were just a stone's throw from Judith Philip's London address at Great Coram Street.

Almost as soon as they arrived, Magdalene Thornton registered the probate for her mother's and her sister's wills at the Prerogative Court of Canterbury, which was then an office in the heart of the city.[26] Both Judith Philip and Ann Rachel Thornton had owned pieces of property across London, and it was a legal necessity for anyone who left more than five pounds and who had property in two parishes in England to have their will read and signed by the court. Once the wills were registered, a family meeting was called to determine what to do with the property in the Caribbean.

By November 1850 the final surveys with the details of the two estates from Blair and Mitchell had arrived, and it was clear that the two executors were having trouble finding buyers for any of it. As a later document made obvious, there was no one in Grenada who wanted the property. With that problem in mind, all the surviving members of the family assembled at the lord mayor's office at Mansion House to put their final seals on yet another document, which they hoped would sell their Caribbean property once and for all.[27] Present at this meeting were Magdalene and Judith Thornton and the children of their dead brother: the twins Jeannette Rose and Ellen Ann, along with Frances Catherine, Magdalene Judith, and the youngest, William Wheeler Thornton. Overseeing the meeting was their attorney, Crawford Davison Kerr of Kensington Gardens, who was one of London's leading lawyers, a board member of the Society of Underwriters for Lloyd's Shipping, and through his property in Demerara probably connected to their grandfather Edmund Thornton.[28] With the early death of his father and now his grandmother, William Wheeler was technically head of the family, but as is clear from the scant surviving documents his aunts still called the shots. Once again, the property was put on the market, with the family and their attorneys managing the sale from London.

At this stage all five of Judith Philip's grandchildren were unmarried, like their newly arrived aunts. The girls, then mostly in their twenties, all lived together at Montagu Square, while William Wheeler Thornton was working as a clerk in the Church of England in the Nottinghamshire village of Beeston, just over a hundred miles from London.[29] All of the Thornton children were well educated, with no expense spared, particularly in the case of William Wheeler, who had more ambitious plans than being a clerk. His first-class education included a degree from Trinity College, Oxford, and a master's degree in divinity, which he completed the year his aunts arrived in the country.[30]

If the family had hoped to be rid of their Caribbean property in 1850, they were disappointed; it would be another five years until the property was sold. In 1855 most of the family gathered again to sign their names to an indenture to appoint yet another attorney. This time they enlisted the help of Edward Francis Parry of Hillsborough in Carriacou to manage the estates until a buyer was found. Jeannette Rose, Frances Catherine, and William Wheeler Thornton put their signatures on the document, which was witnessed by two family servants. All of Judith Philip's grandchildren were there, and this time the new husbands of Ellen Ann and Magdalene Judith featured prominently in the proceedings. Magdalene and Judith Philip signed separately, in the house at Montagu Square where they too now lived, as perhaps befitted their position and their seniority in the family.[31] Given the large amounts of wealth listed in the probate calendar when various family members later died, it appears that this attempt to be rid of their Caribbean past was successful and that sometime after this document was signed their Grenada property was eventually sold, finally closing the chapter on the Caribbean inheritance of Judith Philip.

By this time William Wheeler Thornton was nestled into the Church of England establishment and putting his learning to good use. In 1851 he had been promoted to curate and sent to work at St. George's Church in Benenden, a small village in the heart of the Kent countryside.[32] The local minister, Daniel Boys, was a well-respected member of the church who had been in his position for almost fifty years.[33] Benenden's importance to the church was greater than suggested by the size of the village; the see of the vicar covered a large area of a busy diocese. William Wheeler, aged twenty-eight, married the minister's daughter, the twenty-five-year-old Susannah Catherine Boys, on October 18, 1852; the marriage ceremony was witnessed by William's sister Ellen Ann Thornton and a family friend. Over the next five years the couple would have four children together. The connections between the Thornton and the Boys families were further underscored when, just nine months later, thirty-four-year-old Ellen Ann married Daniel Boys's son Thomas.[34] For the next twenty years Thomas Boys was the Anglican curate at nearby Ivychurch, and the couple lived in the village of New Romney, just a few miles from their in-laws at Benenden.[35]

William Wheeler and Ellen Ann Thornton were not the first of Judith Philip's grandchildren to marry. In 1850 their older sister Magdalene Judith Thornton had married Henry Amedroz, who was, as his father had been before him, a secretary for the navy, working for the first sea lord.[36] Thanks to his position, his family was allowed to live in one of the few exclusive "grace and favour" apartments at Admiralty House.[37] Later, the couple would move to Blandford Square in Marylebone. Their son (also named Henry Amedroz) would become a noted academic whose seven-volume history of the Abbasid caliphate is still on history reading lists.[38]

The strong bonds that kept this family together are evident in the repeated appearances of members of the family at various events in the nineteenth century. The new partners of the Thornton children also took an active part in these events. The witnesses at Ellen Ann's wedding were her twin, Jeannette Rose Thornton, and her new brother-in-law, Henry Amedroz. In 1855, when the Amedrozes' first child was born, William Wheeler Thornton presided over the baptism.[39] Aside from William Wheeler Thornton and Ellen

Ann Boys and their families, the rest of the family lived in London within walking distance of the house on Montagu Square.

What is striking about this family and their maneuverings is just how far and how quickly they became embedded in the English middle class. Their wealth and education bought them an accepted place in middling British society, and two of the siblings married into the heart of the rural Anglican establishment. Far from the Caribbean, this was a staid and genteel world that stuck resolutely to its high church roots against the pressures of the evangelicals. Writing in the 1850s Anthony Trollope, who coincidentally lived almost next door to the Thorntons' property on Great Coram Street, chronicled the fictional town of Barchester to wonderfully describe the world that William Wheeler Thornton and Ellen Ann Boys had embraced by midcentury.[40] In addition to Sunday services, their work would have involved a relentless round of community activities and afternoon teas, unobtrusive pastoral work in a place marked by order, respect, and tradition, enlivened only by the local petty jealousies and intrigues of country living. Magdalene Judith Amedroz, married to a senior government clerk and living under the nose of the admiralty, was never reduced to waiting in the kitchen, hidden from her husband's social world. She was openly accepted as Henry Amedroz's wife and she behaved as such. Aunts Magdalene and Judith Thornton never did marry, but they lived in the style expected of wealthy English spinsters in the busy multicultural capital. Brief mentions of them in the census show two women of sophistication, living out their remaining years surrounded by the trappings of comfortable society, including servants.[41] At least until her death, it was Magdalene Thornton, living in London as a grande dame, rather than the Reverend Thornton, who remained the head of the family, both in private and on official documents.

William Wheeler Thornton was eventually promoted to be the rector of St. John the Evangelist in the quiet Surrey village of Blindley Heath, and in this role he published religious texts.[42] He and his family lived in nearby Godstone along with their three servants and a Swiss governess. With his retirement in 1877 and the death of his wife, William Wheeler moved back to London and took up residence at Montagu Square with his elder sister Jeannette who, in the 1891 census, was listed as the "head" of the family. Into the 1880s and 1890s living with them at this house was their sister Frances and later Ellen Ann Boys who, like her brother, moved back to London following the death of her spouse. The family employed two housemaids and a French cook, Sylvie, whose brother Eugene acted as a footman.[43] The Amedrozes lived for most of their married life in nearby Blandford Square, with their servants and a Swiss butler.[44]

Magdalene Thornton died in Islington in 1857, just two years after the sale of her family's property.[45] Her sister Judith died at her Portland Street address in 1869.[46] No wills have been found for the two women, but it appears from the probate of their nieces and nephew that they bequeathed considerable wealth. When their eldest niece died in 1891, she was worth in present money over £1.8 million.[47] Eight years later, William Wheeler Thornton would pass away worth a similar amount. This was not the kind of wealth one acquired from being a country parson.

How concerned the Thornton family were about their mixed-race heritage is hard to gauge, since we have no letters or diaries to provide insight into their inner lives. It looks like they completely rejected any hint of their Caribbean heritage, and they laundered themselves effectively into a white English world. All of the children and, as far as it can be known, the grandchildren had excellent educations that they used to secure ongoing stability and fortune. William Wheeler Thornton and his sisters were light in color, making assimilation much easier, while their children doubtless passed as white and English.

At first glance it is tempting to see this family as betrayers of their Caribbean roots and of their racial heritage, but that would ignore the weight of their English heritage and the severe limitations operating in the Caribbean, even for such elite people of color. The children of Judith Philip and Edmund Thornton were born into a capricious world that threw up powerful barriers to those who were "illegitimate" and not of the proper skin color. This inheritance was not really qualified by money. Unlike many mixed-race families, Judith Philip's children had plenty of money, ensuring the kind of prosperity that most free colored people could only dream about, but money did not trump race in the Caribbean. Free colored elites had to make a choice. The choice Judith Philip made in Grenada was to not side with the radical republicans, like her brother Joachim, nor to identify with the French party. She could have had the pick of the francophone community as a husband, yet she chose to take up with an English merchant and cleave to the British side. Her choice to have her children educated in England, and to engage effectively in the business life of the city of London, ensured that the great metropolis at the heart of British power would exert a powerful pull on her children.

It is worth considering the very different choices made by Judith Philip's brother J. B. Louis Philip, who moved to Trinidad in the late eighteenth century to take up the offer of free plots of land made by the Spanish government. Within just a few years he had amassed a considerable fortune in plantations and slaves.[48] By the time of his death in the early 1820s, he was one of only a handful of free colored proprietors who could be classed as part of the elite.[49] J. B. Louis chose to send his two sons, Jean-Baptiste and St. Luce, to Britain for their education, where after years of study at Edinburgh University they qualified as doctors.[50] Both sons would eventually inherit the fortune made by their parents, and they received a large compensation payout when slavery ended. While in London, these nephews lived with their aunt Judith at the Great Coram Street address, but unlike their cousins they returned to the Caribbean where Jean-Baptiste especially used his education to advance their sectional interests in the face of white opposition.

In Trinidad Jean-Baptiste Philippe was active in the agitation evolving across the British Caribbean in the early nineteenth century, protesting discrimination and abuse against free people of color. This increasing level of political activity led to commissioners being appointed in 1822 to investigate the injustices and to make recommendations to the British Parliament and the Colonial Assemblies.[51] Jean-Baptiste organized a nonviolent opposition against the governor, Sir Ralph Woodford, in Trinidad and collected signatures for petitions that were sent to England. In 1823, he headed a two-man delegation to London and presented his case directly to the Colonial Office, describing how the British governors from Picton to Woodford abused the civil rights of free colored people in Trinidad. He signed his petition not with his name, but with "A Free Mulatto."[52]

An Address to Lord Bathurst was published by Jean-Baptiste Philippe in 1824 but has come down to us with the more arresting title of *A Free Mulatto*.[53] This small book is probably the most famous early text to come out of Trinidad, and is certainly one of the most important books written by a free colored man during the Age of Revolutions. His manifesto cites all the slights and misfortunes of the free colored slave-owning community in Trinidad and argues for civil equality, particularly in the ownership of private property. His descendant (possibly his nephew) Michel Maxwell Philip would inherit a sense of justice along with the family wealth, which afforded him an expensive education at St. Mary's College and at a university in Scotland. In 1854 he was called to the bar and in 1866 became one of the first men of color to be elected to an imperial legislative council, eventually becoming the solicitor general and mayor of Port of Spain in 1867.[54]

FOR SOME MIXED-RACE PEOPLE with fewer resources at their disposal than the children of Judith Philip or her brother, imperial service was an avenue for those with the right connections. Often, the white fathers bought a commission for their mixed-race sons or otherwise assisted them in gaining a foothold. This was certainly the case for Thomas Picton Jr., the eldest son of Rosetta Smith and the former governor of Trinidad. Although the elder Thomas Picton left the colony in disgrace in 1803, he made provision for his four Trinidadian children: Thomas, Richard, Augusta, and Frederick, leaving each of them £1,000 in his 1815 will.[55] Since Picton left the island never to return, their stigmatized mother raised the children. Rosetta Smith could never count herself among the very wealthy of the island, as J. B. Louis Philip did. She owned land and slaves and was far from poor, but she never had the kind of resources available to the Philips, and her children were not nearly as wealthy as the Philip children. We therefore need to be careful of the epithet "elite." Not all families enjoyed the same levels of influence and wealth.

Augusta Picton remained on Trinidad, but she disappears from the record after inheriting some of her mother's slaves in the 1820s. The last notice for her is in the 1825 register, which indicates her ownership of just two slaves.[56] Frederick Picton cannot be located at all. Thomas and Richard Picton, however, were sent to be educated in Wales at a private school, which was arranged for them by their uncle the Reverend Edward Picton. Richard Picton returned to Trinidad but, like his sister, he disappears from the record at the time of emancipation, after he married into a well-established and affluent white family of French descent. The last entries for him are in the slave registers for 1833, which show him owning land and chattel with his new wife, Maria Pietry.[57] It is probable that Richard Picton died soon after, since it is his wife who is listed as the owner of their three slaves in the later compensation records.[58] Thomas Picton Jr. capitalized on his education as a medical doctor, gaining a post with the Colonial Corps. In 1822 he was sent to the west coast of Africa. Tragically, within just a few months of his first appointment he caught a fever and died somewhere off the coast of Sierra Leone.[59] He was unmarried and had no children.

Had he not died, the colonial service would have been a pathway to legitimacy and success in the empire for Picton, as it was for several other mixed-race sons. Perhaps the most outstanding case was a grandson of Rebecca Ritchie, a close friend of Dorothy Thomas and also a prominent free woman of color in the business and social life of Demerara. Originally from Barbados, Ritchie came to Demerara with her daughter Mary Ann at the end of the eighteenth century. Later, Mary Ann became the common-law wife of the Scottish planter John Douglas, with whom she had several children.[60] When John Douglas decided to return to Scotland to make a legitimate marriage in 1809, he took his three mixed-race children with him. Rather than have them live with his white bride, however, he sent them to board at the Lanark Grammar School. His second son, James Douglas, born in 1803, received further training from a French Huguenot tutor at Chester, England, gaining a language skill that would put him in good stead for his future career.

At age sixteen, his schooling complete, Rebecca Ritchie's grandson James traveled to Canada and gained a junior post with the Northwest Company, a frontier business known for its motley collection of employees and its trade in fur. When that company merged with the Hudson Bay Company, James Douglas quickly moved up the ranks, managing a series of remote fur-trading settlements throughout Canada. He married the half-indigenous daughter of one of the company's senior factors, and by 1840 he was appointed as a chief factor in the company. When Vancouver Island was made a colony, Douglas was one of only a handful of men with the skills and experience necessary for the position of governor. In 1851, Douglas got the job and in 1858, when the British government created the colony of British Columbia, James Douglas became the governor of the greatly enlarged territory. Overseeing a dangerous frontier and managing one of the world's largest gold rushes marked his time as the chief administrator in this difficult and unruly province. Upon his retirement in 1864, for his eminent services Queen Victoria made him a knight commander of the Bath.[61]

To rise from the taint of illegitimacy and mixed-race parentage to be a knighted governor of one of the largest territories in the British empire, largely by his own wits, was an astonishing feat. James Douglas was undeniably a self-made man who felt at home in the empire, and he traveled not only through the Caribbean and the Atlantic world but across the great expanse of North America. Douglas, the son of a white Scottish planter and a mulatto woman from Barbados, had perhaps the most successful career of any mixed-race child from the Caribbean.

Somewhat less distinguished, but still notable, was the career of Dorothy Thomas's last grandchild, Huntly Gordon, the son of her youngest daughter, Dorothea Christina Thomas, and Major John Gordon. He was the child at the heart of the legal battle to determine marriage by habit and repute in Scotland in 1828–29. Since Dorothea Christina never did succeed in having her son declared legitimate, it appears that part of her out-of-court settlement with Gordon was a requirement to relinquish the child to his father's custody and return to her mother in Demerara.[62] Huntly grew up in an elite Scottish household, accepted by his stepmother and stepbrothers as part of the family. He was educated by a tutor, then studied medicine at Edinburgh University, and went on to secure a commission as an assistant surgeon in the Ninety-Fifth Foot, stationed in Ceylon.[63] He had the advantage of elite Scottish connections, but he had no money. Inheriting a tenth share of Dorothy Thomas's considerable estate after her death in August 1846 was the fillip that allowed him to marry Julia Grantham, the daughter of an officer in his regiment, in February 1847. His happiness was short-lived, however. Five years later they were divorced on the grounds of her adultery.[64] A scandal of that kind, in addition to his illegitimacy and his racial heritage, might have been expected to eliminate any hope of advancement, yet Huntly Gordon eventually rose to become the surgeon general of the British army.[65] His promotion was doubtless helped by the prominence of his eldest half brother, who was elevated to the peerage to become Baron Gordon of Drumearn. One of the many ironies of Dorothy Thomas's story is that the Gordon connection, sordid as it was in its particulars, has meant that this ex-slave woman can be found rubbing shoulders with nobility in peerage records.[66]

The wayward and unlucky Dorothea Christina Thomas returned to her mother's sphere of influence in Demerara, where she finally succeeded in making an appropriate match. The indomitable Dorothy Thomas was determined that her daughters and granddaughters should return to the Caribbean, but since the opportunities for free colored men were severely limited there, her university-trained son and grandsons were encouraged to stay in Britain to pursue their professions. Her grandson Gavin Fullerton was an accountant who became a merchant working with his namesake uncle, and he also had a plantation in Berbice. Gavin went to live near his uncle at Kerelaw Castle in Scotland, where he married a white Scottish woman; they had five children. He died in Scotland on June 14, 1894. Henry "Harry" Robertson became a doctor and was listed in the census as an apothecary and general practitioner in London in 1841 and 1851. He married an Englishwoman in 1858 and was recorded in Staffordshire in 1871 and Shrewsbury in 1881. The Coxall grandsons cannot be located.[67] The exception to this trend was the son of Dorothea Christina's daughter Ann in Grenada. Joseph Garraway was the beneficiary of an excellent education in Scotland, where he was trained in law, but unlike his cousins who chose to stay in Britain, Joseph returned to the Caribbean. He had the advantage that his prominent father acknowledged him as a legitimate son, and he had substantial property that had been given to him by his grandmother. Joseph Garraway did very well at the law and in 1836 became one of the first free men of color in the Caribbean to be appointed as a stipendiary magistrate, overseeing the apprenticeship scheme. He was appointed a judge of the Court of Appeal in 1839, and he continued to act as a magistrate until his early death in 1852.[68]

ANOTHER PATH TO ACCEPTANCE within the imperial fold was artistic. Social status was inherently flexible in the bohemian world of the theater, arts, and letters, so one's racial heritage could be subsumed into the exotic persona of the artiste. This was the route taken by the most notable of Dorothy Thomas's many grandchildren, Henrietta Catherina Florentina Simon, who became a celebrated diva on the London stage. She was the daughter of the failed Demerara planter D. P. Simon, the eldest grandchild of Thomas, and the first to be sent to school in London, apparently at her father's instigation. In that sense she was the child least subject to her grandmother's influence, which may explain why she was completely left out of Dorothy Thomas's will.

The rather unreliable memoirs of her son (Thomas's great-grandson), George Augustus Sala, claim that Henrietta Simon was sent to the Kensington House academy when she was very young, traveling to London in the company of a rich merchant-planter, Charles McGarel.[69] A letter from D. P. Simon sent to his daughter in London in 1803 suggests that she was under ten years old. Charles McGarel was a lobbyist on behalf of

Demerara planters, who came from a prominent Catholic family, so he may have had contact with the Kensington House academy, which was a Catholic school. It was originally a school for boys run by the Scottish educator James Elphinstone and then became a Jesuit school run by the French émigré nobleman and cleric Prince Charles Victor de Broglio. Kensington House catered to the children of French aristocrats living in London in exile from the revolution, but it was also popular with Caribbean planters. At the time that Henrietta was there the school was run by the Reverend de Theil and Melchier Strickler. From 1815 to 1825 Kensington House was a Catholic boarding establishment under the proprietorship of Mr. and Mrs. Antonio Salterelli. There is a mysterious period between 1825 and 1830 when no tenant was named in the rate books, and the building was said to be "in private tenure."[70]

Henrietta might have begun her schooling at Kensington, but soon she was a live-in pupil at a school in Marylebone run by the widow of Augustus Sala, an Italian dancer at the King's Theatre who had died in 1800. Augustus Sala had an undistinguished career dancing at the King's Theatre and other London venues with his first wife, who was also Italian, between 1781 and 1790 and then alone till 1798. He was buried on January 8, 1800, at St. Giles in the Field.[71] After her husband's death, Susannah Sala established a well-regarded school in her house in Lissom Street in Marylebone, where her son Augustus John James Sala also taught. In June 1812, when Henrietta was sixteen or seventeen, she married Augustus John James Sala, age twenty-three, probably with a dowry furnished by her grandmother.[72]

The newlyweds moved just around the corner to a house in New Street, to what became an extension of Susannah Sala's school. Henrietta was a talented singer and musician, and she began to teach. According to her own account, between the births of her many children she continued to study music and dance as a pupil of the Italian tenor Diomiro Tramezzani and the celebrated choreographer James Harvey D'Egville, both of whom were engaged at the King's Theatre. She also took lessons with the controversial Italian castrato Giovanni Velluti, who arrived in England in 1825 but was greeted with much distaste. She paid for her lessons with Velluti by teaching at his academy.[73] As befitted the young mother of several children, she performed discreetly at private musical soirees and also gave private lessons to "the first families of the kingdom."[74] Evidence from the memoirs of her son and newspaper reports suggest that these elites included the family of the

Duke of Clarence, the future King William IV. Lady Augusta Fitzclarence, the daughter of William IV, was said to be the godmother of Henrietta's youngest child.[75] Notices of Henrietta's concerts in the London and Brighton newspapers indicate that Queen Adelaide, the wife of William IV, was a patron, and the king may also have been, as was the Duke of Cambridge (the king's brother), the Duchess of Cambridge, and their elder daughter. It seems that Henrietta Sala also taught music to the Duke of Cambridge and his daughters.

Next to nothing is known about Henrietta Sala's husband, but problems with gambling and drinking are suggested in a thinly disguised novel written much later by their youngest son.[76] It was not long before there was trouble in the marriage. With the family in a desperate financial situation, Henrietta Sala was forced onto the public stage in December 1827, taking the role of Countess Almaviva in *The Marriage of Figaro* at Covent Garden. She was introduced to the public in an artfully contrived biographical sketch published in the *Lady's Monthly Museum*, which emphasized her delicacy and ladylike manners. Madame Sala may not have had a great voice, the piece concluded, but she was a welcome addition to the theater. In a world where to be an actress was interchangeable with being a courtesan, a wife and mother such as Henrietta Sala brought "a private respectability," which might help to "redeem the stage from the folly, imprudency and immorality of its professors."[77]

Her theatrical debut was hardly a triumph. The performance of the star diva, Lucia Elizabeth Vestris, drew sharp ridicule and, while the reviewers were respectful about the sweet voice of the new talent—"an Englishwoman of a foreign name"—it was clear that Henrietta Sala was no great opera singer.[78] She was no great paragon of domestic virtue either.[79] Exactly one year after Henrietta Sala first trod the public stage, her youngest son was born. Christened George Augustus Henry Sala, he was subsequently revealed to be the son of his godfather, Captain Henry Fairfield, one of the many louche men who were habitués of the "green rooms" of London theaters.[80] Eight months later the cuckolded and debt-ridden husband of Henrietta, Augustus John James Sala, died. George Augustus Sala is ambiguous about the cause of death, but his novel *The Baddington Peerage* points to suicide. The main character, Philip Leslie, marries a "dark dancing girl" who becomes the mistress of Captain Gervase Falcon. Leslie is ruined by drink and gambling and throws himself into the murky Thames. One might wonder about the parentage of Henrietta's other children, such as Henrietta De Egville Sala, named for the famous choreographer James Harvey D'Egville, with whom she studied dance, and Charles Kerrison Sala, the godson of another of her military admirers, Sir Edward Kerrison. George Augustus Sala's disingenuous homage to his mother refers pointedly to her special relationships with army officers, especially those from the Dragoon guards, and says that she came to be known as the "mother of the guards."[81]

The death of her husband left Henrietta Sala penniless, with no home and six children to support. She soon became a fixture on the London stage, and she lived with her children in various rented rooms in the city. During the winter she rented a house on Manchester Street in Brighton, where she gave music and singing lessons to the children of the elite, returning to London in the late spring for "the season."[82] In her mid-thirties she was a statuesque and beautiful woman with many admirers, one or two of whom could be relied upon to assist with her living costs. As well as performing and giving lessons, she kept a sort of salon, according to the account of her boastful youngest son, that was much frequented by all kinds of gentlemen, especially young military officers, "whom she diligently schooled in that *grande maniere* of which she was the undoubted possessor."[83] One of the more constant of her intimate friends was a Captain Gage, who was such a persistent habitué of the green room of the St. James Theatre that his nickname was "Greengage." Another habitué of the green room was "a very young and eminently handsome man" named Charles Dickens, who also became a friend and admirer of Madame Sala.[84] Dickens wrote the play *The Strange Gentleman* in 1836 in which Henrietta Sala had great success in the role of Julia Dobbs. The production ran for so long that his next libretto, *The Village Coquettes*, also with Madame Sala, had to be postponed till the end of the year.[85] Another risqué comedy written by Dickens, *Is She His Wife?*, was staged at the St. James Theatre from early March 1837 till the end of May, and Madame Sala was much acclaimed in the role of the wife.

Henrietta Sala was a flexible performer, able to act many parts, dance, and sing. When asked to perform a Spanish flamenco she was so impressive that the audience demanded three encores. When she finally left the stage she almost fainted from exhaustion in the wings, only to be caught in the arms of "a lieutenant in a crack regiment" who, as her son remembered, "carried her as though she had been a feather up two flights of stairs to her dressing-room."[86] Sala's mother had "indomitable energy" and such versatility that the manager of the St. James suggested she take the title role in a play called *The Slave*. She declined, of course, "naturally reluctant to assume a part, the costume of which necessitated not only the blacking of the hands and face, but the donning of a full suit of black tights."[87] In addition to her performances at the St. James Theatre and at the Haymarket, Madame Sala was a regular soloist at musical soirees and concerts. Every June there was her annual concert in the Hanover rooms, or at the Quadrant in Regent Street, patronized by the Duchess of Cambridge and her daughter.[88]

It must have been a constant struggle for Henrietta Sala to keep her family from penury. In 1838 she was forty-two years old and needed all her indomitable energy to meet the demands of multiple roles in both the Haymarket and the St. James Theatres from January through June. She was billed to perform in two plays at the St. James in July when she was struck by a virulent strain of smallpox. As a colonial from the Caribbean she did not have any resistance to this terrible disease, and the virus hit her very hard. She recovered, thanks to the attention she received from the medical elite who lived in Brighton, including one of Queen Victoria's own doctors, but was blind for some time and never fully regained her sight.[89] Her face, which was as much her meal ticket as her voice, was horribly pockmarked.

With no way to make money, she was dependent on charity for the next two years. Charles Dickens wrote in response to her appeal for publicity for a hastily arranged benefit concert that he had "not the remotest influence with any daily or weekly paper," but he had mentioned it to a friend at the *Morning Chronicle*. The benefit was a success, with some of her illustrious musical friends, such as Vincenzo Bellini, donating their talents to the cause. The queen herself was in attendance.[90] Dickens had been unable to help on this occasion, but his letter was heartfelt. "Should there be any mode by which, either now or at any future time, I can advance your interest or be of service to you," he wrote, "I pray you to command me."[91] Later in 1839 the Royal Society of Musicians, whose patron was the Duke of Cambridge, donated sixty pounds.

It was more than a decade before Madame Sala found a way for Dickens to be of service to her. In the meantime her theatrical career descended into a desperate, tawdry business. Her attempt to make a new career in Paris in 1840 failed utterly, and she returned to England in 1841, but had only enough money to get to Dover, where she and her family were engaged at the Dover Theatre Royal. Madame Sala and all her children appeared in a

French play translated as *The Yellow Rose*, which received catcalls from the meager audience, and then she played Queen Gertrude to her son Charles Kerrison Sala's prince in a threadbare production of *Hamlet*. When the Theatre Royal closed down later that year, there was so little money that she had to resort to the business of her grandmother Dorothy Thomas, organizing two masquerade balls for the local gentry that were attended by all the officers of the nearby garrison. This yielded enough money to get her back to London for the season in 1842. Her youngest son remembered them staying at a boardinghouse in Haymarket where they were all "horribly bitten by fleas."[92] Unable to attract enough fashionable music pupils, Madame Sala returned to the stage at the Princess Theatre, another threadbare establishment with cavalier management.

By 1843 all but the youngest of her children were off her hands. Her daughter Henrietta Sala had died ten years before, and Augusta Sala was employed as a governess in the family of a member of Parliament. Albert Sala had gone to sea, while Frederick Sala was a teacher of piano in Buckinghamshire, and Charles Kerrison Sala was engaged as an actor at the Theatre Royal in Dublin. Her youngest child, George Augustus Sala, was left with the responsibility of looking after his mercurial mother, who had by now a drinking problem: he brought her home from the theater, cooked her meals, put her to bed, and endured her rages. When he turned fourteen he was told he must go out and earn a living, but this was no easy matter since Henrietta Sala had not been able to afford to send her youngest to school. He did have a facility with drawing, and she found him a brief apprenticeship with a miniature painter in London. After a few months he was taken on at the Princess Theatre to paint scenery for fifteen shillings a week. It was a pittance, but enough to allow him to rent a tiny garret where he could escape from his mother.

With her sight still very poor and her health ruined, Madame Sala quit the theater in 1844 and went to live permanently in Brighton, where she continued to take pupils and give her annual concert until she became too infirm.[93] Doubtless, she and her son had high hopes for a windfall legacy when Dorothy Thomas died in 1846. George Augustus Sala was extremely bitter to discover, however, that "she never left me a penny ... bequeathing all her money to some twenty-five uncles and aunts I have the honour to possess [in Demerara]."[94] He resented his connection to Thomas and resented his mother even more. For some years Henrietta Sala remained estranged from her youngest son, who was living in dire poverty, working at the Princess Theatre and writing stories in his spare time. There was a thaw in the relationship in 1851 when she came up to London to take her son to the Euston Hotel for tea with her dear friend Charles Dickens, who had once promised Madame Sala to be of service to her if he could.[95] True to his word, Dickens accepted a story for his magazine *Household Words*, and the career of George Augustus Sala as Dickens's protégé was launched.[96]

Throughout Sala's long and often notorious career he unwittingly provided glimpses of the extreme bitterness he felt toward his racially compromised mother and his repugnance at sharing a biological connection to a vulgar ex-slave woman. Misogyny and racism flowed through his writing as a toxic undertow. He wrote a great deal about the beautiful and talented Madame Sala as the grande dame, but his most transparent pieces of writing provided revealing glimpses of his impoverished and tawdry early life with his mercurial mother, who was dependent on the vagaries of marginal theater productions and the dubious patronage of her gentlemen friends. Such a shabby background suited him in the role of notorious bohemian and as a founder of the Savage Club, and he liked to cast himself as a sort of gypsy outsider. In his fiction, however, the bitterness toward his mother was given full rein.

Sala's novel *Quite Alone*, published in 1864, after his mother's death, provided a typical portrayal of the stock female villain in his fiction. She was "the wild woman" first seen at a Paris fairground, where she promised to reenact "scenes of her native Madagascar taking refuge in the branches of a banyan tree from the pursuit of hunters." Instead of this exotic entertainment, however, the reader was treated to a description of a woman "thinly clad in an absurd and tawdry costume" attacking her stage assistant in a drunken rage. She was described as "lithe and shapely but of what age it was impossible to discover through the paint and sham tattoo marks with which her face and arms were riddled.... There was something in her eyes that struck infinite horror and terror."[97] This depraved, alcoholic woman used the theatrical name "Madame Ernestine," but her close associates knew her by the common name of Polly. A young woman, she was very beautiful and elegant, yet untamed and dangerous like a sleek, black panther. Bewitching to men, she was revealed to be cruel, unprincipled, grasping, and ultimately riddled with rage and alcohol. This she-devil appeared again and again in Sala's fiction in various guises, but she was always a theatrical performer and courtesan of ambiguous ethnic lineage who employed exotic aliases. The persistence of this vile female character in his novels showed a strong misogynist streak in George Augustus Sala's perverse personality, fueled, no doubt, by the psychological damage caused by his appalling childhood and a lifetime of striving to be a white person in a racially determined world. In his journalism his virulent racism was on open display.

His most famous work, *My Diary in America in the Midst of War*, written when he was a foreign correspondent during the American Civil War, offered his readers a warm appreciation of the institution of chattel slavery, which he based on his familial connection to slave plantations. "I come, on my mother's side, from a long line of West Indian planters who owned slaves," he wrote. He believed he knew Africans and understood them to be naturally inferior to whites and "ten thousand times better off" as slaves in America than as free people in Africa.[98] "The enslaved African," he claimed, was inherently "lazy, indolent, slovenly . . . willing and obedient only when he feels the eye or hand of his master; inconceivably vain, trivial and puerile; always lecherous as a monkey and often savage as a gorilla."[99] As for free people of color, they were "a listless, decrepit, drowsy, cowering race, always going to the wall, always sliding and slinking away, always ragged, always dirty . . . cretins whose goiters are on their brain instead of their throats."[100] As he penned these hateful words, Sala knew he was speaking of his mother and grandmother, as well as "some twenty-five uncles and aunts" he had "the honour to possess." He knew that he too was a carrier of those despised racial characteristics.

George Augustus Sala was a literary luminary in his day, the natural successor to his mentor, Charles Dickens. While his reputation has faded somewhat, he remains the subject of biography and social history.[101] His career leaves no doubt about the success of Dorothy Thomas's strategy of inserting her grandchildren into the heart of empire. Equally there can be no doubt that his success came at a great psychological cost. His bohemian lifestyle was marked by addiction to alcohol, gambling, and flagellation, which suggests a deep self-loathing fueled by a lifelong denial of self as he strove to expunge his sole inheritance from the fantastic old black woman he had visited many years before at the red brick mansion in Kensington.

CONCLUSION

I N JUNE 1821 A YOUNG ENGLISHMAN stepped across the mudbank of the Demerara River and strode along the flimsy wharf toward the warehouse and offices of John and William Pattinson. John Castelfranc Cheverley was fresh from England and had come to work as a clerk for this merchant company. He had taken a second-class berth out of Liverpool on the merchant brig *Sir John Cameron*—little more than a "pigsty"— so it had not been an easy voyage.[1] He had shared the rigors of the journey with another clerk who was also going to Demerara to join the family firm.

There were two other passengers on the grubby ship: Mr. Irish, a youthful, quarrelsome American man from the colony of Nova Scotia, who was prone to alcoholism and "very sensitive about nationality," and Benjamin James Hopkinson, a refined and well-educated man, who was smartly attired and had a "very agreeable" manner. Hopkinson was a native of the colony, from an old Demerara family, and was the owner of two large cotton plantations. Cheverley was puzzled that a wealthy, well-educated man would travel on such a ship so patently not up to his standard. The passage had been booked by his agents, Hopkinson explained, and he had reluctantly resigned himself to the voyage, although he admitted to apprehension at the prospect of sharing a dilapidated cabin with the "ruffian" Mr. Irish. Cheverley thought Hopkinson might be of French extraction and was glad of his "intelligence and gentlemanly feeling" on such a long journey.[2]

As they approached Demerara, Cheverley was astonished to see a young mulatto man jump on board "full of airs and impudence . . . to shew unmistakably he was not a slave" and proceed to take over the ship and guide it into port. Shouting instructions to the captain and contemptuous answers to questions from the anxious passengers, the young pilot took complete control, directing the sailors without any further reference to the captain, who meekly accepted the affront. Cheverley was "not a little surprised at this first specimen of free-coloured manners."[3] Many more such surprises were to come.

Hopkinson surprised Cheverley just prior to stepping ashore, by appearing with a full head of tight curly black hair. Hopkinson confided that he had been wearing a wig on the ship, but in the extreme humidity of Georgetown he could no longer tolerate wearing it. Declining to come ashore with Cheverley, Hopkinson disembarked alone a little later. Cheverley's next surprise was the discovery that his amiable shipboard companion was not white at all but was a free man of color. Cheverley was astonished when he realized that the elegant and highly educated Hopkinson had chosen to travel in such a low state on such a mean ship in order to avoid difficult altercations with white people. "I was not aware," he naïvely wrote, "of the prejudices of the West India whites against the slightest taint of negro blood."[4] Strange as it was, Hopkinson meekly accepted his compromised position, which in Cheverley's mind was quite out of keeping for a major planter, which Hopkinson undoubtedly was.

Cheverley saw no reason not to remain friends with Hopkinson and continued to see him regularly, including on the militia days when they both had to turn out for monthly drill. Hopkinson lived with his mother, Joanna Hopkinson, in a large house in the center of town. She explained that she regretted "the difference that education had produced between her and her son." She thought he should have been a carpenter, but his white father had taken the boy to England. "Ben must be a gentleman," the senior Hopkinson had insisted, as she caustically lamented. Although Cheverley's observations suggested that Joanna Hopkinson had been left well provided for by her deceased white husband, he had left the colony nearly thirty years before. Since that time she had become a self-made businesswoman with nearly forty slaves she employed as hucksters.[5] He thought that despite her lack of learning she was "a very worthy and respectable woman of her class," far more respectable than many people he visited in the course of his employment.

Cheverley encountered numerous other free colored women in addition to Joanna Hopkinson, many of them quite wealthy and richly attired. On his first Sunday in Demerara he observed a bevy of free colored women on their way to church, each with a retinue of two or three slaves walking behind, carrying their prayer book or an umbrella. He was intrigued by the formality of these colored women and the strong attachment they all had to their gilt-edged prayerbooks, "although they could not read a word." One of these old women, Molly Lemon, who was revealed to be the aunt of his employer's wife, was delighted to meet Cheverley since she was "on the lookout to form good white connections" for her daughters.[6] Like Joanna

Hopkinson, most of these free colored women owned a number of young women whom they deployed as hucksters. He observed that these black and mulatto women were completely immersed in the Atlantic economy, keeping tabs on orders from Europe, on the merchants who organized the transport of goods, and on the captains who oversaw delivery. It was quite an operation. He was able to observe the way they worked at close quarters, since a neighbor in Georgetown, Norah Leeds, was one such entrepreneur. Sunday was her settling day, and before she set off for church she could be seen sitting "in great state" in her shop with her slaves drawn up before her, making sure that they all accounted for every penny they had made in sales that week. Nothing escaped her careful scrutiny.

One woman in particular drew Cheverley's attention. He described "Miss Dorothy Thomas usually styled Miss Doll" as "a dark mestizo ... with the deportment of an empress." Cheverley noted that she was very wealthy and was acknowledged to be "quite the head of the coloured class" in the colony. She lived in "a splendidly furnished, handsome house in Georgetown" and also owned a cotton estate up the coast called "Kensington." Her slave workforce was either employed on the plantation or worked for her as hucksters. Cheverley noted that Dorothy Thomas was very strict and made sure her hucksters made good on every sale. Once again, Cheverley was surprised to find that Thomas, "like most of her contemporaries," had a white man in her employ "who was not rich but who submitted to the degradation of being domineered by this imperious old dame." He recounted a visit he paid to Thomas to inquire about some cotton due to be delivered to the Pattinsons that had failed to arrive. Imperiously she called up her white factotum, who arrived with a "meek and chastened aspect" and submitted to a tongue-lashing about his laxity. "When Mr. Thomas was alive things were different," she admonished, and the man scurried off to fix the problem.[7]

Cheverley was also impressed that Dorothy Thomas ran the grand entertainments in the colony. Her balls were particularly noteworthy, and he compared them to the kinds of balls given by women back in England, noting that they were places where white men could mix with women of color. He was quick to add that had Benjamin James Hopkinson gone there, as a colored man he would not have been welcome, no matter how wealthy he was. Cheverley may also have encountered Mary Ostrehan Brett in this role, although she is not specifically mentioned in his memoir. He did include an unflattering account of his encounter with Thomas's friend Lucy Van Den

Velden, whom he described as "a coloured lady of indifferent reputation at the other end of town" who apparently tried to extort money from him.[8]

Cheverley continued to see his friend Hopkinson until he left the colony in October 1823. As members of the militia, both men were caught up in the suppression of the slave rebellion that broke out in July that year, and both were appalled by the indiscriminate brutality meted out to any enslaved person the militia encountered.[9] Interestingly, it did not strike Cheverley as incongruous that his free colored compatriot was not allowed equal participation in the social and political life of the colony, yet would stand shoulder to shoulder with white men inflicting violence on rebellious slaves. Hopkinson may have found the violence of the slave system as unpalatable as Cheverley did, but it was an economic imperative for him. As the owner of well over a thousand slaves, Hopkinson had as great a commitment to maintaining the slave economy as anyone in Demerara. Cheverley returned to England almost as soon as the rebellion was suppressed, but Hopkinson stayed on to become a member of the Court of Policy of the colony. When slavery was finally abolished, Benjamin James Hopkinson was well rewarded with a massive compensation payout of £56,272. His mother, Joanna Hopkinson, received £1,783, which was about half the sum awarded to Dorothy Thomas.[10]

CHEVERLEY'S RARE ACCOUNT OF HIS two years in Demerara came into our possession just as we sat down to write the conclusion to this book. A colleague in London gave us a copy of this little-known memoir, thinking it might add some details to our research.[11] Such generosity has occurred time and time again throughout this project. We have been blessed, repeatedly, by the insights and knowledge of a variety of scholars and enthusiastic genealogists, who have unstintingly shared their findings with us and suggested books or diary accounts from the southern Caribbean. The snippets of memory from Cheverley's brief stay in the colony provided us with more tantalizing glimpses of the lives of the women we discuss in this book and gave us yet more women to track down. This experience reminded us that this research is ongoing, and that the formality of a "conclusion" is probably premature for a project in which new details keep arriving. The more we look for women like Elisabeth Samson, the more we find.

The world of Demerara on the eve of a slave rebellion, as described by Cheverley, was in some ways a world turned upside down: a place where a refined and educated gentleman of color had to share a cabin with a disreputable white drunkard and where all the specie of the colony came through the hands of imperious black women, who managed their slaves with keen sharpness. His insights turn the notion of total white control on its head: he describes grand entertainments run by black women for the benefit of white men, and white men scurrying around after their domineering black employers. His image of an intimidated white man obsequiously taking orders from a black woman also turns on its head our received notions of gender relations. Even in his naïve telling, the world of slavery and slaveholding becomes so much more complicated and confounded.

In this respect, Cheverley's memoir provides a good way for us to conclude a book that seeks to unsettle easy assumptions about race, about gender, and about power. The enterprising women whose micro-biographies form the core of this book undoubtedly sought advantages from a slave economy at the expense of enslaved Africans and other people of African descent. While we found these women to be admirably resourceful, we do not hesitate to acknowledge that their impressive enterprises were thoroughly complicit in the dehumanizing slave culture of the Atlantic world. Their stories can be troubling, even disturbing, and will be inevitably disappointing for people who are seeking positive agency in the stories of people of color. In the course of this research we have found many scholars who are enthusiastically supportive of our project, but we also have faced recurring critical questions about whether we are valorizing women whose businesses served to further entrench the slave system. We have also faced questions about the politics of the time from people who look to find a connection between self-emancipated descendants of enslaved Africans and the emancipatory struggles and fight for civil equality. To be sure, political activity can be found in these stories, but with the possible exception of Marie Rose Fedon, who fought with her husband as a revolutionary, this is not the kind of "agency" that researchers are seeking.

Much of what these women did was a performance of politics, from skirting the law in a fundamentally racist society that sought to castigate and limit the opportunities of colored people, to trying to work within the ever-changing rules of a colonial slave society. Elisabeth Samson's canny manipulation of the Dutch legal system, with which this book began, was just the first of a series of tactical maneuvers that could be described as profoundly political. Dorothy Thomas's visit to the Colonial Office is another case in point. Her political motivation was to seek equality through the elimination of the discriminatory tax on slaveholders like herself, not to improve the lot of the people she owned. Similarly, Judith Philip made political decisions in the wake of the activities of her brother in the Fedon Rebellion, but her politics were the polar opposite of Marie Rose Fedon's. Judith Philip remained resolutely with the British party and actively engaged with the British plantocracy. Other women in this book ran hotels, brothels, and bars that catered to the white male elite and provided them with bastions of power. For the women in this book, who were just one remove from chattel slavery, their everyday experience was an exercise in political engagement in a fluid, unpredictable world.

It is nonsense to assume that the only agency allowed enslaved Africans and their descendants is action that pits the individual against the system, slave against master, victim against victimizer. All historical subjects have agency, for good or ill or, invariably, a mixture of both. One does not have to valorize self-emancipated slaves who became slave owners and helped perpetuate the system that held them in bondage—or even admire them. However, we would argue it is important to know that such women existed in all their complexity and contradictions.In trying to grasp the complexities of slavery and slave societies, it is necessary to understand the all-encompassing economic system that made slaveholders of women who were themselves the children of enslaved Africans. How was a self-emancipated slave woman to thrive and not slide back into a form of bondage if not by engaging in the slave economy? It is also important not to invert the logic of the slave system to presume a natural racial divide in the ownership of people. From the outset the Atlantic slave trade relied on indigenous slavery in Africa, and while the industrial demand for slaves in the Americas profoundly and detrimentally changed the slave societies and economies of Africa, the historical reality of black people holding other black people in bondage—in Africa and in the New World—is long-standing and has proved tenaciously persistent.

Women like Elisabeth Samson, Dorothy Thomas, Susannah Ostrehan, Rosetta Smith, and Judith Philip were entrenched in the system of slavery, and they added to it. They did not emancipate slaves in large numbers, and they lived with chattel for their whole adult lives. While Rachael Pringle Polgreen manumitted several slaves upon her death, the other women in our study kept hold of most of their chattel and seemed only to emancipate members of their own family. That said, we must not underestimate the importance of these filial manumissions, or the lengths these women went to first secure and then free their mothers, sisters, sons, daughters, nieces, and nephews.

Judith Philip, Dorothy Thomas, Susannah Ostrehan, and Mary Ostrehan Brett all received compensation for the emancipation of their slaves upon the abolition of slavery.[12] But as free colored people they had fewer opportunities than most and, as women, they were doubly disadvantaged. While many of them engaged with white men in business, what stands out is how much they did business among themselves. Transaction after transaction was recorded where free colored women engaged financially with one another, repeatedly buying and selling property, including slaves. These facts make their presence in the archive even more extraordinary, especially when their lives are compared to poor white women—particularly in Barbados—who were less able to navigate a slaveholding society.

Many of the mixed-race children and grandchildren of these women went to live in Britain, and in the process they helped to solidify imperial networks that spanned the Atlantic. It was not just that the children were educated in the heart of the empire; very often their mothers visited for long periods. Judith Philip spent over ten years in her London home. Similarly, on repeated occasions Dorothy Thomas visited London for long periods. Thomas and Philip had extensive business dealings with merchants and financial institutions in Britain, maintaining ongoing and fruitful relationships with powerful law firms on which they relied to oversee their affairs in the metropole. The ubiquitous Baillie family had commercial and legal arrangements with more than one of these entrepreneurial women, extending the web of empire even further.

Not all the women in this book interacted with the empire in the same way or followed the model of a metropolitan education. Benjamin Hopkinson's mother was extremely dubious about education and its supposed benefits. For her, the education of her son served no useful purpose: it artificially widened his horizons in an ultimately futile effort to place him on par with whites. None of the Ostrehan children appear to have gone to Britain to be educated. The heirs of Susannah Ostrehan traveled between colonies, from Barbados to Grenada, Demerara, and Berbice, and back to Barbados, but no further. The Ostrehans dealt generally with local merchants, as did Rosetta Smith. Yet each of these women in her own way was a key player in the economic life of the southern Caribbean.

These micro-biographies work to destabilize the dominant narrative of predatory white men and their transient concubines. The nuances of the intimate relationships demonstrated by these biographies are perhaps one of the most arresting features of this research. Until now Rosetta Smith existed as a known historical subject only as the manipulative mistress of Governor Picton in Trinidad. Clearly she benefited from her relationship with Picton, but that only lasted five years, and with the governor's spectacular fall from grace after 1803 she was on her own. Since Picton never married, it remains a matter of speculation what kind of relationship these two people actually had. They did stay connected after he left Trinidad, but she was economically independent of him, and her transactions all reveal her to be a woman capable of and confident in managing her own affairs.

The other known historical subject, Rachael Pringle Polgreen, has been the victim of many salacious anecdotes, yet the nature of her relationships with white men is not clear at all. While her business was set up to provide for white elites, her personal and business relationships with white men remain largely a mystery, and it appears that she married a man of color. The partners of the Ostrehan women cannot be located, but they appear to have partnered in both intimate and business arrangements with merchant mariners and ship captains, emphasizing their connections to a wider maritime world. Neither Elisabeth Samson, nor Judith Philip, nor Dorothy Thomas resemble a concubine. All of them had long-standing relationships with prominent white men, and each woman was at least as wealthy, if not more so, than her partner, and each independently managed successful business enterprises.

In this respect our research dovetails very nicely with research on New Orleans separately undertaken by Emily Clark and Kenneth Aslakson, both of whom have persuasively demonstrated that marriage, not concubinage, was the tradition that free people of color established and perpetuated in New Orleans. Hidden in plain sight in church and notarial records, the stories of dozens of such partnerships have now been recovered and described so extensively as to leave no doubt that they were widespread and well known among contemporaries.[13] In the case of biracial relationships, where legal marriage was not permitted, the intimate partnerships have the hallmarks of marriage in all but legal formality. Just as we found in our research in the southern Caribbean, the systematic search of the archives in New Orleans has revealed that the supposed permanent bachelorhood of white men in New Orleans was in actuality something quite different. Many men who formed relationships with free women of color took pains to create families that closely resembled conventional contemporary families. Shared households, notions of paternal duty, the recognition of filial obligations, and attention to extended families characterized many of these men's lives. They did not abandon their free black partners to make legitimate marriages with white women but instead found ways to constitute the ideals of patriarchal responsibility in a family form that was otherwise illicit.

As in the southern Caribbean colonies we have studied, the historical invisibility of such stable, de facto marriages, as well as the biracial families they created, is a disquieting reflection of the power of expectation. As Emily Clark has observed in the North American context, "Women of African descent were supposed to be hypersexual Jezebels, beings whose libidinous essence inexorably roused white male lust." Not just in New Orleans, but throughout the Atlantic world, "the exploitation of black women by white men turned on this convenient trope."[14] Clark reminds us that "the subjection of eroticized women of color by white men is one of the key mechanisms and metaphors of colonialism."[15] This is something of which all historians of the Atlantic world must be well aware, yet literature past and present has locked the free woman of color into a deeply entrenched erotic narrative from which deviation is virtually unimaginable, and some historians continue to depend on the same nineteenth-century sources that inspired the fantasy.

At the same time a whole cohort of men is bound tightly to a narrative that diminishes the humanity and decency of white males. It surely is time for historians of the slave societies of the Atlantic to shift their gaze from a concentrated focus on white exploitative patriarchs, such as Thomas Thistlewood, and consider as well the variety of patriarchal manifestations exemplified by such diverse characters as Carl Creutz in Suriname, Robert Collymore in Barbados, John Garraway in Grenada, and William Fraser in Berbice.

However significant such white men were in the lives of our subjects and their children, it is the matrilineal legacy of the free women of color in this book that most impresses. The determination of the women to provide their children with a route to legitimacy is remarkable. Through the descendants of these women we are able to examine the webs of connections throughout the empire. The journeys made by children and grandchildren added to the burgeoning Atlantic mobilities and power networks. The lives of these descendants do not only link metropole and colony but underscore a complex, intracolonial dynamic that was as much a part of their mothers' and grandmothers' lives as it was part of theirs.[16] Even though in the postemancipation world the gendered realities for the female descendants grew more stark, we found them to be extraordinarily resilient and competent at navigating the nineteenth century's patriarchal resurgence, in spite of both their racial inheritance and their gender.[17] In this respect our research echoes Rebecca Scott and Jean Hébrard's multigenerational history of Rosalie Vincent and her descendants.[18]

The dynamics of this increasingly complex world are highlighted by the micro-biographies in this book. Each of our subjects and her descendants navigated a difficult milieu that was less about the emanations of metropolitan power and more about the shifting ways that interconnected colonies responded to fluid events. Nor is this just a case of British colonies; all of our subjects, with the possible exception of Rachael Pringle Polgreen, engaged in a multicultural colonial world. Opportunity is key here. As colonies were destabilized and exchanged as a result of war or revolution, occasions arose in which free women of color could exercise more local power. Competing legal, property, tax, and social regimes opened new avenues to free women of color adept at moving across borders. If the legislature in Suriname refused the right to marry, one could go to the heart of the empire in The Hague and appeal to a higher power. If authorities in Barbados introduced punitive emancipation regulations for enslaved women, one could find innovative strategies to circumvent these new restrictions. If revolution tore through a colony, as in Grenada, an empowered free woman could move on to new frontiers. One striking thing about these women is the connections that each maintained between different locations. A key attribute of entrepreneurialism is flexibility, which our subjects displayed admirably in responding to dramatically changed circumstances, be it in the political sphere or within the intimacy of their own families.

One of the strongest elements to this research is not just that these women had families with their white partners but also that they worked hard to maintain their original black family networks—very often blending the two. Ensuring the well-being of their descendants through their white partners was only one aspect of these women's lives; manumitting siblings and parents was as important, if not more so, than any metropolitan concerns.

Our research underscores the power of the free colored moment that we highlighted in chapter 1. From the emergence of entrepreneurial free colored women in the early eighteenth century, to the death throes of slavery and the introduction of apprenticeship, these enterprising women were able to overcome the system, by nimbly navigating the system. Their ability to turn the economic and social circumstances to their own advantage, rather than being circumscribed and controlled by white patriarchal power, indicates that at this crucial juncture in Atlantic history, the categories of race and gender were decidedly protean.

The most compelling aspect of these women's life experience is the variety of responses that each made to shifting times, and the different ways they navigated the Age of Revolutions. Their life experiences, we believe, confound any attempt to make generalizations that situate these women within the metanarratives too readily invoked in contemporary discussions of the Atlantic world. We feel the study of these particular women is too new and raw, too destabilizing, to fit neatly into any of the metanarratives. Judith Philip and Marie Rose Fedon, for example, came from the same colony, the same ethnic group, and the same social class, but overall they exercised their agency in very different ways and effected different outcomes. This diversity is not comfortably encompassed under the same rubric.

That said, there are powerful links to an older African heritage that many of the mothers and grandmothers of these women shared. Judith Philip's mother, Jeanette, we know, was African, as was Elisabeth Samson's mother, Nanoe. So too was Priscilla Ostrehan and the mother of Marie Rose Fedon, and all the rest were at least close to the older African traditions. As Pamela Scully and Diana Paton have illuminated, Africa was home to several intersecting cultures that once in the New World undercut "European bourgeois conventions."[19] And while the scholarship on women in a variety of African traditions is still thin, the research makes a powerful argument for the continuation of this inherited female agency in the New World. In parts of West Africa, women were far more publicly and economically active and engaged more directly with systems of rule than in a slave society. Our micro-biographies reveal that these authoritative roles appear to have persisted in the Caribbean context. The free colored women of our study are therefore much closer to the ebullient Métis women of Senegal, as documented by Hilary Jones, or the powerful Ashanti women, as researched by Beverly Stoeltje.[20]

We can detect connections to the wider Atlantic context in the way that free black women could reformulate their identity and subtly subvert white colonial power relations. It is patently clear that free women of color can no longer be discussed in the reductive terms that scholars have so often used. It is our belief that the evidence we have unearthed about the lives of our subjects, in the full knowledge that there are many others like them, means that historians can no longer tell the same macro-history of the slave Caribbean. Nevertheless, we lay no claim to creating an alternative narrative for free women of color in the Atlantic world. The claims we make in recovering these lives are tentative; we have no interest in rewriting the macro-history of the Anglo-Caribbean colonial experience, let alone of the slave economies of the Atlantic world. Micro-biographies of a handful of free colored women cannot produce a new reading of the slave Caribbean, but they can demonstrate that the history of Caribbean slave society was more topsy-turvy than we have hitherto understood.

NOTES

INTRODUCTION. *Elisabeth and Her Sisters*

1. We acknowledge our indebtedness to the research of Cynthia McLeod in recovering the biography of Elisabeth Samson as presented here.
2. Qtd. by McLeod in "Celebrating the Extraordinary Life of Elisabeth Samson," 2.
3. McLeod is the author of an academic study, *Elisabeth Samson, Een Vrije, Zwarte Vrouw in het 18e Eeuwse Suriname*, and a novel, *The Free Negress Elisabeth*.
4. McLeod, "Celebrating the Extraordinary Life of Elisabeth Samson," 1–2.
5. Pybus, "Tense and Tender Ties."
6. Candlin, *The Last Caribbean Frontier*.
7. See Ginzburg and Poni, "The Name and the Game."
8. Gaspar and Geggus, *A Turbulent Time*.
9. This stands in contrast to the kinds of fortune that Linda Colley uncovered for her global history of Elizabeth Marsh. See Colley, *The Ordeal of Elizabeth Marsh*.
10. Higman, *Slave Populations*, 66–72.
11. Welch, *"Red" and Black over White*; Welch, "Crimps and Captains"; Kerr, "Victims or Strategists."
12. Scott and Hébrard, *Freedom Papers*.
13. Bhabha, "White Stuff," 24.
14. We are building on the work of Daniel Livesay and others who have explored this phenomenon. Livesay, "Children of Uncertain Fortune"; Stoler, "Tense and Tender Ties."
15. See Wheeler, *Complexion of Race*; Wilson, *The Island Race*; Nussbaum, *Limits of the Human*; Pybus, *Black Founders*.
16. Ogborn, *Global Lives*.
17. Equiano, *Narrative of the Life*; Walvin, *An African's Life*; Carretta, *Equiano, the African*.

CHAPTER ONE. *The Free Colored Moment*

1. Murdoch, "Land Policy." For an individual case, see Quintanilla, "Mercantile Communities in the Ceded Islands."
2. India continued to be a major investment but settlers were forbidden access; see Bowen, *Business of Empire*, 41; Lawson, *East India Company*, esp. ch. 6, "The Fall from Grace 1763–84," 103–26. See also Bryant, "Scots in India in the Eighteenth Century." For the enthusiasm the cession created, see Hamilton, *Scotland, the Caribbean and the Atlantic World*.
3. Davis, *The Problem of Slavery*, 52.

4. O'Shaughnessy, "Formation of a Commercial Lobby."

5. Melvill is sometimes spelled with an *e* as in Melville. For consistency, we have used Melvill throughout, since that was the most common spelling. He would later be impeached; see Mackillop and Murdoch, *Military Governors and Imperial Frontiers*, 188; Melville, *A Narrative of the Proceedings upon the Complaint Against Governor Melvill*, 1–132; see also A Grenada Planter, *A Full and Impartial Answer*; and "Memoirs of the Late General Melville."

6. The phases argument is one advanced by Barry Higman in *Slave Populations*, 43.

7. Candlin, *The Last Caribbean Frontier*, 29.

8. "Memoirs of the Late General Melville," 65; see also Hancock, *Citizens of the World*, 43–71.

9. Burke, *The State of the Nation*, 12.

10. Occasionally lots of up to five hundred acres were allowed but only rarely; see Murdoch, "Land Policy," 556.

11. Abstract of Several Informations and Plans Relative to the Settling of Grenada, Tobago, St. Vincent and Dominica, April 1763, box 12/12, Stowe Collection, Grenville Papers, Henry E. Huntingdon Library; Some Hints About Settling the Lands in the New Sugar Islands, undated, box 12/19, ibid., qtd. in Murdoch, "Land Policy," 554.

12. Marshall, "The Black Caribs."

13. Beginning with C. L. R. James in 1938, the scholarship on free colored people is now quite extensive. Here are some of the key texts though this is not an exhaustive list: James, *The Black Jacobins*; Dunker, "The Free Coloured"; Brathwaite, *Development of Creole Society in Jamaica*; Greene and Cohen, *Neither Slave, nor Free*; Berlin, *Slaves Without Masters*; Handler, *The Unappropriated People*; Sio, "Race, Colour and Miscegenation," 5–21; Heuman, *Between Black and White*; Cox, *Free Coloureds*; Sio, "Marginality and Free Coloured Identity"; Campbell, *Cedulants and Capitulants*; Landers, *Atlantic Creoles in the Age of Revolutions*; and Newton, *Children of Africa in the Colonies*.

14. Scott, "The Common Wind."

15. Beginning shortly after the conclusion of the Seven Years' War, the colonial authorities, urged by the Comte d'Estaing in St. Domingue, began to limit the freedoms of free colored people in the colony; see Dubois, *Avengers of the New World*, 66.

16. Candlin, *The Last Caribbean Frontier*, 43.

17. Hamilton, *Scotland, the Caribbean and the Atlantic World*, 20–21.

18. Mackillop and Murdoch, *Military Governors and Imperial Frontiers*, xxv–xxx; see also Donaldson, *The Scots Overseas*; Fry, *The Scottish Empire*; and Hamilton, *Scotland, the Caribbean and the Atlantic World*, 140–69; Sheridan, "The Role of Scots in the Economy and Society of the West Indies"; Addo et al., *Caribbean Scottish Relations*. For a history of the Johnstones, see Rothschild, *Inner Life of Empires*.

19. Hamilton, *Scotland, the Caribbean and the Atlantic World*, 5–7.

20. Hamilton, "Robert Melville and the Frontiers of Empire," esp. 191.

21. The best work on this topic, which builds on the work of Jack Greene, is O'Shaughnessy, *An Empire Divided*.

22. Mackillop and Murdoch, *Military Governors and Imperial Frontiers*, 191.

23. Melville, *A Narrative of the Proceedings upon the Complaint Against Governor Melvill*.

24. See *The New Jamaica Almanac*; Tobler, *Almanack*; Tobler and Tobler, *Carolina and Georgia Almanack*; Pitman, "Slavery on British West Indies Plantations"; Ashley, *Memoirs and Considerations Concerning the Trade and Revenues of the British Colonies in America*.

25. Hamilton, *Scotland, the Caribbean and the Atlantic World*, ch. 4. See also Quintanilla, "Mercantile Communities in the Ceded Islands."

26. O'Shaughnessy, *An Empire Divided*, 111, 121, 193.

27. Taylor, *The Black Carib Wars*. The earliest source on this conflict is Young, Account of the Black Charaibs, which is also interesting because of his perspective as a governor of Dominica and the chief commissioner for the ceded islands.

28. O'Shaughnessy, *An Empire Divided*, 117, 186, 192.

29. Handler, *The Unappropriated People*, 32–33.

30. Dull, *The French Navy and the Seven Years' War*.

31. The main works for this period in Grenadian history are Devas, *The History of the Island of Grenada*; Brizan, *Grenada, Island of Conflict*; and Steele, *Grenada*. For the disenfranchisement of the French settlers, see Devas; despite being quite old, it is still the best on this subject. See also Cox, *Free Coloureds*.

32. Candlin, *The Last Caribbean Frontier*, 11–12.

33. Julien Fedon to Francois Philip for the Sale of "Lancer," June 18, 1791, Deeds C4, 282–85, Supreme Court Registry of Grenada (hereafter cited as SRG).

34. See Fedon to Campbell for the Sale of "Lancer," June 18, 1791, Deeds C4, 275–82, SRG. The money for "Lancer" must have come from Fedon's jeweler father, Pierre. Curtis Jaocbs has done much to recover the history of the family; see Jacobs, "The Fedons," 2–5.

35. Jacobs, "The Fedons," 8; see also Freedom Certificate of Marie Rose Fedon, 1787, Deed Book W1, 166–67, SRG.

36. An Act to Require All Free Mestives, Cabre's Negroes and Other Coloured Free Persons Residing in or Who May Hereafter Arrive in These Islands to Register Their Names for the Purpose Herein Mentioned, CO 103/8, 93–96, National Archives of the United Kingdom (hereafter cited as NAUK).

37. See Jacobs "The Fedons," 5, citing information found in the Register for the Parish of Grand Pauvre, 1779–83, unnumbered box, 2, SRG.

38. Jacobs, "The Fedons," 4, citing the marriage entries found in the Grenada files: Etienne Fedon married Elizabeth Cavelan, French Deeds 1787–89, 74–78, SRG; Jean Fedon married Marguerite Cavelan, Deed Book E2, 401, SRG; Etienne and Elizabeth Fedon sold two quarreys of land to Julien and Marie Rose Fedon, French Deeds 1787–89, 74–78, SRG; Charles and Marie Louise Nogues sold land in Gouyave to Julien Fedon, Deed Book X3, 98, SRG.

39. Jacobs, "The Fedons," 8. See also various measures increasingly applied to restrict free colored people on the island, such as An Act to Prevent the Further Sudden Increase of Free Negroes and Mulattos, 1786, CO 103, NAUK.

40. Jacobs, "The Fedons," 8.

41. Certificate of Freedom for Marie Rose Cavelan, 1787, Deed Book W1, 166–67, SRG.

42. The Fedon Rebellion is covered by a range of authors from the period. All of them are from the British perspective, but nevertheless they do differ in their interpretations. Dr. John Hay's is particularly interesting and observant. See Garraway, *A Short Account*; Turnball, *Narrative of the Revolt and Insurrection*; Wise, *Review of the Events*; A Grenadian Planter, *A Brief Enquiry*; Hay, *Narrative of the Insurrection*; Thornhill, *Narrative of the Insurrection*; and finally the chilling report sent to the Duke of Portland from the president of the council in the days after the insurrection broke out: Mckenzie to the Duke of Portland, March 1795, CO 101/34/9, folios 22–39, NAUK.

43. Hay, *Narrative of the Insurrection*, 76–84.

44. Gaspar and Geggus, *A Turbulent Time*. For the revolution on St. Domingue, see Dubois, *Avengers of the New World*.

45. Duffy, *Soldiers, Sugar and Seapower*. See also Buckley, *Slaves in Redcoats*.

46. Gaspar and Geggus, *A Turbulent Time*, 66.

47. Although, as Gaspar and Geggus have explored, the upsurge in unrest predated in some cases these decrees and rumors of emancipation; see Gaspar and Geggus, *A Turbulent Time*, 7–8.

48. Ibid., 24.

49. Duffy, *Soldiers, Sugar and Seapower*, 5, 19, 25.

50. Ibid., 113–14, 119; Gaspar and Geggus, *A Turbulent Time*, 107–8. For an alternative and positive vision of the man, see Midgett, "West Indian Version."

51. See Gaspar and Geggus, *A Turbulent Time*, 110.

52. Ibid., 85.

53. Duffy, *Soldiers, Sugar and Seapower*, 255, 337. See also Moore, *Life of Sir John Moore*.

54. Duffy, *Soldiers, Sugar and Seapower*, 54–55.

55. Ibid., ch. 6.

56. Ibid., 257.

57. Ibid., ch. 6.

58. Steele, "The Arrival and Strange Death of Brigadier-General Colin Lindsay," in her *Grenada*, 123–25; see also the suicide of Captain Vaughan in Trinidad in Joseph, *History of Trinidad*, 175–80.

59. Duffy, *Soldiers, Sugar and Seapower*, 77, 281, 347.

60. See a note on the St. George's Militia of Grenada and its commander, the free colored man Louis La Grenade, in Garraway, *A Short Account*, 79.

61. Taylor, *The Black Carib Wars*, 4.

62. Duffy, *Soldiers, Sugar and Seapower*, 59–88; Gaspar and Geggus, *A Turbulent Time*, 109–10.

63. Dubois, *Avengers of the New World*, 178–79. See also, more generally, Bell, *Toussaint L'Ouverture*; Foix, *Toussaint L'Ouverture*; and James, *The Black Jacobins*.

64. See the details in the chapter "Second Maroon War 1795–1796" in Campbell, *The Maroons of Jamaica*; Craton, *Testing the Chains*, 211–24.

65. McDaniel, "The Philips." See also Campbell, "Rise of the Free Coloured Plantocracy"; Jacobs, "The Fedons," 20–21; Joseph, *History of Trinidad*, 186.

66. Candlin, *The Last Caribbean Frontier*, 51–75.

67. Gaspar and Geggus, *A Turbulent Time*, 25–28.

68. Handler, *The Unappropriated People*, 18–19.

69. Trinidad Questionnaire on Population and Climate, 1830 report for the Royal College of Physicians, 1829–31, RCP/OFFIP/4022/1–2, NAUK.

70. Brizan, *Grenada, Island of Conflict*, 118.

71. Higman, *Slave Populations*, 77.

72. Ibid.

CHAPTER TWO. *Bars, Brothels, and Business*

1. For details on the economic strength of this community, see Brathwaite, *Development of Creole Society in Jamaica*; Greene and Cohen, *Neither Slave, nor Free*; Welch, *"Red" and Black over White*; Welch, "Crimps and Captains"; Campbell, *Cedulants and Capitulants*; see also Cox, *Free Coloureds*; Sio, "Race, Colour and Miscegenation"; Heuman, *Between Black and White*; Sweet and Nash, *Struggle and Survival in Colonial America*; Shepherd, Brereton, and Bailey, *Engendering History*; and Gaspar and Hine, *Beyond Bondage*.

2. For details on manumission, see Handler, *The Unappropriated People*, 26–66.

3. Marryat, *Peter Simple*, is a case in point but there are many others where negative images abound. See Orderson, *Cursory Remarks and Plain Facts*; Waller, *Voyage in the West Indies*, 93; McCallum, *Travels in Trinidad*, 148; Fullarton, *A Statement, Letters and Documents Respecting the Affairs of Trinidad*; Coleridge, *Six Months in the West Indies*, 129; Poyer, *History of Barbados*, 639; Bayley, *Four Years Residence*, 495; Day, *Five Years' Residence*, 90.

4. Poyer, *History of Barbados*, 639.

5. Ibid., 640–41.

6. Ibid., 640.

7. Waller, *Voyage in the West Indies*, 19–20; see also Bayley, *Four Years Residence*, 493.

8. Welch, "Unhappy and Afflicted Women?"; Aspinall, "Rachel Pringle of Barbados"; Connell, "Hotel Keepers and Hotels in Barbados"; Beckles, "Property Rights in Pleasure"; Alleyne, *Historic Bridgetown*, 68–75; Welch, *"Red" and Black over White*, 60–63; Waller, *Voyage in the West Indies*, 6–7; Bayley, *Four Years Residence*, 28; Pinckard, *Notes on the West Indies*, 245; St. Clair, *A Soldier's Recollection*, vol. 2, 373–74.

9. Pinckard, *Notes on the West Indies*, vol. 1, 245.
10. Day, *Five Years' Residence*, 37.
11. Trollope, *The West Indies and the Spanish Main*, 206.
12. Brace, *The Blind African Slave*, 140.
13. Long, *History of Jamaica*, vol. 2, 354; Moreton, *Manners and Customs of the West India Islands*, 132; see also Beckles, "Property Rights in Pleasure," 169–88.
14. Bayley, *Four Years Residence*, 494–95.
15. Ibid., 155.
16. Coleridge, *Six Months in the West Indies*, 134.
17. Clark, *The Strange History of the American Quadroon*; Aslakson, "The 'Quadroon-Plaçage' Myth"; Hoefte and Vrij, "Free Black and Colored Women."
18. For example, see Fuentes, "Power and Historical Figuring."
19. For further information on this contentious issue, see Candlin, "Empire of Women." For examples of this blind spot, see Beckles, "On the Backs of Blacks"; Newton, *Children of Africa in the Colonies*. This work expands on Jerome Handler's thesis in *The Unappropriated People*.
20. Inventory of Rachael Pringle Polgreen, St. Michael, 1791, 1–3, Barbados Department of Archives (hereafter cited as BDA).
21. Ibid., 4–6.
22. Handler, "Joseph Rachell and Rachael Pringle Polgreen," 383. For an early mention of Barbadian hotels, see Oldmixon, *The British Empire in America*, vol. 2, 80.
23. Last Will and Testament of Rachael Pringle Polgreen, July 25, 1791, Probate Records, BDA.
24. See Poyer, *History of Barbados*, 639.
25. See Welch, *"Red" and Black over White*, 10, 75, 112.
26. Alleyne, *Historic Bridgetown*, 71–73.
27. See Handler, *The Unappropriated People*, 121; Last Will and Testament of Robert Collymore, October 13, 1824, RB4/65, Probate Records, BDA; Last Will and Testament of Amaryllis Collymore, January 5, 1829, RB4/65, Probate Records, BDA.
28. Newton, *Children of Africa in the Colonies*, 38.
29. This problem was first elucidated by Shepherd, *Women in Caribbean History*. For this problem in Barbadian historiography, see Newton, *Children of Africa in the Colonies*; Beckles, "On the Backs of Blacks." See also, more generally, Heuman, *Between Black and White*; Cox, *Free Coloureds*; Campbell, *Cedulants and Capitulants*.
30. See the Barbados Slave Registers, Plantation and Personal, 1817, T-71/520–65, NAUK.
31. Newton, *Children of Africa in the Colonies*, 50–51; see also Shepherd, *Women in Caribbean History*, 76, for an argument made by Carl C. Campbell and Jerome Handler.
32. Newton, *Children of Africa in the Colonies*, 66.
33. Rate Books, St. Michael Vestry, parts 1 and 2, 1770–80, BDA; see also Deed Record Books, RB3/40, 442, BDA.
34. *Barbados Gazette; or, The General Intelligencer*, January 26–30, 1788; Febru-

ary 4–7, 1788; January 31–February 4, 1789, all at Bridgetown Public Library; *Barbadian* (1842), qtd. in Connell, "Prince William Henry's Visits"; Lambert, *House of Commons Sessional Papers*, 203. We are grateful to Marisa Fuentes for this research.

35. Rowlandson, *Rachel Pringle of Barbados*.
36. Orderson, *Creoleana*, 75–82.
37. See Paul Baines, "William Lauder (Forger)," *Oxford Dictionary of National Biography*, http://www.oxforddnb.com/view/article/16121?docPos=3 (accessed February 5, 2013); Handler, "Joseph Rachell and Rachael Pringle Polgreen," 33; see also John Gilmore's introduction to *Creoleana* by Orderson, 1–19. For the Milton forgery scandal, see Henderson, *Furius*; Hunt, "William Lauder," 111.
38. Orderson, *Creoleana*, 76.
39. Ibid., 77.
40. Ibid., 78. Some, such as Rowlandson, have written her name as Rachel; however, in the archives her name is written as Rachael. We have maintained this spelling. We have also not used a hyphen for her two last names because, similarly, her name in archival sources was not hyphenated.
41. Sugden, *Nelson: A Dream of Glory*, 351.
42. See Welch, "Crimps and Captains," 98.
43. See English Settlers in Barbados, RL1/3, 91, Church of Latter-day Saints Archives, Utah, available at http://www.ancestry.com (hereafter cited as CLS).
44. The argument is made by Welch, *"Red" and Black over White*, 91, following Handler, *The Unappropriated People*, 34–138.
45. Orderson, *Creoleana*, 59.
46. Ibid., 79.
47. Connell, "Prince William Henry's Visits," 157–64. See also, more generally, Hans Rollmann, "Prince William Henry in Newfoundland," *Anglicans in Newfoundland and Labrador*, http://www.mun.ca/rels/ang/texts/pwh.htm (accessed February 5, 2013).
48. *Barbadian*, May 21, 1842, qtd. in Connell, "Prince William Henry's Visits," 157–64.
49. Madden, *A Twelvemonth's Residence in the West Indies*, 17–21. See also Lloyd, *Letters from the West Indies*, 7.
50. For details of this relationship, see Tomalin, *Mrs Jordan's Profession*.
51. "Advertisement by Rachael Pringle-Polgreen for a Lost Gold Ring," *Barbados Gazette; or, The General Intelligencer*, January 31–February 4, 1789, at Bridgetown Public Library. We are grateful to Marisa Fuentes for this research.
52. See Ziegler, *King William IV*, 102; see also Connell, "Prince William Henry's Visits," 157–64.
53. Lambert, *House of Commons Sessional Papers*, 203, qtd. in Fuentes, "Power and Historical Figuring," 575.
54. Fuentes, "Power and Historical Figuring," 575–77.
55. This argument was first outlined in Patterson, *Sociology of Slavery*, 160. See also Beckles, "Property Rights in Pleasure," 169–87.

56. There are many books on prostitution in London; the most pertinent for this study is Hitchcock, *English Sexualities*, 94–98.

57. Being enslaved added its own dimension though and changed fundamentally the right of consent; see Beckles, "Property Rights in Pleasure," 169–71.

58. See Fuentes, "Power and Historical Figuring," 564; Handler, "Joseph Rachell and Rachael Pringle Polgreen," 33; and Beckles, "Property Rights in Pleasure," 180.

59. Pinckard, *Notes on the West Indies*, vol. 1, 110–18; Madden, *A Twelvemonth's Residence in the West Indies*, 16–22; Bayley, *Four Years Residence*, 148–50; Lloyd, *Letters from the West Indies*, 24–27.

60. Winfield, *British Warships of the Age of Sail*.

61. Several male free colored Polgreens existed and could well be related. See "Edward Polgreen," "John Polgreen," and "James Polgreen," St. Michael Vestry Levy Books, 1768–82, RB3/50–51, BDA.

62. "Rachel Polgreen," St. Michael Vestry Levy Books, 1779–88, RB3/50–51, BDA.

63. "Ann Polgreen," "Mary Ann Bellamy," "Katherine Payne," St. Michael Vestry Levy Books, 1779–88, RB3/50–51, BDA.

64. The firm owned several properties, including land on Back Church Street and Cheapside. See the entries for "Adwin" and "Firebrace" in St. Michael Vestry Levy Books, 1779–88, RB3/50–51, BDA.

65. Nelson, *Benedict Arnold's Navy*, 160.

66. Candlin, *The Last Caribbean Frontier*, 51–75; see also Naipaul, *Loss of El Dorado*, 129–31.

67. Robinson, *Memoirs of Sir Thomas Picton*, vol. 1, ch. 2.

68. See Candlin, "The Torture of Louisa Calderon," in her *The Last Caribbean Frontier*, 118–38; see also Epstein, "The Politics of Colonial Sensation."

69. Fullarton, *A Statement, Letters and Documents Respecting the Affairs of Trinidad*; Fullarton, *A Refutation of the Pamphlet Which Colonel Picton Lately Addressed to Lord Hobart*; McCallum, *Travels in Trinidad*. See also Epstein, "The Radical Underworld Goes Colonial."

70. Howell, *Complete Collection of State Trials and Proceedings*, esp. ch. 676: "Proceedings Before the King's Bench Westminster in the Case Against Sir Thomas Picton *Esq.*" See also Candlin, *The Last Caribbean Frontier*, 118–37.

71. McCallum, *Travels in Trinidad*, 148.

72. Naipaul, *Loss of El Dorado*, 279–84; Epstein, "The Politics of Colonial Sensation," 712–41.

73. Howell, "Deposition of Maria Calderon," in *Complete Collection of State Trials and Proceedings*, 244.

74. Fullarton, *A Statement, Letters and Documents Respecting the Affairs of Trinidad*, 67. For more on the idea of domestic titles used freely, see Kerr, "Victims or Strategists."

75. Joseph, *History of Trinidad*; Millette, *Genesis of Crown Colony Government*; Campbell, *Cedulants and Capitulants*, 101, 142; Brereton, *Introduction to the History of Trinidad and Tobago*. To be fair, however, Brereton was writing a short history.

76. Myatt, *Peninsular General*; Havard, *Wellington's Welsh General*; Robinson, *Memoirs of Sir Thomas Picton*.

77. Book of Spanish Protocols, "S" and "P," Index 1787–1813. For example, see her entries in 1799–1801 at nos. 1161/198, 256, 502; Trinidad Slave Registers 1813–15 (Personal and Plantation), T-71/501-6, NAUK.

78. McCallum, *Travels in Trinidad*, 146.

79. Ibid.

80. McCalman, *Radical Underworld*; Epstein, "The Radical Underworld Goes Colonial."

81. Fullarton, *A Statement, Letters and Documents Respecting the Affairs of Trinidad*, 189.

82. McCallum, *Travels in Trinidad*, 133.

83. Book of Spanish Protocols, "P," 1810, 1023/252, Index 1787–1813; Will of Sir Thomas Picton, Prob. 11/1571, NAUK.

84. Richard Rose Picton's education and his ultimate fate is recorded in Return of the Services and Professional Education—Thomas Rose Picton, 1813–23, WO 15/3908, NAUK.

85. The best notice is from 1825 when Augusta Picton and Richard Picton received slaves from Rosetta Smith; see Trinidad Personal Slaves, 1825, T-71/512, NAUK; see also Richard Rose Picton and his [new?] wife, Marie Adelaide Pietry, in Trinidad Personal Slaves, 1834, T-71/518, NAUK.

86. Morris, "Progenitors and Coloured Elite Families"; see also Cumberbatch, "Amaryllis Collymore and Her Son Ren." For the Congnets, see Campbell, *Cedulants and Capitulants*, 108, 215.

87. The meat contract was operated by Smith; see McCallum, *Travels in Trinidad*, 85. See also Rosette Picton residing in St. George's to John Gloster Garraway, March 26, 1810, M2 105, SRG.

88. *Port of Spain Gazette*, July 1821; see also Book of Spanish Protocols, "P" 1813, 1037/311, Index 1787–1813.

89. Trinidad Slave Registers 1813–15 (Personal and Plantation), T-71/501-6, NAUK.

90. Ibid.

91. Handler, "The Economic System: Occupations Wealth and Property," in his *The Unappropriated People*, 117–53.

92. Book of Spanish Protocols, "P" and "S," 1799–1801, 1161, Index 1787–1813.

93. Ibid., 1161/198, 256, 502.

94. Book of Spanish Protocols, "P" (Smith to James Douglas and James Blandin), 1809, 1023/873, and 1810, 1023/313.

95. For example, see Lushington and Law to Julien Fedon for sale of property, December 20–21, 1790, Eighteenth and Nineteenth Century Deeds, unnumbered box, 1763–1804, SRG.

96. Fullarton, *A Statement, Letters and Documents Respecting the Affairs of Trinidad*, 67, 91, 93; McCallum, *Travels in Trinidad*, 148. The lawyer's report of the case

and the letter Griffiths and Lilburne wrote to the colonial secretary can be found in CO 295/4/159 and CO 295/4/161, both in Trinidad Correspondence, 1803, NAUK.

97. Joseph, *History of Trinidad*, 175–80.

CHAPTER THREE. *By Labors and Fidelity*

1. There are only two studies of this family. This chapter greatly expands and amends this work but is no less indebted. The first is McDaniel, "The Philips"; and the second is Candlin, "What Became of the Fedon Rebellion?" in his *The Last Caribbean Frontier*, 1–23.

2. Judith Philip's slave wealth can be seen both in her plantation entries in the slave registers published triennially from 1818 onward and in the planter compensation reports beginning in 1836; see Carriacou Plantation Slave Registers, 1833, T-71/319, 2–12, NAUK, and "Judith Philip," 1836, no. 780, NDO 4/10, Grenada Compensation, NAUK.

3. Some of the details about the location can be gleaned from transactions recorded in the Supreme Court Registry of Grenada, such as Indenture between Susannah Philip and Judith Philip, October 5, 1807, Deeds S4, 349–50, SRG. See also two maps of the island drawn in the late eighteenth century: Fenner, *A New and Accurate Map of the Island of Cariacou*; and *Map of Carriacou, 1795*, from the personal files of Frances Brinkley, cited in McDaniel, "The Philips," 180.

4. Slaves were routinely moved around depending on the season. This was especially so on Carriacou, where a diverse array of crops were grown on relatively small lots. See Higman, *Slave Populations*.

5. The entries (or "slave returns") for J. B. Louis Philip can be found at Trinidad Plantation Slave Registers, 1833, T-71/501, 213–17 ("Concorde" estate) and 430–32 ("Philippine" estate), NAUK; for Susannah's presence, see her transactions in Book of Spanish Protocols (Trinidad), 1812, Index "P," Port of Spain.

6. See, for comparison, the Carriacou Plantation Slave Registers, 1833, T-71/319, NAUK.

7. For slavery in the French Caribbean, see Dubois, "Slavery in the French Caribbean."

8. Judicial Report of the Evidence in the Case of Jose, 1834, CO 101/78, 136–38, NAUK.

9. Ibid., 137.

10. Ibid.

11. Dr. Duncan Blair was the estate surgeon; ibid., 137–38.

12. Indenture Between the Heirs of Honore Philip and Pierre Charbonne, August 19, 1788, Book of French Deeds Grenada, 1780–90, 284–300, SRG. See also Judith Philip Appoints Joseph Newton and Pierre Charbonne as Her Executors and Attorneys, May 30, 1803, Grenada Deed Books I2, 492–93, SRG.

13. See the entries in the slave registers for Marinette "Mary Bell" Charbonne, 1833, 17, T-71/319, Grenada Plantation Slave Registers, NAUK.

14. This is now the site of the Grenada National Museum on the corner of Young and Monckton Streets and should not be confused with the current jail on Richmond Hill, which was built in the 1880s.

15. Attorneys Report, CO 101/78, 134, NAUK.

16. Judicial Report, ibid., 137.

17. Ibid., 138.

18. Ibid., 130–49.

19. Major General George Middlemore was an experienced soldier, a hero of the Napoleonic wars. See James Falkner, "George Middlemore," *Oxford Dictionary of National Biography*, http://www.oxforddnb.com/view/article/18664 (accessed March 10, 2013).

20. The Humble Petition of Judith Philip and of the Undersigned Inhabitants of Carriacou in the Government of Grenada, CO 101/78, 147–48, NAUK.

21. Middlemore to Smith, June 24, 1834, CO 101/78, 133, NAUK.

22. Green, *British Slave Emancipation*, esp. ch. 3, "Law and Government," 65–98.

23. For more on this idea, see the introduction to Candlin, *The Last Caribbean Frontier*, xvi–xxvi.

24. Spring Rice to Smith, 1834, CO 101/78, 131–32, NAUK.

25. The details of Honore's will, his family, and his occupation can be found at Judith Philip to Michel Philip Release, May 26, 1789, unnumbered box, Eighteenth and Nineteenth Century Deeds, SRG. Details of Catherine's inheritance can be found at Catherine Philip to the Heirs of Honore Philip Deceased, June 15, 1786, Deeds V1, 560–62, SRG; for details of the brothers Jean-Pierre and François's donation to the heirs of Honore Philip, see Magdalen Philip to the Heirs of Honore Philip, Deeds Y, 153–58, SRG. In this document Honore is described as a "merchant"; see 153.

26. Felix and Tallet, "The French Experience"; see also Kennedy, *Rise and Fall of the Great Powers*, 97.

27. Moogk, "Reluctant Exiles."

28. Blanning, "Louis XV and the Decline of the French Monarchy"; see also Swann, *Parliaments and the Political Crises under Louis XV*.

29. Banks, "Official Duplicity."

30. Judith Philip to Michel Philip Release. For specifics about François's property on Grenada and St. Lucia, see Marie-Magdalaine Vigi Philip to Henry Hilaire de Moussacq, January 27, 1807, Deeds S4, 61–66, SRG; Julien Fedon to Francois Philip, Sale of Property, June 18, 1791, Deeds C4, 282–88, SRG. For Jean-Pierre (and others), see Magdalaine Philip Gives Power of Attorney to James Lair, June 23, 1789, Deeds Y1, 153–58, SRG.

31. Judith Philip to Michel Philip Release; Articles of Agreement Between the Heirs of Honore and Jeanette Philip (Deceased), September 7, 1778, unnumbered box, Eighteenth and Nineteenth Century Deeds, SRG; see also the presence of Honore Sr. in the records, such as Peter Simmond to Honore Philip, May 10, 1768,

no. 2903, French Deeds 1768–69, SRG; Honore Philip and Joseph Flandant to James Bishop, May 20, 1768, no. 2949, ibid.; Honore Philip to Daniel Daudier, March 7, 1769, no. 3292, ibid.

32. John D. Garrigus, trans., *The Code Noir* (1685), http://les.traitesnegrieres.free.fr/39_esclavage_code_noir_agl.html (accessed March 10, 2013); see also Breathett, "Catholicism and the Code Noir in Haiti."

33. Brinkley, "Analysis of the 1750 Carriacou Census."

34. Ibid., 44–60.

35. Devas. *A History of the Island of Grenada*, 57–73.

36. Jeannett [*sic*] Philip and Honore Philip the Younger with Charlotte de Nesmes Dechanteloupe, April 25, 1774, no. 2871, Grenada Record Book, 1774, SRG; Honore Philip to the Heirs of Honore Philip, September 10, 1785, Deeds K3, 50, SRG.

37. Catherine Philip to the Heirs of Honore Philip Deceased, June 15, 1786, Deeds V1, SRG.

38. Indenture Between the Heirs of Honore Philip, September 10, 1785, Deeds K3, 53, SRG.

39. S. V. Morse, *Description of the Grenadines*, 1778, CO 101/16, NAUK.

40. Fenner, *A New and Accurate Map of the Island of Cariacou*.

41. Most transactions in the Grenada files point to the trades of each of the children, for example Indenture Between Michel Philip, Carpenter, and Judith Philip, February 11, 1792, unnumbered box, 1792, French Deeds 1972, 106–7, SRG; Indenture Between the Heirs of Honore and Jeannette Philip, September 10, 1785, Deeds K3, SRG (in this document all the trades are listed: mason, carpenter, shoemaker, and so on); see 53.

42. McDaniel, "The Philips," 179–80.

43. Catherine Philip to the Heirs of Honore Philip Deceased, June 15, 1786, Deeds V1, 560–62, SRG.

44. See, for example, Judith Philip to Honore Philip, Lease for a Year, May 25, 1789, unnumbered box, Eighteenth and Nineteenth Century Deeds, 49–51, SRG; Philip Family Indenture, September 10, 1785, Deeds K3, SRG; Articles of Agreement Between the Philip Family, September 10, 1785, Deeds K3, 51–61, SRG.

45. Indenture Between Marie-Magdalaine Philip and Henry Mousacq (for Francois Philip), 1807, Deeds S4, 61–68, SRG; Philip Family Indenture, September 10, 1785, Deeds K3, 49–64, SRG. This document not only lists Jean-Pierre's property with the family but also many of the lots and houses in St. George's and the names of those who rented property from them.

46. See Lessly, "The Laws of Grenada and the Grenadines," 187.

47. Joseph, *History of Trinidad*, 178; and Candlin, "Paper Tigers and Crooked Dispositions," in her *The Last Caribbean Frontier*, 51–70.

48. Scott, "The Common Wind."

49. Lessly, "The Laws of Grenada and the Grenadines," 187.

50. Although his will has not survived, the details are found in Articles of Agreement Between the Philip Family, September 10, 1785, Deeds K3, 51–61, SRG.

51. Philip Family Indenture: The Will of Nicholas Regis Philip, June 24, 1794, Deeds E2, 150–55, SRG; Magdalaine Philip Appoints Jeanne Rose Fotheringham to Be Her Attorney, June 26, 1794, Deeds E2, 159–61, SRG.

52. Magdalaine Philip to the Heirs of Honore Philip, Deeds Y1, 153–58, SRG. For the details concerning Louis Mongre, see 155.

53. Honore Philip to Judith Philip, Sale of Land, February 11, 1792, and March 7, 1793, unnumbered box, Eighteenth Century Deeds, 1792–99, 106–7, SRG.

54. See Joseph, *History of Trinidad*, ch. 9, 168; and Naipaul, *Loss of El Dorado*, 129–30.

55. Indenture on Behalf of the Children of Michel, Magdalen, and Susannah Philip, January 25, 1790, French Deeds 1782–92, 97–103, SRG.

56. Devas, *A History of the Island of Grenada*, 173.

57. Last Will and Testament of Judith Philip, November 25, 1848, 11/2105, Probate Records, NAUK. The will can also be found at the Supreme Court Registry of Grenada; see Last Will and Testament of Judith Philip, November 25, 1848, Deeds B3, 558–61, SRG.

58. Magdalaine Philip Appoints Jeanne Rose Fotheringham to Be Her Attorney; and Philip Family Indenture: The Will of Nicholas Regis Philip, June 24, 1794, Deeds E2, 155, SRG.

59. Magdalaine Philip Appoints Jeanne Rose Fotheringham to Be Her Attorney.

60. The Children of Edmund Thornton and Judith Philip to Their Attorneys, April 9, 1855, Deeds W-C3, 289–92, SRG; see also Philip Thornton to Stacey Grimaldi witnessed by Edmund Thornton, February 15, 1816, Court of the King's Bench: Plea Side: Affidavit of Due Execution of Articles of Clerkship, ser. I, class KB105, piece 26, UK Articles of Clerkship 1756–1874, NAUK.

61. See Slade, "Craigston and Meldrum Estates," 481–537.

62. Baillie, Campbell, and Thornton Indenture, February 25, 1810, Deeds M2, 463–67, SRG. Also, he is found in many other partnerships, such as Indenture Between Edmund Thornton with William Gillach and John Lang, April 28, 1788, Deeds Q3, 174–84, SRG.

63. Edmund Thornton appears in a number of places, such as Demerara, where he had extensive business dealings. See Return of Edmund Thornton and the Lady Saltoun, T-71/391, Demerara Slave Registers (Plantation), 1817, 85–96, NAUK.

64. Doll Thomas and her daughters, for example, are discussed in the following chapter.

65. Marriage Banns of Edmund Thornton and Jane Butler, December 28, 1796, Lancashire Anglican Parish Registers, Lancashire Archives, Preston, England.

66. Devas, *A History of the Island of Grenada*, 121. For details on clandestine marriages and Gretna Green romances, see Stone, *Family, Sex and Marriage in England*, which is still in many ways the benchmark text. See also Meteyard, "Illegitimacy and Marriage Law in Eighteenth Century England."

67. Register for the Parish of Grand Pauvre, 1779–83, 2, SRG. See also Jacobs, "The Fedons."

68. See Judith Philip About to Depart for England and May be Absent for Some Time Appoints Duncan Campbell, James Baillie, and Susannah Philip as Her Attorneys, June 24, 1794, Deeds E2, SRG. Campbell and Baillie were the business partners of Thornton. Details of the house are found in McDaniel, "The Philips," 182; see also Last Will and Testament of Judith Philip.

69. See Judith Philip About to Depart for England Appoints Pierre Charbonne and Joseph Newton as Attorneys, May 30, 1803, Deeds I2, 492–93, SRG. For Thornton's address and his marriage to Jane Butler, see Edmund Thornton Sale of Morne Rouge, July 9, 1814, Deeds Y2, 448–51, SRG.

70. See Duffy, *Soldiers, Sugar and Seapower*; and Gaspar and Geggus, *A Turbulent Time*.

71. Devas, *A History of the Island of Grenada*, 120–28.

72. Aside from the works by Raymund Devas, two other modern histories of Grenada cover the rebellion: Brizan, *Grenada, Island of Conflict*; and Steele, *Grenada*. See also A Grenadian Planter, *A Brief Enquiry*; Wise, *Review of the Events*; Hay, *Narrative of the Insurrection*; Turnball, *Narrative of the Revolt and Insurrection*; Thornhill, *Narrative of the Insurrection*. A neat synthesis of all their views from later in the nineteenth century was written by a descendant: Garraway, *A Short Account*.

73. Judith Philip Appoints Duncan Campbell, James Baillie and Susannah Philip as Attorneys, June 24, 1794, Deeds E2, SRG.

74. See Candlin, "What Became of the Fedon Rebellion?" in his *The Last Caribbean Frontier*.

75. See Duffy, *Soldiers, Sugar and Seapower*, 119–20.

76. McDaniel, "The Philips," 187. See also Campbell, "Rise of the Free Coloured Plantocracy"; Jacobs, "The Fedons," 20–21; Hay, *Narrative of the Insurrection*.

77. We are grateful to Curtis Jacobs for this information.

78. Garraway, *A Short Account*, 12; see also Wise, *Review of the Events*, 9–10.

79. See Gaspar and Geggus, *A Turbulent Time*, 105, 107–8.

80. Steele, *Grenada*, 129.

81. Garraway, *A Short Account*, 79.

82. Several transactions attest to his engagement with prominent British merchants and landowners; for example, see Joachim Philip with William Scott, no. 3288, Court of Common Pleas 1794–96, SRG. For white French connections, see Joachim Philip to Rondeau, 1787, French Deed Book 1780–90, 170, SRG.

83. Joachim Philip with William Scott; Joachim Philip with Harrison, no. 3280, Court of Common Pleas 1794–96, SRG; Joachim Philip with Munro, no. 3284, ibid.

84. Garraway, *A Short Account*, 4.

85. Ibid., 12. See also Thornhill, *Narrative of the Insurrection*, 5–7.

86. Thornhill, *Narrative of the Insurrection*, 7.

87. See Susannah Philip Appoints M. Gahagan and Duncan Campbell as Her Attorneys, July 25, 1795, Deeds E2, 562–64, SRG.

88. This division is elucidated by C. L. R. James in *The Black Jacobins*; see also Cox, "Fedon's Rebellion," 11. Nogues's family transactions point to his lack of real wealth;

see Charles Nogues to the Pinel Family Indenture, December 4, 1792, Deeds F4, 102–5, SRG.

89. Ninian Home to Colonial Office, April 1793, in Frances Brinkley, personal files, and Grenada Governors Letter Books, both qtd. in McDaniel, "The Philips," 187.

90. Garraway, *A Short Account*, 80. See also Statement of Public Expenditure, March 1795–June 1796, Governors in Letters Grenada, CO 101/34, 257, NAUK.

91. The details of the Act of Attainder can be found at Record Book of the Court Oyer and Terminer, June–November 1796, unnumbered file, 1–39, SRG; see also extensive coverage in Governors in Letters Grenada.

92. Minutes of the Council, March 17, 1803, Grenada, qtd. in Jacobs, "The Fedons," 20.

93. Secretary of State Portland to Houston, Governors in Letters Grenada, CO 101/34, 238–42, NAUK.

94. Green to Portland, May 27, 1797, CO 101/35, NAUK; Grenada Act, December 27, 1797, CO 103/10, NAUK. For earlier examples of this attitude, see also Governor Melvill to the Earl of Hillsborough, May 10, 1768, CO 101/12, NAUK; Vagabond Act, 1794, SRG; Cox, "Fedon's Rebellion," 16; and Treaties of 1763 and 1784.

95. Joseph, *History of Trinidad*, 187. For Chacon's fears, see Chacon to the Prince de la Paz, May 16, 1796, no. 56, Trinidad and Tobago Historical Society Collection, Port of Spain, 1935, 2, qtd. in Millette, *Genesis of Crown Colony Government*, 28.

96. Green to Portland, May 27, 1797.

97. Record Book of the Court Oyer and Terminer, 1796.

98. *St. George's Chronicle and Grenada Gazette*, April 29, 1803; Susannah Philip Sale of "La Trinite" to Judith Philip, October 5, 1807, Deeds S4, SRG.

99. Return of Judith Philip, T-71/503, Trinidad Slave Registers: Personal Slaves, 1813, NAUK.

100. Slave return of J. B. Louis Philip for Philippine and Concord[e] Plantations, T-71/501, Trinidad Slave Registers: Plantation Slaves, 1813, NAUK.

101. Ibid. See also Campbell, *Cedulants and Capitulants*.

102. Judith Philip to Ann-Rachel Thornton Indenture, November 20, 1828, Deeds W2, SRG.

103. See Children of Judith Philip: Intention to Sell, April 9, 1855, Deeds W-C3, SRG.

104. Children of Judith Philip Appoint Duncan Blair and George Abercrombie Mitchell as Attorneys, July 3, 1849, Deeds B4, SRG.

105. Last Will and Testament of Ann-Rachel Thornton, April 4, 1849, Deeds B4, SRG.

106. Cited in McDaniel, "The Philips," 11.

107. Judith Philip, no. 780, NDO 4/10, Details of Planter Compensation Commission, Grenada, 1836, NAUK.

108. The amount of £6,000 was equivalent to almost £321,000 in 2005. See Cur-

rency Converter, National Archives, http://www.nationalarchives.gov.uk/currency/results.asp#mid (accessed March 10, 2013). The details of the compensation commission have been explored in Draper, *The Price of Emancipation*, and are available online at the *Legacies of British Slave-Ownership* project, http://www.ucl.ac.uk/lbs. See the entry for Judith Philip at http://www.ucl.ac.uk/lbs/person/view/11042 (accessed March 10, 2013).

109. Last Will and Testament of Judith Philip.

CHAPTER FOUR. *A Lasting Testament of Gratitude*

1. Last Will and Testament of Susannah Ostrehan, February 22, 1809, Wills and Inventories, St. Michael, 1800–1850, BDA; Inventory of Susanna [sic] Ostrehan, February 27, 1809, Inventories, St. Michael, BDA.
2. Handler, *The Unappropriated People*, 41; see also Seaforth to the Duke of Portland, July 27, 1810, 46/7/4, Seaforth Papers, National Archives of Scotland.
3. Welch, "Unhappy and Afflicted Women?"
4. Handler, "Manumission and the Validation of Free Status," in his *The Unappropriated People*, 29–65.
5. Handler, *The Unappropriated People*, 59–63.
6. Seaforth hoped to "induce the legislature to . . . establish a register for the Free coloured People." Seaforth to Alton, July 14, 1802, 46/7/7, Seaforth Papers, National Archives of Scotland. We are grateful to Jerome Handler for this research. See Handler, *The Unappropriated People*, 63–64.
7. Handler, *The Unappropriated People*, 60–61.
8. Ibid., 44–47.
9. Beckles, *History of Barbados*, 85.
10. See entry for Susey Ostrehan, no. 372, Deeds, part 2, 1779, St. Michael Vestry Levy Books, BDA; Susy Ostrehan, no. 420, Deeds, part 2, 1780, St. Michael Vestry Levy Books, BDA.
11. Last Will and Testament of Susannah Ostrehan, item 2, 1, BDA.
12. Christian Blackman would also die a relatively well-off woman after spending time in Demerara. See Last Will and Testament of Christian Blackman, February 2, 1835, Wills and Inventories, St. Michael, 1800–1850, BDA.
13. Last Will and Testament of Priscilla Ostrehan, November 3, 1810, item 6, Wills and Inventories, St. Michael, 1800–1850, BDA.
14. Ibid., 1.
15. Ibid.; Last Will and Testament of Susannah Ostrehan; Last Will and Testament of Mary Ostrehan, May 30, 1829, Wills and Inventories, St. Michael, 1800–1850, BDA; Last Will and Testament of Mary Ostrehan Brett, 1847, ibid.
16. Newton, *Children of Africa in the Colonies*, 27–28.
17. Ibid., 24; Craton, "Proto-Peasant Revolts?"; Beckles and Watson, "Social Protest and Labour Bargaining," 273.
18. See Colonel Codd to Governor Leith, April 25, 1816, CO 28/84, NAUK; Rear Admiral Harvey to J. W. Croker, Secretary of the Admiralty, April 30, 1816, ibid. We

are grateful to Craton, "Proto-Peasant Revolts?," 101–5, for the above research. See also Schomburgk, *History of Barbados*, 395–99.

19. Petley, "Gluttony, Excess, and the Fall of the Planter Class"; Heuman, "The Social Structure of the Slave Societies of the Caribbean," in Knight, *General History of the Caribbean*, vol. 3, 138–68; Pinckard, *Notes on the West Indies*, vol. 2, 97–106; Waller, *Voyage in the West Indies*, 15.

20. Handler, *The Unappropriated People*, 17–20.

21. See Moore, *The Public Acts in Force*, 226–27; Coleridge, *Six Months in the West Indies*, 291; Beckles, "Black over White"; Beckles, *History of Barbados*, 46–50; Sheppard, *The "Redlegs" of Barbados*, 41–55; Schomburgk, *History of Barbados*, 382–83.

22. Newton, *Children of Africa in the Colonies*, 28–30.

23. Census of Barbados, 1829, qtd. in Sheppard, *The "Redlegs" of Barbados*, 55; Sheppard regards this figure as "rather low."

24. Waller, *Voyage in the West Indies*, 19–22, 96–97.

25. Handler, "Memoirs of an Old Army Officer," 22.

26. Newton, *Children of Africa in the Colonies*, 30.

27. Waller, *Voyage in the West Indies*, 4; Handler, "Memoirs of an Old Army Officer," 25; Bayley, *Four Years Residence*, 36; Pinckard, *Notes on the West Indies*, vol.1, 295–98, and vol. 3, 266–67.

28. Qtd. in Handler, "Memoirs of an Old Army Officer," 23. See also Waller, *Voyage in the West Indies*, 4.

29. Poyer, *History of Barbados*, 95, 639. See also Handler, "Memoirs of an Old Army Officer," 21–30; Waller, *Voyage in the West Indies*, 3–4; Madden, *A Twelvemonth's Residence in the West Indies*, 261–62.

30. For example, see the Susannah Ostrehan display at the George Washington House, Bridgetown, by an unknown author.

31. See Hoefte and Vrij, "Free Black and Colored Women," 145–68.

32. Berbice Slave Registers, Plantation and Personal, 1817, T-71/439, 139, NAUK; and Last Will and Testament of Susannah Ostrehan, item 4, bequest to Susan [*sic*] Ostrehan.

33. For Thomas Ostrehan's property in the Fontabelle area, see Barbados Deeds, RB3/42, 404–5, BDA. We are grateful to Pedro Welch for this research; see Welch, "Crimps and Captains," 97.

34. Entries for Susannah Ostrehan, Susey Ostrahan [*sic*], and Thomas Ostrehan Sr. and Jr. in St. Michael Vestry Levy Books, part 2, 1779, BDA.

35. Susan Ostrehan Formally of Grenada but Now of Barbados Through Her Attorney John Swein Sells Land Formally Occupied by David Clunce to Alexander Fraser, Two Lots, January 10, 1799, Deeds M4, SRG.

36. Fraser was heavily involved with, and indeed married into, the Baillie family. See Alston, "Slaves and Highlanders"; see also Hamilton, *Scotland, the Caribbean and the Atlantic World*, 67, 200.

37. See English Settlers in Barbados, 1613–88, RL1/5, CLS.

38. Manumission of Elizabeth Bannister with Her Son Francis, RB3/41, 20,

BDA; Susannah Ostrehan's 1809 will gives to Christian Blackman "my mulatto man William in trust and confidence that she will emancipate him agreeable to the laws of Great Britain."

39. English Settlers in Barbados, 1613–88, RL1/5, 384, CLS.

40. Ibid.; Mary Ostrehan was also listed as "Molly" Ostrehan in the baptismal records of St. Michael's, Barbados, in 1792, and in Demerara as "Polly" Ostrehan in the *Essequibo and Demerary Royal Gazette*, April 9, 1817; transaction, August 10, 1793, Deeds, O2, SRG.

41. Manumission of Elizabeth Bannister, Henry Magee and Mary Ostrehan Brett, RB3/41, 20, BDA.

42. Occasionally she is confused with Suzy Austin, but they were different women; see Alston, "Slaves and Highlanders."

43. Matthew King of Basse Terre Guadeloupe Sells to Mary Nicholls, March 2, 1814, Barbados Deeds, RB1/262, vol. 2, 484, BDA.

44. Inventory of Susanna Ostrehan, 1; Alleyne, *Historic Bridgetown*, 52, 72.

45. Inventory of Susanna Ostrehan, 1–5.

46. Morris, "Progenitors and Coloured Elite Families," 52–65; see also Cumberbatch, "Amaryllis Collymore and Her Son Ren"; Handler, *The Unappropriated People*, 121; Last Will and Testament of Robert Collymore, October 13, 1824, RB4/65, Probate Records, BDA; Last Will and Testament of Amaryllis Collymore, January 5, 1829, ibid.

47. Baptism of Elizabeth Daughter of Lydia Baptised 1785; Baptism of William Son of Lydia 1790, Parish St. Michael, RL1/5, English Settlers of Barbados, CLS.

48. Last Will and Testament of Susannah Ostrehan, item 3; Last Will and Testament of Priscilla Ostrehan, item 2.

49. Last Will and Testament of Susannah Ostrehan, items 3 and 4.

50. Handler, "Memoirs of an Old Army Officer," 23. See also St. Clair, *A Soldier's Recollection*, vol. 1, 373–99.

51. Pinckard, *Notes on the West Indies*, vol. 1, 246–47.

52. Ibid., 393.

53. Welch, "Crimps and Captains," 108, citing Ostrehan for Mary Ann, RB3/40/501, Deed Record Books, BDA.

54. Welch, "Crimps and Captains," 108, citing deeds RB1/229/90 and RB1/220/322.

55. Mary Ostrehan alias Mary Warner from Barbados, Free Negro; Ann Cook and Mary Best from the Parish of St. Michael Appoint Rev. Walter Carew and Armey Smith of Grenada as Attorneys to Set Free Jenny Mingo, October 7, 1793, Deeds, O2, SRG.

56. Welch, "Crimps and Captains," 98–99, citing the Last Will and Testament of Elizabeth Swain Bannister, 1828, Wills and Inventories, St. Michael, 1800–1850, BDA.

57. Welch, "Crimps and Captains," 113, citing Deed RB1/259/16.

58. Last Will and Testament of Priscilla Ostrehan, item 1.

59. Bayley, *Four Years Residence*, 28, 150, 155; see also entries in the Rate Books for St. Michael, St. Michael Vestry Levy Books, 1810, BDA, for Sabinah Braid on Bay Street, Cumberland Street, and so on; Alleyne, *Historic Bridgetown*, 72; and the Last Will and Testament of Sabinah Brade, 1829, Wills and Inventories, St. Michael, 1800–1850, BDA.

60. Bayley, *Four Years Residence*, 28.

61. A deed of manumission for "Polly" in 1814 refers to her being with Susannah Ostrehan in Barbados; see deed RB1/259/17.

62. See Candlin, *The Last Caribbean Frontier*, 26–29; Higman, *Slave Populations*, 67; Sheridan, "Condition of the Slaves on the Sugar Plantations of Sir John Gladstone"; Dalton, *History of British Guiana*; Costa, *Crowns of Glory*, 55–56; see also Stedman, Price, and Price, *Narrative of a Five Years Expedition*; McDonnell, *Considerations on Negro Slavery*; Quintanilla, "Mercantile Communities in the Ceded Islands."

63. Higman, *Slave Populations*, 77.

64. See the speech by George Canning on the future of Trinidad in Hansard, *Parliamentary History of England*, vol. 36, cols. 864–66. For similar theories on economic growth and defense, see Stephen, *Crisis of the Sugar Colonies*, 151–97; see also Drescher, *Econocide*, 96.

65. The three main sources about Demerara at this time all speak of the difficulties in farming this region and of the water. See Pinckard, *Notes on the West Indies*, vols. 1–3; Bolingbroke, *Voyage to Demerary*; St. Clair, *A Soldier's Recollection*.

66. Bolingbroke, *Voyage to Demerary*, 50.

67. Ibid., 83.

68. Ibid., 25, 79.

69. Ibid., 54.

70. St. Clair, *A Soldier's Recollection*, vol. 1, 104.

71. Pinckard, *Notes on the West Indies*, vol. 2, 172.

72. Bolingbroke, *Voyage to Demerary*, 63.

73. Pinckard, *Notes on the West Indies*, vol. 2, 172.

74. St. Clair, *A Soldier's Recollection*, vol. 1, 354–55.

75. Bolingbroke, *Voyage to Demerary*, 42–43.

76. Ibid., 41.

77. Daly, *Short History*, 103.

78. Bolingbroke, *Voyage to Demerary*, 44.

79. Pinckard, *Notes on the West Indies*, vol. 1, 346.

80. "List of Free-Coloured Persons Who Have Paid Their Colonial Tax Levied on Slaves for the Year 1808—Published by Order of the Honble. Court of Policy. Ann Cook Seven Slaves," *Essequibo and Demerary Royal Gazette*, September 25, 1810.

81. Blackman would later affix her name to a memorial of thanks to Dorothy Thomas. See Rodway, *Timehri*, vol. 10, 241.

82. Dorothy Thomas's first recorded mention in the sources for Demerara is in the *Essequibo and Demerary Royal Gazette*, October 31, 1807.

83. See Vickery, *The Gentleman's Daughter*; and Murray, *Elegant Madness*.
84. Bolingbroke, *Voyage to Demerary*, 44.
85. Recent scholarship casts doubts on this whole narrative; see Clark, *The Strange History of the American Quadroon*; Aslakson, "The 'Quadroon-Plaçage' Myth."
86. Daly, *Short History*, 104.
87. "List of Free-Coloured Persons Who Have Paid Their Colonial Tax, 1808," *Essequibo and Demerary Royal Gazette*, September 25, 1810.
88. Demerara Slave Registers (Plantation and Personal), 1817–34, T-71/391–436, NAUK; Berbice Slave Registers (Plantation and Personal), 1817–34, T-71/437–46, NAUK.
89. For example, see Pinckard, *Notes on the West Indies*, vol. 3, 267–68; Bolingbroke, *Voyage to Demerary*, 15, 170; Waller, *Voyage in the West Indies*, 6.
90. In 1796 George Pinckard saw none at all. See Pinckard, *Notes on the West Indies*, vol. 1, 452. Six years later Bolingbroke noticed two. See Bolingbroke, *Voyage to Demerary*, 169–70.
91. Berbice Slave Registers (Plantation and Personal), 1817, T-71/437, NAUK; Welch, "Crimps and Captains"; *Legacies of British Slave-Ownership*, www.ucl.ac.uk/lbs/person/view/7545.
92. Smith, *British Guiana*, 27.
93. Bolingbroke, *Voyage to Demerary*, 185.
94. Daly, *Short History*, 125.
95. Smith, *British Guiana*, 21.
96. Thompson, *Unprofitable Servants*, 99; see Berbice Slave Registers (Plantation and Personal), 1817–34, T-71/437–46, NAUK.
97. Welch, "Crimps and Captains," 99, citing the Last Will and Testament of Elizabeth Swain Bannister, 1828, Wills and Inventories, St. Michael, 1800–1850, BDA; see also Alston, "Slaves and Highlanders."
98. See the complaints from "Old Stingo" and "New Temperence" in Rodway, *Timehri*, vol. 10, 233–34.
99. Scholarship by both Emily Clark and Kenneth Aslakson on the "Quadroon balls" in antebellum New Orleans, where a white man would choose an attractive woman of color, then negotiate the financial arrangements with her mother in order to take the woman as his temporary mistress, has shown them to be a myth. See Clark, *The Strange History of the American Quadroon*; and Aslakson, "The 'Quadroon-Plaçage' Myth."
100. Rodway, *Timehri*, vol. 10, 236.
101. Ibid., 232.
102. Thurn, *Timehri*, vol. 4, 104.
103. Rodway, *Timehri*, vol. 10, 236.
104. *Essequibo and Demerary Royal Gazette*, November 18, 1815.
105. Last Will and Testament of Mary Ostrehan, 1829.
106. Ibid., item 6.
107. The best work on this rebellion is Costa, *Crowns of Glory*.

108. "A Memorial of Gratitude," *Essequibo and Demerary Royal Gazette*, October 9, 1824.

109. Rodway, *Timehri*, vol. 10, 241–42.

CHAPTER FIVE. *The Queen of Demerara*

1. S. T. Masters, "Some Facts About British Guiana," *Auburn Morning News: Official Paper of the County*, January 6, 1874, 191.

2. Costa, *Crowns of Glory*; Bryant, *Account of an Insurrection of the Negro Slaves*; Steele, *Grenada*.

3. The *Essequibo and Demerary Royal Gazette* (Georgetown), January 18, 1823.

4. Ibid., October 1824.

5. The observation about mercantile activity in Dominica is recorded in the Parliamentary Register for 1784, House of Commons Parliamentary Papers, http://parlipapers.chadwyck.com.

6. Dominica Deed, July 10, 1784, transcribed March 2, 1787, Grenada Deed Book W1, SRG.

7. Dorothy Thomas's will indicates that there was at least one sister.

8. See Zaceck, *Settler Society in the English Leeward Islands*.

9. For John Kirwan and family in Montserrat, see Kirwan Family Papers, accession no. M 1991-13, Records 1780–1900, University of West Florida Archives; see also the sale notice for the plantation on Antigua in the *Whitehall Evening Post; or, London Intelligencer*, September 14, 1756.

10. Evidence of Doll Thomas being a staunch Catholic in her old age comes from Lloyd, *Letters from the West Indies*.

11. Elizabeth Kirwan is named as the free mulatto partner of John Coxall in Grenada Church Records, October 10, 1796, July 2, 1797, March 3, 1798, December 12, 1801, August 14, 1803, MF 1523656, CLS; and in his will entered August 26, 1818, 1563329, CLS. Catherina Simon is also called Catherina Cells in the *Essequibo and Demerary Royal Gazette*, December 14, 1805, and February 13, 1813. It is clear from the lot no. 155 in Cumingsburg that was sold that this is the same woman as Catharina Simon, who was named in a previous ad as the owner of lot 155. The burial of Edward Iles is registered in Grenada Church Records, October 14, 1792, MF 1523656, item 2, folio 101, CLS.

12. Montserrat Deed of Manumission for Ned, July 24, 1781, transcribed in Grenada, March 2, 1787, Grenada Deed Book WI, SRG.

13. Akenson, *If the Irish Ran the World*, 162. See also Sheridan, *Sugar and Slavery*.

14. See report of Governor Burt to Lord Germain, March 17, 1778, CO 152/57, NAUK; Mulcahy, *Hurricanes and Society*, 108; O'Shaughnessy, *An Empire Divided*, 69–71, 161.

15. For a comprehensive discussion of the hurricane's devastation, see Neely, *Great Hurricane of 1780*.

16. Dalton, *History of British Guiana*, vol. 1, 193–223, and chs. 6, 7, and 8.

17. See "Naamen der Eijgnaaren van een ofte meer Plantagien," July 1785, in

the Netherlands National Archives in Amsterdam, http://www.vc.id.au/fh/pl1785transcript.html (accessed March 10, 2013). Cells's presence in Demerara is discussed by George Pinckard in *Notes on the West Indies*, vol. 3, 278.

18. Williams, *From Columbus to Castro*, 244; see also Baker, *Centering the Periphery*, 67.

19. Baptized as "infant daughter" in Grenada, December 20, 1789, MF 1523656, item 2, 35, CLS.

20. Joseph Thomas Witness to the Manumission of "Sally" in Dominica on August 28, 1786, transcribed in Grenada Deed Book E2, SRG.

21. Manumission transactions for Dorothy and her children were entered on March 2, 1797, Grenada Deed Book WI, SRG.

22. Baptism of Eliza Thomas, June 1, 1787, MF 1523656, item 2, folio 14, CLS.

23. Cox, *Free Coloureds*, ch. 4, "Free Coloureds in the Economy."

24. Burial of Edward Isles [sic], October 14, 1792, MF 1523656, item 2, folio 101, CLS.

25. Report on the loss of the *Jack*, 1797, Liverpool Registry of Merchant Ships, Abolition and Slavery Collection, Merseyside Maritime Museum.

26. Born June 26, 1797, baptized, September 9, 1797, MF 1523656, item 2, CLS.

27. Bill of Advocation: Mrs. Dorothea Gordon v. Major John Gordon, 1829, CS 271/66510, National Archives of Scotland.

28. Transactions between Benjamin Webster and Dolly Kirwan, December 1, 1794, and September 10, 1795, Grenada Deed Book, E2, SRG.

29. Land transfer in Grenville, dated July 13, 1829, entered December 20, 1830, Grenada Register: Wills, Indentures, Etc., MF 1563329, 1829–31, 449, CLS.

30. October 24, 1797, MF 1523656, item 2, 55, CLS.

31. The Act of December 1797 was aimed at preventing "too frequent and indiscriminate manumission" and was repealed in 1806, although the tax of £100 continued. See House of Commons Parliamentary Papers, April 5, 1816, 74–75, http://parlipapers.chadwyck.com.

32. Gov. Green to Portland, May 27, 1797, CO 101/35, NAUK. See also Grenada Act, December 27, 1797, CO 103/10, NAUK. This point is also made by Edward Cox in "Fedon's Rebellion," 7–19.

33. Testimony of Dorothea Christina Thomas, CS 271/66510, National Archives of Scotland.

34. Last Will and Testament of John Garraway, August 10, 1812, Prob. 11/1537, 387–89, NAUK; Garraway's descendant wrote a book in the late nineteenth century on the Fedon Rebellion.

35. John Coxall and Elizabeth Kirwan died together in a maritime disaster in 1818. See Will of John Coxall Esq., August 28, 1818, MF 15633929, 374–75, CLS.

36. "Names of Free Coloureds, Extracted from Bridgetown Levy Books, 1808," compiled by Pedro Welsh, posted on H-Slavery discussion log, March 23, 2005, http://h-net.msu.edu; Parish of St. Michael, RL1/5, English Settlers of Barbados, CLS.

37. It is not clear when John Fullerton moved to Demerara from Grenada after

1801. Both he and his brother Gavin Fullerton, along with Gilbert Robertson, are listed in "An Address Has Been Presented to His Honor Lt. Col. Nicholson, by the Planters and Merchants of these Colonies, Demerary," *Essequibo and Demerary Royal Gazette*, June 10, 1805. After Charlotte's death Fullerton returned to Scotland and married. See Fullerton's genealogical record at http://www.thepeerage.com/p555253.htm#i555227 (accessed June 20, 2013).

38. Joseph Thomas was listed as a free colored subscriber, as was Dorothy Thomas, in *Essequibo and Demerary Royal Gazette*, April 10, 1813. The notice for the sale of "Kensington" appeared in *Essequibo and Demerary Royal Gazette*, March 22, 1816.

39. The "Kensington" plantation was later referred to in the memoirs of John Castelfranc Cheverley as the property of Dorothy Thomas; see Thornburn, *No Messing*.

40. Marianne Pemberton Holmes, "Notes on Demerara," accession no. 14748, box 3.1, 1837–59, Special Collections, University of Virginia Library.

41. *Essequibo and Demerary Royal Gazette*, June 15, 1811, July 18, 1812, August 15, 1812, February 11, 1815, August 8, 1815, July 1, 1815.

42. Last Will and Testament of Dorothy Thomas, Prob. 11/2007, NAUK.

43. For more information on the company of Robertson, Sandbach and Parker, as well as Gilbert Robertson, see the Parker Family Papers, 920 PAR I–IV, Liverpool Record Office (hereafter cited as LRO). The merchant George Robertson's mulatto son George Robertson was one of Dorothy's attorneys and an executor of her will.

44. *Essequibo and Demerary Royal Gazette*, October 6, 1804, December 27, 1806, January 10, 1807.

45. *Essequibo and Demerary Royal Gazette*, August 15, 1807 (letter dated August 8, 1807).

46. Henrietta Simon went to England in 1810; see Letter of D. P. Simon to Henrietta Simon, March 25, 1813, in personal possession of Cassandra Pybus.

47. *Essequibo and Demerary Royal Gazette*, December 14, 1805, May 30, 1807, February 10, 1810, January 7, 1812.

48. C. S. Parker to E. Parker, June 28, 1810, 920 PAR 1/53, LRO.

49. Sale of plantation to C. S. Parker is in the *Essequibo and Demerary Royal Gazette*, March 21, 1818; Kensington Plantation—Gilbert Robertson and Charlotte Fullarton—56 slaves, Demerara Slave Returns, 1820, T-71/407, NAUK.

50. The Coxall will is dated 1817 and was entered into the Grenada Deed Book in August 1818, MF 1563329, 374, CLS. A belated report of the last voyage of Coxall's ship can be found in the *London Gazette*, 1845, 613.

51. Deed Book R2, SRG.

52. The slave registers of Grenada are available at www.ancestry.com.

53. Transaction of August 29, 1837, entered April 4, 1839, in Grenada Deeds, 1839–61, MF 1563330, 2–4, 447, CLS.

54. See Livesay, "Children of Uncertain Fortune."

55. We know about this school from the reminiscences of George Augustus Sala, who met Dorothy Thomas there in the late 1820s. See Sala, *Temple Bar*, 246–47.

56. See Gerzina, *Black England*, 13.

57. Long, *History of Jamaica*, vol. 2, 274.

58. See Livesay, "Children of Uncertain Fortune."

59. The journal of an anonymous Glasgow merchant, held in the National Archives of Scotland, lists consistent payments from John Robertson over several years.

60. See C. S. Parker to J. Parker, June 28, 1791, Parker Family Papers, LRO. The career of Gilbert Robertson Jr. is the subject of a forthcoming book by Cassandra Pybus.

61. The announcement for the convoy "in 14 days or six weeks" was made in *Essequibo and Demerary Royal Gazette*, April 29, 1810, and was repeated again in May of that year.

62. C. S. Parker to E. Parker, August 11, 1810, Parker Family Papers, 920 PAR 1/53, LRO.

63. There were a number of schools taking in mixed-race children at that time, including the Paisley Grammar School, the Tain Academy, and the Inverness Royal Academy.

64. *Essequibo and Demerary Royal Gazette*, May 6, 1817. The lion was on display for about eight months, leaving in February 1818.

65. Dorothy Thomas—82 Slaves, no. 834, Demerara Slave Returns, 1826 Index, T-71/420, NAUK.

66. The case is recounted in graphic detail in the pamphlet "An Appeal to the Good Sense and Justice of the Inhabitants of the British Empire," written and published by Joseph Henry Holmes, advocate, Demarara, in 1823; he was the husband of Marianne Pemberton Holmes.

67. "Protector of Slaves Report: Part 1 Demerara," December 15, 1830, House of Commons Parliamentary Papers: Accounts and Papers, vol. 16, 262, http://parlipapers.chadwyck.com.

68. Dorothy Thomas, Guiana Slave Holder Compensation, nos. 1400, 1402, NDO 4/8, NAUK.

69. There are several white women listed, including Louise Goppy, Sarah and Mary-Ann Rogers, Sarah Alleyne, and Jane Thornton, who each received over £7,000. Guiana Slave Holder Compensation, NDO 4/8, NAUK.

70. "Report of St. George's Day."

71. "The Climate of Demerara," 542–43.

72. Marianne Holmes's "Notes on Demerara" are held in the papers of their son George Frederick Holmes at the University of Virginia.

73. Ibid.

74. Barker, *The Victory*, 191.

75. Lady Augusta Fitzclarence was the godmother to Henrietta's youngest son, George Augustus Sala.

76. Connell, "Prince William Henry's Visits."

77. Sala, *Temple Bar*, 246.

78. Kensington House was sold by Thomas Wetherall in 1830 and reopened as a private lunatic asylum; see prospectus by William Corbin Finch, *Kensington House Asylum* (London: J Mallett 1830). For several years prior to that, it was listed in the rate books as being "in private tenure."

79. Sala, *Temple Bar*, 246.

80. Ibid.

81. Holmes, "Notes on Demerara."

82. Masters, "Some Facts About British Guiana," 191.

83. Lloyd, *Letters from the West Indies*, 24–26. The planters from Berbice were probably John Lucie Smith Jr. and Gavin Fullerton, who were close friends and executors of her estate.

84. Schomburgk, *Description of British Guiana*, 22.

85. "Notices from British Guiana," *Edinburgh Gazette*, March 6, 1849. John Lurie Smith was an assistant judge advocate in the trial of missionary John Smith; see Costa, *Crowns of Glory*, 253. He went on to become advocate general.

86. Last Will and Testament of Dorothy Thomas, Prob. 11/2007, NAUK.

87. Sala, *Temple Bar*, 246.

CHAPTER SIX. *By Habit and Repute*

1. Bond of Robert Garraway, August 11, 1813, MF 1563328, 230, CLS.

2. See MF 1523656, folio 369, CLS; Will of Robert Garraway, August 17, 1817, MF 1563329, 290, CLS.

3. Stone, *Uncertain Unions*; Gillis, *For Better, for Worse*.

4. Moreton, *Manners and Customs of the West India Islands*, 125. Farley, "The Shadow and the Substance," states that in the tiny colony of Berbice it was not legal for white men to marry their free colored partners until 1818.

5. Bill of Advocation: Mrs. Dorothea Gordon v. Major John Gordon, CS271/66510, National Archives of Scotland.

6. Will of Robert Garraway, August 17, 1817, proved June 6, 1822, MF 1563329, 290, CLS.

7. Baptism of Ann Garroway [sic] Thomas Daughter of Dorothy C. Thomas, January 12, 1816, Records of Parish of St. Michael, Barbados, CLS.

8. Will of Robert Garraway.

9. *Essequibo and Demerary Royal Gazette*, March 21, 1817.

10. Tendered as evidence in the Bill of Advocation: Mrs. Dorothea Gordon v. Major John Gordon.

11. The Queen's Royal Regiment of Foot was stationed in Trinidad after the peace in 1816; they moved to Demerara in 1818. See "The Queen's Royal Regiment Living History Group," http://www.allthequeensmen.co.uk (accessed March 12, 2013).

12. Barker, *The Victory*, 191, explains how visitors to Demerara hired their slaves from "the well-known Doll Thomas."

13. See "The Queen's Royal Regiment Living History Group."

14. Letter from Major John Gordon to Mrs. Dorothea Gordon, December 9, 1826, CS217/66510, National Archives of Scotland.

15. Major John Gordon to Mrs. Dorothea Gordon, April 15, June 9, and July 2, 1823. This and all the subsequent quotes are taken from Bill of Advocation: Mrs. Dorothea Gordon v. Major John Gordon.

16. The parish register of St. Mary's, Chester, shows the baptism of Huntly Gordon on June 21, 1822, registered as the son of John Gordon and Dorothea Christina Thomas.

17. Barker, *The Victory*, 191.

18. See "Letter to the Editor," *Essequibo and Demerary Royal Gazette*, December 22, 1813.

19. C. S. Parker to E. Parker, June 28, 1810, 920 PAR 1/53, LRO.

20. Gilbert Robertson died in Edinburgh on March 10, 1840. His will has not been found.

21. Dorothy Thomas's purchase of Garraway's Grenada property and her gift of it to her daughter and grandson in 1837 are recorded in Grenada Deed Book, April 2, 1839, MF 1563330 447, CLS.

22. Poyer, *History of Barbados;* Waller, *Voyage in the West Indies*, 19–20; Bayley, *Four Years Residence*, 493.

23. Waller, *Voyage in the West Indies*, 19–20.

24. Ashe, *Travels in America*, vol. 2, 344–46.

25. Aslakson, "The 'Quadroon-Plaçage' Myth of Antebellum New Orleans," 710.

26. Dorothea Christina was legally married when Dorothy wrote her will in 1843, and is probably the woman described by Matthew Henry Barker as "married to a highly respectable merchant of Demerara"; see Barker, *The Victory*, 192.

27. Candlin, *The Last Caribbean Frontier*, 75–96; Poyer, *History of Barbados*, 639.

28. Candlin, *The Last Caribbean Frontier*, 143–56.

29. McDaniel, "The Philips," 182; Devas, *A History of the Island of Grenada*, 173.

30. Julien Fedon and Marie Rose Cavalan [sic], Register for the Parish of Grand Pauvre, 1779–83, 2, SRG.

31. Pinckard, *Notes on the West Indies*, vol. 1, 245.

32. Welch, "Unhappy and Afflicted Women?"; Handler, "Joseph Rachell and Rachael Pringle Polgreen."

33. Barker, *The Victory*, 191.

34. Candlin, *The Last Caribbean Frontier*, ch. 2, 24–51; and Pybus, "Tense and Tender Ties."

35. Dominica deed, July 10, 1784, Grenada Deed Book W1, SRG.

36. Barker, *The Victory*, 191.

37. Joseph Thomas did make a bequest of a slave to a niece a couple of years before he died; see deed, November 11, 1798, MF 1563328 458, CLS. He may also have bequeathed a slave to his youngest daughter, since John Gordon's letters refer to "the slave your father left you." See Bill of Advocation: Mrs. Dorothea Gordon v. Major John Gordon.

38. Berbice Slave Registers, 1817, 1819, 1822, in Slave Registers of Former British Colonial Dependencies, 1812–34, at http://www.ancestry.com.

39. Pedro Welch reports that Elizabeth Swain Bannister's manumission was secured by Susannah Ostrehan. Welch, "Crimps and Captains," 98.

40. The evidence about the children's schooling comes from Petition from William Fraser, October 19, 1823, CO 111/96, NAUK; and Alston, "Slaves and Highlanders."

41. Petition from William Fraser.

42. Alston, "Slaves and Highlanders."

43. Welch, "Crimps and Captains," 98–99, citing the Last Will and Testament of Elizabeth Swain Bannister, 1828, Wills and Inventories, St. Michael, 1800–1850, BDA.

44. William Fraser purchased the plantation "L'Esperance" in Suriname from Henry Davidson in 1829 for £13,500, to be paid over eight years, CS96/2131, National Archives of Scotland. See also Alston, "Slaves and Highlanders."

45. Anna Maria Fraser was the daughter of Mary or Polly Stewart, "a free mulatto" in Barbados in 1775; see RL1/5 P 48, CLS.

46. She received a modest £3, according to Alston, "Slaves and Highlanders."

47. Manumissions dated August 25, 1818, March 23, 1821, and October 18, 1821, MF 1563329, 37, 163, 373, CLS.

48. Registers for Parish and Town of St. George, Grenada, in the Slave Registers of Former British Colonial Dependencies, 1812–34, at www.ancestry.com.

49. Reference to Garraway as the master of the Chancery Court is in *London Gazette*, 1844, 15.

50. Joseph Garraway was appointed the stipendiary magistrate in 1836 and went on to become judge of the Assistant Court of Appeal.

51. Ann Garraway married Roger Sweeny on April 15, 1847.

52. Last Will and Testament of Dorothy Thomas, Prob. 11/2007, NAUK.

CHAPTER SEVEN. *Uncertain Prospects*

1. Last Will and Testament of Judith Philip, November 25, 1848, Prob. 11/2105, NAUK. The will can also be found at the Supreme Court Registry of Grenada; see Last Will and Testament of Judith Philip, November 25, 1848, Deeds B3, 558–61, SRG.

2. Last Will and Testament of Ann-Rachel Thornton, published April 4, 1849, Deeds B3, 578–79, SRG. See also Thornton Family Indenture, April 9, 1855, Deeds W-C3, 286–92, SRG.

3. Burial Notice of Louis Edmund Thornton at Ancestry.com from information found in Saint Marylebone, Register of Burials, call no. 89/mry1/333, London Metropolitan Archives.

4. Marriage banns of Louis Edmund Thornton and Elizabeth Charlotte Western, St. Pancras, November 18, 1813, at Ancestry.com from information collated from the Church of England Parish Registers, 1754–1921, London Metropolitan Archives.

5. Louis Edmund Thornton for Philip Thornton to Stacey Grimaldi, at Ancestry.com from information found originally at Court of King's Bench: Plea Side: Affidavits of Due Execution of Articles of Clerkship, ser. I, class KB 105, piece 26, NAUK.

6. Last Will of Judith Philip, 1848; Last Will of Ann-Rachel Thornton, 1849; and Heirs of Judith Philip Indenture, Deeds B3, November 14, 1850, 689–95, all at SRG.

7. Burial Record of Magdalene Thornton, July 15, 1857, from information collated by Ancestry.com from information found in Highgate Cemetery of Saint James, Transcript of Burials, January 1857–December 1857, call no. DL/T/063/016, London Metropolitan Archives. See also Judith Thornton, 1851 census data, at Ancestry.com from information collated from the Census of the United Kingdom, 1851, class HO107, piece 1507, folio 269, 7, GSU roll 87841, NAUK.

8. Magdalene and Judith Thornton Intention to Depart, 1849, Deeds B3, 684–85, SRG.

9. Ibid., 685.

10. Heuman, "The British West Indies," 470–95.

11. Last Will of Ann-Rachel Thornton, 1849, 579.

12. See *Legacies of British Slave-Ownership* at http://www.ucl.ac.uk/lbs. See also Draper, *The Price of Emancipation*; Livesay, "Children of Uncertain Fortune" and "Extended Families."

13. See *Legacies of British Slave-Ownership* at http://www.ucl.ac.uk/lbs/person/view/12954 and http://www.ucl.ac.uk/lbs/person/view/8816.

14. For example, see Welch, *"Red" and Black over White*; Welch, "Crimps and Captains"; Newton, *Children of Africa in the Colonies*; Handler, *The Unnappropriated People*; Sio, "Marginality and Free Coloured Identity."

15. See McDaniel, "The Philips"; Candlin, *The Last Caribbean Frontier*, ch. 1, "What Became of the Fedon Rebellion?" 1–23; Philippe, *A Free Mulatto*, and the introduction to the 1996 edition by Selwyn R. Cudjoe, v–xxiii. See also the Plantation Slave Registers for the Philip Family on Trinidad. The returns for J. B. Louis Philip can be found at Trinidad Plantation Slave Registers, 1833, 213–17 ("Concorde" estate) and 430–32 ("Philippine" estate), T-71/501, NAUK.

16. Wheeler, *Complexion of Race*; Beasley, *Victorian Reinvention of Race*.

17. Sala, *Life and Adventures*, vol. 1, 3–4.

18. Shyllon, "The Black Presence and Experience in Britain"; Fryer, *Staying Power*; File and Power, *Black Settlers in Britain*; Dabydeen, Gilmore, and Jones, *The Oxford Companion to Black British History*.

19. Livesay, "Children of Uncertain Fortune," 1–13.

20. Aslakson, "The 'Quadroon-Plaçage' Myth."

21. Heuman, *The British West Indies*, 483–84.

22. Magdalene and Judith Thornton Intention to Depart, 1849, Deeds B3, 684–85, SRG.

23. Judith Thornton, 1851 census data, collated by Ancestry.com from information

found at the Census of the United Kingdom, 1851, class HO107, piece 1507, folio 269, 7, GSU roll 87841, NAUK

24. Census details for 8 Montagu Square collated by Ancestry.com from information found at the Census of the United Kingdom, 1851, class HO107, piece 1489, folio 494, 4, GSU roll 87816, NAUK.

25. The archives for William Cavendish-Scott-Bentinck, the fifth Duke of Portland, are kept at the University of Nottingham Library's Special Collections Department.

26. Heirs of Judith Philip Indenture, Deeds B3, November 14, 1850, 689–95, SRG.

27. Ibid.

28. See Kerr's entry at the *Legacies of British Slave-Ownership* website, http://www.ucl.ac.uk/lbs/person/view/42110. See also Society for the Registry of Shipping, ed., *Register of Shipping for the Year 1831* (London: W. Merchant, 1831), 1. Another man, Samuel Mitcham, was also present but his role is unclear.

29. William Wheeler Thornton, 1851 census data collated by Ancestry.com from information found at the Census of the United Kingdom, 1851, class HO107, piece 2127, folio 16, 24, GSU roll 87757, NAUK.

30. We thank Julia Collar, archivist at St. George's Church, Benenden, for her invaluable assistance in tracing William Wheeler Thornton in Kent. See also Haslewood, *Parish of Benenden*, 163.

31. Thornton Family Indenture, April 9, 1855, Deeds W-C3, 286–92, SRG.

32. Haslewood, *Parish of Benenden*, 163.

33. Ibid., 155.

34. Ancestry.com, England and Wales, Free BMD Marriage Index, 1837–1915, vol. 2a, 1853, 671; see also the Marriage and Baptism Index and Records, St. George's Parish Church, Benenden, July 13, 1853.

35. Thomas Boys, 1861 census data, collated by Ancestry.com from information found at the Census of the United Kingdom, 1861, class RG9, piece 555, folio 84, 3, GSU roll 542660, and class RG11, piece 911, folio 38, 36, GSU roll 1341217, NAUK. See also Boys, *A Key to the Book of Psalms*.

36. London, England, Register of Marriages and Banns 1850, Saint Mary, Bryanston Square, Register of Marriages, P89/MRY2, item 065, London Metropolitan Archives.

37. Sainty, *Office-Holders in Modern Britain*.

38. Henry Frederick Amedroz, 1871 census data, collated by Ancestry.com from information found at the Census of the United Kingdom, 1871, class RG10, piece 175, folio 9, 9, GSU roll 823304. See also Amedroz, *Eclipse of the Abbasid Caliphate*.

39. Marriage and Baptism Index and Records, St. George's Parish Church, Benenden, 1855.

40. Trollope, *Barchester Chronicles*.

41. When she died Magdalene was listed as living at the smart address of 11 King Edward Terrace, Islington, while her sister was living on Great Portland Street;

see Transcript of Burials, January 1857–December 1857, London Metropolitan Archives, call no. DL/T/063/016, NAUK. See also Death Notice of Judith Thornton, March 20, 1869, England and Wales, National Probate Calendar (Index of Wills and Administrations), 1858–1966, at www.ancestry.com.

42. William Wheeler Thornton, 1871 census data, collated by Ancestry.com from information found at the Census of the United Kingdom, 1871, class RG10, piece 837, folio 13, 18, GSU roll 827752, NAUK.

43. William Wheeler Thornton, 1891 census data, collated by Ancestry.com from information found at the Census of the United Kingdom, 1891, class RG12, piece 96, folio 88, 14, GSU roll 6095206, NAUK.

44. Henry Frederick Amedroz, 1871 census data, collated by Ancestry.com from information found at the Census of the United Kingdom, 1871, class RG10, piece 175, folio 9, 9, GSU roll 823304, NAUK.

45. Transcript of Burials, January 1857–December 1857, London Metropolitan Archives, call no. DL/T/063/016, NAUK.

46. Death Notice of Judith Thornton, March 20, 1869, England and Wales, National Probate Calendar (Index of Wills and Administrations), 1858–1966, at www.ancestry.com.

47. Death Notice of Jeannette Thornton, December 30, 1891, ibid.

48. Returns of J. B. Louis Philip for Philippine and Concord[e] Plantations, Trinidad Slave Registers: Plantation Slaves, 1813, T-71/501, NAUK. See also Philip Family Indenture, Deeds K3, September 10, 1785, 49–52, SRG.

49. For more on the prominent free colored families of Trinidad, see Campbell, *Cedulants and Capitulants*, esp. ch. 2, "Free Coloured Proprietors."

50. See the introduction by Selwyn R. Cudjoe to Philippe, *A Free Mulatto*, i–xxi.

51. Commissioners of Legal Enquiry in the West Indies, 1822–28, unnumbered volume, Free People of Colour: Disabilities and Grievances, CO 318/76, NAUK.

52. See Wesley, "Emancipation of the Free Colored Population."

53. Philippe, *A Free Mulatto*.

54. McDaniel, *The Philips*, 178–94.

55. Last Will and Testament of Sir Thomas Picton, 1815, Prob. 11/1571, NAUK.

56. Return of Augusta Picton, Trinidad Slave Registers, T-71/511, NAUK.

57. Return of Richard Picton and Maria Pietry, Trinidad Slave Registers, T-71/518, NAUK.

58. Marie Adelaide Picton, Trinidad claim no. 53, August 29, 1836, for "3 Enslaved" received £172, 3s., 11d.; see *Legacies of British Slave-Ownership* database, http://www.ucl.ac.uk/lbs/claim/view/29772 (accessed April 26, 2013).

59. Thomas Picton Jr.'s education and his ultimate fate are recorded in WO 15/3908, Return of the Services and Professional Education—Thomas Rose Picton, 1813–23, NAUK.

60. Girard, "Sir James Douglas's Mother and Grandmother."

61. Adele Perry, biography of James Douglas, *Canadian Dictionary of Biography*, forthcoming.

62. This is deduced from the proposal in regard to his son made by John Gordon before the court case discussed in chapter 6.

63. His graduation from Edinburgh University is listed in *Edinburgh Medical and Surgical Journal* 56 (1841): 48.

64. Information on Huntly Gordon's marriage to Julia Grantham is from http://www.lincolnshire-wolds.org/all-lincolnshire/23743.htm (accessed May 20, 2013).

65. His military promotion to surgeon general can be found in *London Gazette*, August 11, 1876.

66. For example, see the entry for Edward Strathearn Gordon, Baron Gordon of Drumearn, at http://thepeerage.com/p17018.htm#i170174 (accessed May 20, 2013).

67. See http://www.helensburgh-heritage.co.uk.

68. See Newton, *Children of Africa in the Colonies*, ch. 6. He is described as "Mr. Galloway [*sic*] a colored gentleman highly respected for his talents" in Thome and Kimball, *Emancipation in the West Indies*, 66. His appointment is noted in House of Commons Parliamentary Papers, 1837, vol. 53, 384–421, http://parlipapers.chadwyck.com.

69. Sala, *Life and Adventures*, vol. 1. See also the Will of Charles McGarel, T528/38, NAUK.

70. See Certificate of de Broglio to Run Kensington House Boarding School, 1802, MR/RH/1/034; Abbe Jean Simon Pierre Rouelle and Nicholas Francis de Thiel, school prospectus, 1805, MR/RH1/42, MS 11936/498/1001047, MS 11936/507/1061060, all in London Metropolitan Archives.

71. The brief biography supplied by George Augustus Sala for his grandfather is a complete fabrication.

72. Their marriage certificate is dated June 22, 1812. The witnesses were his mother, Susannah Sala; his sister Sophia Sala; and a man named Charles Hinde.

73. *Quarterly Musical Magazine and Review* (December 15, 1827).

74. *Lady's Monthly Museum* 27 (1828): 120–26.

75. See Sala, *Life and Adventures*, 7.

76. Sala, *The Baddington Peerage*, is a novel about men who impetuously marry women who are not what they seem.

77. *Lady's Monthly Museum* 27 (1828): 126. However, as Tracy Davis points out, "the similarities between the actress's life and the prostitute's or *demi-mondaine*'s were unforgettable and overruled all other evidence about respectability" (*Actresses as Working Women*, 69).

78. *Morning Chronicle*, December 15, 1827; see also *Morning Post*, December 15, 1827; *Evening Standard*, January 6, 1828.

79. Most actresses and singers in late Georgian and early Victorian England were also courtesans. See Davis, *Actresses as Working Women*; and Auerbach, *Woman and the Demon*. Auerbach notes that the term "public woman" for performer and prostitute alike was a social liability, but "it endowed the actress with the fallen woman's incendiary glory without dooming her to ostracism and death" (205).

80. According to one of Sala's biographers, G. A. Sala removed Henry from his

name after discovering his true parentage. See Edwards, *Dickens' Young Men*; and "George Augustus Sala and His Panorama," 13.

81. Sala, *Life and Adventures*, 25.

82. See the announcement of Madame Sala's return in the *Court Journal*, March 14, 1835.

83. Sala, *Life and Adventures*, 22.

84. Sala, *Life and Adventures*, 50; Sala, *Things I Have Seen*, 47–50.

85. Pope-Hennessy, *Charles Dickens*, 76.

86. Sala, *Life and Adventures*, 70.

87. Ibid., 72–74.

88. *Court Journal*, June 27, 1835.

89. According to G. A. Sala, among her "intimate friends" was Sir Matthew Tierry, who had been the doctor to William IV, and she was attended by Sir James Clark when she contracted smallpox.

90. *Theatrical Observer and Daily Bills of the Play*, January 2, 1839 (which includes the quotation from Dickens).

91. Charles Dickens to Henrietta Sala, July 23, 1838, in House et al., *Letters of Charles Dickens*, 420.

92. Sala writes candidly about Dover in *Life and Adventures*, 121–23. His account of the trip to Paris in *Things I Have Seen*, 133–35, is much more fanciful.

93. See notices for her concerts in *Musical World*, March 8, 1856; and *Journal of the Society of the Arts*, June 19, 1857. Her death in Brighton is recorded in *Gentleman's Magazine*, April 10, 1860, where she is said to have been sixty-six; her death certificate from Brighton states her age as sixty-seven, but she was closer to seventy-five. G. A. Sala was with her when she died.

94. Sala, *Temple Bar*, 247.

95. Sala writes about his mother's relationship with Dickens in *Things I Have Seen*, 47–50, 56.

96. See Blake, "Charles Dickens, George Augustus Sala and Household Words."

97. Sala, *Quite Alone*, 29; see also Sala's story "The Wild Woman" in *Harpers*.

98. Sala, *My Diary*, 38.

99. Ibid., 39.

100. Ibid., 420.

101. Straus, *Sala*; Mackenzie, *Letters of G. A. Sala to Edmund Yates*; Edwards, *Dickens' Young Men*; Blake, "George Augustus Sala."

CONCLUSION

1. Thornburn, *No Messing*, 52–56.

2. Ibid., 52–53. Benjamin James Hopkinson was the eldest son of the planter Benjamin Hopkinson, who had been in Tobago before moving to Demerara; he died in Bath in 1801 (Prob. 11/1360, NAUK). Benjamin James Hopkinson was born in Tobago in November 1785, baptized in London in 1798, and attended Oriel College, Oxford (1802), and Trinity College, Cambridge (1804). By 1816 he was established as

a merchant in Throgmorton Street, London (Guild Hall Records, MS 11936/466/922569, London Metropolitan Archives).

3. Thornburn, *No Messing*, 61.

4. Ibid., 62.

5. Ibid., 63. Benjamin Hopkinson had left the colony in 1898 and returned to England, where he married a white woman. In the slave compensation records, Joanna Hopkinson was said to be the owner of thirty-seven slaves.

6. Thornburn, *No Messing*, 66. Lemon is the name of a free colored family of women from Barbados. It is highly likely that Molly Lemon's sister, a grandmother of Cheverley's employer, was the Betsy Lemon who was once enslaved by Rachael Polgreen; see chapter 2.

7. Thornburn, *No Messing*, 76–77.

8. Ibid., 119.

9. Costa, *Crowns of Glory*; Craton, *Testing the Chains*.

10. *Legacies of British Slave-Ownership* website, www.ucl.ac.uk/lbs (accessed June 20, 2013).

11. We are much indebted for this to Nick Draper and especially to C. C. Thornburn, the editor who drew it to Nick's attention.

12. *Legacies of British Slave-Ownership* website, www.ucl.ac.uk/lbs (accessed June 20, 2013).

13. Aslakson, "The 'Quadroon-Plaçage' Myth"; Jones, *The Métis of Senegal*.

14. Clark, *The Strange History of the American Quadroon*, 96.

15. Ibid., 9.

16. Here the work of David Lambert and Alan Lester, along with that of Zoe Laidlaw, is pertinent because of their discussions of imperial careers. See Laidlaw, *Colonial Connections*; Lambert and Lester, *Colonial Lives Across the British Empire*.

17. Mohammed, *Gendered Realities*, xiv–xxiii.

18. Scott and Hébrard, *Freedom Papers*.

19. Scully and Paton, *Gender and Slave Emancipation*, 1–34.

20. Stoeltje, "Ashanti Queen Mothers"; Jones, *The Métis of Senegal*.

BIBLIOGRAPHY

MANUSCRIPT SOURCES

Barbados Department of Archives
  Deeds, 1770–1830
  Levy Books, 1768–82, 1779–88
  Probate Records, 1791, 1800–1850
Church of Latter-day Saints Family History Center
  England and Wales, Free BMD Marriage Index, 1837–1915
  English Settlers in Barbados, 1613–1880
  Grenada Church Records, 1792–96
  Grenada Deeds, 1798–1861
  National Probate Calendar (Index of Wills and Administrations), 1858–1966
London Metropolitan Archives
  Church of England Parish Registers, 1754–1921
  Rate Books and Insurance Records for Kensington and Westminster, 1795–1830
  Register of Burials, 1830
  Transcript of Burials, January–December 1857
National Archives of Scotland
  Court of Sessions Records, 1828–29
National Archives of Trinidad and Tobago
  Book of Spanish Protocols, "S" and "P," Index 1787–1813
  Trinidad and Tobago Historical Society Collection, 1796
National Archives of the United Kingdom
  Census of the United Kingdom 1851, 1861, 1871, 1881, 1891
  Colonial Office Records, 1768–1834
  Court of King's Bench Records, 1816
  National Debt Office Records, 1836
  Probate Records, 1812–49
  Royal College of Physicians Records, 1830
  Treasury Records, 1817–34
  War Office Records, 1813–23
Supreme Court Registry of Grenada
  Court of Common Pleas 1794–96
  Deed Books, 1763–1855
  Receipt Book, 1813–22
  Record Book of the Court Oyer and Terminer, 1796
  Register for the Parish of Grand Pauvre, 1779–83

Collections
  Henry E. Huntingdon Library: Stowe Collection
  Lancashire Archives, Preston, England: Lancashire Anglican Parish Registers
  Liverpool Record Office: Parker Family Papers
  National Library of Scotland: *St. George's Chronicle and Grenada Gazette*, 1789–1810
  Netherlands National Archives: *Naamen der Eijgnaaren van een ofte meer Plantagien*, 1785
  Harry Ransom Center, University of Texas: George Augustus Sala Collection
  St. George's Parish Church: Marriage and Baptism Index and Records
  University of Florida Library: *Essequibo and Demerary Royal Gazette*, 1802–24
  University of Nottingham Library Special Collections: Archives of William Cavendish-Scott-Bentinck, Fifth Duke of Portland
  University of Virginia Library Special Collections: George Frederick Holmes Collection
  University of West Florida Archives: Kirwan Family Papers,

PRINTED PRIMARY SOURCES

Ashe, Thomas. *Travels in America, Performed in 1806*. 3 vols. London: William Sawyer, 1808.

Ashley, John. *Memoirs and Considerations Concerning the Trade and Revenues of the British Colonies in America with Proposals for Rendering Those Colonies More Beneficial to Great Britain*. 2 vols. London: C. Corbett, 1740.

Barker, Matthew Henry. *The Victory; or, The Ward Room Mess*. London: Henry Colburn, 1844.

Bayley, Frederick William Naylor. *Four Years Residence in the West Indies*. London: William Kidd, 1833.

Bolingbroke, Henry. *A Voyage to Demerary Containing a Statistical Account of the Settlements There and Those of the Essequibo, the Berbice and the Other Contiguous Rivers of Guyana*. London: Richard Phillips, 1807.

Boys, Rev. Thomas. *A Key to the Book of Psalms*. London: Printed for L. B. Seeley and Son, 1825.

Brace, Jeffery. *The Blind African Slave; or, The Memoirs of Boyrereau Brinch, Nicknamed Jeffery Brace*, ed. Kari Winter. 1810. Reprint, Madison: University of Wisconsin Press, 2004.

Bryant, Joshua. *Account of an Insurrection of the Negro Slaves in the Colony of Demerara on the 18th August 1823*. Georgetown, Demerara: Printed by A. Stevenson at the Guiana Chronicle Office, 1824.

Burke, Edmund. *The State of the Nation*. London: J. Dodsley, 1782.

Cleland, John. *Fanny Hill; or, A Woman of Pleasure*. 1748. Reprint, New York: Modern Library, 2001.

"The Climate of Demerara." *United Service Journal and Naval and Military Magazine* 3 (1838): 542–43.

Coleridge, Henry Nelson. *Six Months in the West Indies in 1825*. New York: G. and C. Carvill and E. Bliss and E. White, 1826.
Day, Charles William. *Five Years' Residence in the West Indies*, vol. 1. London: Colburn and Co., 1852.
Defoe, Daniel. *The Fortunes and Misfortunes of the Famous Moll Flanders*. 1722. Reprint, Ontario: Broadview, 2005.
Fenner, Walter. *A New and Accurate Map of the Island of Cariacou [sic] in the West Indies 1784*. London: J. Budd, 1784.
Fullarton, William. *A Refutation of the Pamphlet Which Colonel Picton Lately Addressed to Lord Hobart*. London: John Stockdale and Sons, 1805.
———. *A Statement, Letters and Documents Respecting the Affairs of Trinidad*. London: John Stockdale and Sons, 1804.
Garraway, D. G. *A Short Account of the Insurrection That Broke Out in Grenada in 1795*. Grenada: C. Wells and Son, 1877.
A Grenada Planter Now Residing in London. *A Full and Impartial Answer to a Letter in the Gazetteer of October 22, 1768, Relative to the Conduct of His Excellency Governor Robert Melvill*. London: J. Almon, W. Johnston, G. Pearch, and G. Keith, 1768.
A Grenadian Planter. *A Brief Enquiry into the Causes of, and Conduct Pursued by, the Colonial Government, for Quelling the Insurrection in Grenada, 1795. In a Letter from a Grenada Planter to a Merchant in London*. London: J. Budd, 1796.
Hansard, T. C. *The Parliamentary History of England*. 36 vols. London: n.p., 1820.
Haslewood, Rev. Francis. *The Parish of Benenden, Kent: Its Monuments, Vicars and Persons of Note*. Ipswich: Published privately, 1889.
Hay, John. *A Narrative of the Insurrection in the Island of Grenada: Which Took Place in 1795*. London: J. Ridgeway, 1823.
Henderson, Andrew. *Furius; or, A Modest Attempt Towards a History of the Life and Surprising Exploits of the Famous W. L. Critic and Thief-Catcher*. London: H. Carpenter, 1754.
Holmes, Joseph Henry. *An Appeal to the Good Sense and Justice of the Inhabitants of the British Empire*. Georgetown: n.p., 1823.
Howell, T. B. *A Complete Collection of State Trials and Proceedings for High Treason and Other Crimes and Misdemeanors*, vol. 30. London: Hansard, 1823.
Hunt, Leigh. "William Lauder." *Cabinet*, n.s., 1 (February 1809): 111.
Joseph, E. L. *A History of Trinidad*. London: Henry James Mills, 1838.
Lessly, John. "The Laws of Grenada and the Grenadines." 1786. Reproduced in McDaniel, "The Philips," 187.
Lloyd, William. *Letters from the West Indies During a Visit in the Autumn of 1836*. London: Darton and Harvey, 1837.
Long, Edward. *The History of Jamaica*, vol. 2. London: T. Lowndes, 1774.
Madden, Richard Robert. *A Twelvemonth's Residence in the West Indies During the Transition from Slavery to Apprenticeship*. London: James Cochrane and Co., 1835.

Marryat, Frederick. *Peter Simple*. 1834. Reprint, Whitefish, Mont.: Kessinger, 2005.
McCallum, P. F. *Travels in Trinidad During the Months of February, March and April 1803 in a Series of Letters Addressed to a Member of the Imperial Parliament of Great Britain*. Liverpool: Longman, Hurst, Rees and Orme, 1805.
McDonnell, Alexander. *Considerations on Negro Slavery with Authentic Reports Illustrative of the Actual Condition of the Negroes in Demerara to Which Are Added, Suggestions on the Proper Mode of Ameliorating the Condition of the Slaves*. London: Longman, Hurst, Rees, Orme, Brown and Green, 1824.
Melville, Robert. *A Narrative of the Proceedings upon the Complaint Against Governor Melvill*. London: Printed for T. Becket and P. A. De Hondt, 1770.
"Memoirs of the Late General Melville." *Scots Magazine* 72 (1810): 40.
Moore, J. C. *Life of Sir John Moore*. London: John Murray, 1834.
Moore, Samuel. *The Public Acts in Force, Passed by the Legislature of Barbados from May 11th 1762 to April 8th 1800 Inclusive*. London: n.p., 1801.
Moreton, J. B. *Manners and Customs of the West India Islands*. London: Richardson, 1790.
The New Jamaica Almanac, and Register . . . Carefully Computed from the Best Astronomical Tables, and Adapted to the Meridian and Latitude of Port-Royal. Kingston: Printed by Stevenson and Smith.
Oldmixon, John. *The British Empire in America in Two Volumes*, vol. 2. London: John Nicholson, Benjamin Tooke and Richard Parker and Ralph Smith, 1708.
Orderson, J. W. *Creoleana; or, Social and Domestic Scenes and Incidents in Barbados in the Days of Yore and the Fair Barbadian and the Faithfull Black*, ed. John Gilmore. 1842. Reprint, Oxford: Macmillan, 2002.
———. *Cursory Remarks and Plain Facts Connected with the Question Produced by the Proposed Slave Registry Bill*. London: J. M. Richardson, 1816.
Philippe, Jean-Baptiste. *A Free Mulatto*. 1824. Reprint, Port of Spain: Calaloux Publications, 1996.
Pinckard, George. *Notes on the West Indies During an Expedition Under the Command of Sir Ralph Abercromby*. 3 vols. London: Longman Hurst Rees and Orme, 1806.
Poyer, John. *The History of Barbados from the Discovery of the Island in the Year 1605 till the Accession of Lord Seaforth 1801*. London: J. Mauman, 1808.
"Report of St. George's Day." April 23, 1823. Reprint, *Journal of the Royal Agricultural Society of British Guiana* 10 (1896): 232.
Robinson, Heaton. *Memoirs of Sir Thomas Picton in Two Volumes*. London: Richard Bentley, 1836.
Rodway, James, ed. *Timehri: Being the Journal of the Royal Agricultural and Commercial Society of British Guiana*. Georgetown: J. Thomson, 1896.
Rowlandson, Thomas. *Rachel Pringle of Barbados*. London: William Holland, 1796.
Sala, George Augustus. *The Baddington Peerage*. London: Charles Skeet, 1860.
———. *Gaslight and Daylight*. London: Chapman & Hall, 1859.

———. *A Journey Due North*. London: Richard Bentley, 1858.
———. *A Journey Due South*. London: Vizetelly & Co., 1885.
———. *The Life and Adventures of George Augustus Sala*, vol. 1. London: Cassell & Co., 1895.
———. *London Up to Date*. London: A. and C. Black, 1894.
———. *My Diary in America in the Midst of War*. London: Tinsley Brothers, 1865.
———. *Quite Alone: In Three Volumes*. London: Chapman and Hall, 1864.
———. *The Seven Sons of Mammon*. London: Tinsley Brothers, 1864.
———. *The Strange Adventures of Captain Dangerous*. London: C. H. Clarke, 1875.
———. *Temple Bar: A London Magazine for Town and Country Readers*, vol. 1, pt. 2 (January 1861): 246–47.
———. *Things I Have Seen and People I Have Known*, vol. 1. London: Cassell & Co., 1894.
———. *A Trip to Barbary by a Roundabout Route*. London: Tinsley Brothers, 1866.
———. *Twice Round the Clock*. London: John and Robert Maxwell, 1878.
———. *The Two Prima Donnas*. London: Tinsley Brothers, 1881.
———. *Under the Sun: Essays Mainly Written in Hot Countries*. London: Vizetelly & Co., 1886.
———. "The Wild Woman." *Harpers* (August 20, 1864): 535.
Schomburgk, Robert H. *A Description of British Guiana, Geographical and Statistical*. London: Frank Cass, 1840.
———. *The History of Barbados*. London: Frank Cass, 1848.
St. Clair, Thomas Staunton. *A Soldier's Recollection of the West Indies and America*. London: Richard Bentley, 1834.
Stedman, John Gabriel, Sally Price, and Richard Price. *Narrative of a Five Years Expedition Against the Revolted Negroes of Surinam: Transcribed for the First Time from the Original 1790 Manuscript*. Baltimore, Md.: Johns Hopkins University Press, 1988.
Stephen, James. *The Crisis of the Sugar Colonies . . . to Which Are Subjoined Sketches of a Plan for Settling the Vacant Lands of Trinidada*. London: J. Hatchard, 1802.
Thome, James A., and J. Horace Kimball. *Emancipation in the West Indies: A Six Months' Tour in Antigua, Barbadoes, and Jamaica in the Year 1837*. New York: American Anti-Slavery Society, 1838.
Thornhill, Henry. *A Narrative of the Insurrection and Rebellion in the Island of Grenada, from the Commencement to the Conclusion. Introduced with a Summary Discourse on the Excellence of the British Constitution*. Barbados: Printed at Mr. Gilbert Repnel, the Bay, Between the Two Bridges, 1798.
Thurn, E. F., ed. *Timehri*, vol. 4. Georgetown: J. Thomson, 1895.
Tobler, John, ed. *An Almanack, for the Year of Our Lord 1783*. St. Augustine: Printed by William Charles Wells and Charles Wright for and Sold by David Zubly Junior, at His House, 1783.
Tobler, John, and Evan Tobler, eds. *The Carolina and Georgia Almanack, or Ephem-*

eris, for the Year of Our Lord 1783. Charlestown: Printed by R. Keith and J. M'Iver, jun. and Sold at No. 25 1/2, on the Bay, North Side of the Exchange, 1782.

Trollope, Anthony. *The Barchester Chronicles in Six Volumes*. London: Longman, Brown, Green, and Longmans, 1855–67.

———. *The West Indies and the Spanish Main*. London: Chapman and Hall, 1859.

Turnball, Gordon. *A Narrative of the Revolt and Insurrection in the Island of Grenada*. London: Verner and Hood, 1796.

Waller, John Augustine. *A Voyage in the West Indies Containing Various Observations Made During a Residence in Barbados and Several of the Leeward Islands*. London: Richard Phillips and Co., 1820.

Wise, Thomas Turner. *A Review of the Events That Have Happened in Grenada from the Commencement of the Insurrection to the First of May*. Grenada: Printed for the author, 1795.

Young, Sir William. *An Account of the Black Charaibs in the Island of St. Vincent's: With the Charaib Treaty of 1773, and Other Original Documents*. London: Routledge, 1795.

SECONDARY SOURCES

Addo, Joan Anim, Giovanna Covi, Velma Pollard, and Carla Sassi. *Caribbean Scottish Relations: Colonial and Contemporary Inscriptions in History, Language and Literature*. London: Mango, 2007.

Akenson, Donald. *If the Irish Ran the World: Montserrat 1630–1730*. Liverpool: Liverpool University Press, 1997.

Alleyne, Warren. *Historic Bridgetown*. Bridgetown: Barbados National Trust, 1978.

Alston, David. "Slaves and Highlanders." http://www.spanglefish.com/slavesandhighlanders (accessed March 12, 2013).

Amedroz, Henry Frederick. *The Eclipse of the Abbasid Caliphate: Original Chronicles of the Fourth Islamic Century in Seven Volumes*. Oxford: Basil Blackwell, 1920.

Arthur, Paul, ed. *International Life Writing: Memory and Identity in Global Context*. Oxford: Routledge, 2012.

Aslakson, Kenneth. "The 'Quadroon-Plaçage' Myth of Antebellum New Orleans: Anglo-American (Mis)interpretations of a French-Caribbean Phenomenon." *Journal of Social History* (November 2011): 709–34.

Aspinall, Sir Algernon. "Rachel Pringle of Barbados." *Journal of the Barbados Museum and Historical Society* 9, no. 3 (1942): 112–19.

Auerbach, Nina. *Woman and the Demon: The Life of a Victorian Myth*. Cambridge, Mass.: Harvard University Press, 1982.

Baker, Patrick. *Centering the Periphery: Chaos, Order and the Ethnography of Dominica*. Montreal: McGill-Queen's University Press, 1994.

Banks, Kenneth J. "Official Duplicity: The Illicit Slave Trade of Martinique 1713–1763." In Coclanis, *The Atlantic Economy During the Seventeenth and Eighteenth Century*, 229–51.

Beasley, Edward. *The Victorian Reinvention of Race: New Racisms and the Problem of Grouping in the Human Sciences*. New York: Routledge, 2010.
Beckles, Hilary McD. "Black over White: The 'Poor White' Problem in Barbados Slave Society." *Immigrants and Minorities* 7, no. 1 (1988): 1–15.
———. *A History of Barbados: From Amerindian Settlement to Caribbean Single Market*. Cambridge: Cambridge University Press, 1990.
———. "On the Backs of Blacks: The Barbados Pursuit of Civil Rights and the 1816 Rebellion." *Immigrants and Minorities* 3, no. 2 (1984): 167–87.
———. "Property Rights in Pleasure: The Marketing of Slave Women's Sexuality in the West Indies." In McDonald, *West Indies Accounts*, 169–88.
Beckles, Hilary McD., and Karl Watson. "Social Protest and Labour Bargaining: The Changing Nature of Slaves' Responses to Plantation Life in Eighteenth Century Barbados." *Slavery and Abolition* 8, no. 3 (1987): 272–93.
Bell, Madison Smartt. *Toussaint L'Ouverture: A Biography*. New York: Pantheon, 2007.
Berlin, Ira. *Slaves Without Masters: The Free Negro in the Antebellum South*. New York: New Press, 1974.
Bhabha, Homi K. "The White Stuff." *Artforum International* 36, no. 9 (May 1998): 21–24.
Blake, Peter. "Charles Dickens, George Augustus Sala and Household Words." *Dickens Quarterly* 26, no. 1 (2009): 24–41.
———. "George Augustus Sala: The Personal Style of a Public Writer." PhD diss., Sussex University, 2010.
Blanning, T. C. W. "Louis XV and the Decline of the French Monarchy." *History Review* 22 (1995): 20–24.
Bowen, H. V. *The Business of Empire: The East India Company and Imperial Britain 1756–1833*. New York: Cambridge University Press, 2006.
Brathwaite, Edward. *The Development of Creole Society in Jamaica 1770–1820*. Oxford: Oxford University Press, 1971.
Breathett, George. "Catholicism and the Code Noir in Haiti." *Journal of Negro History* 73, nos. 1–4 (1988): 1–11.
Brereton, Bridget. *An Introduction to the History of Trinidad and Tobago, 1783–1962*. Oxford: Heinemann, 1981.
Brinkley, Frances K. "Analysis of the 1750 Carriacou Census." *Caribbean Quarterly* 24, nos. 1–2 (March–June 1978): 44–60.
Brizan, George. *Grenada, Island of Conflict: From Amerindians to People's Revolution, 1498–1979*. Totowa, N.J.: Zed, 1984.
Bryant, G. J. "Scots in India in the Eighteenth Century." *Scottish Historical Review* 64, no. 177 (April 1985): 22–41.
Buckley, Roger Norman. *Slaves in Redcoats: The British West Indian Regiments, 1795–1815*. New Haven, Conn.: Yale University Press, 1979.
Campbell, Carl C. *Cedulants and Capitulants: The Politics of the Coloured Opposition in the Slave Society of Trinidad 1783–1838*. Port of Spain: Paria, 1992.

———. "The Rise of the Free Coloured Plantocracy in Trinidad 1783–1813." *Boletin de Estudios Latinoamericas y del Caribe* 29 (December 1980): 33–53.

Campbell, Mavis C. *The Maroons of Jamaica, 1655–1796*. Trenton, N.J.: Africa World Press, 1990.

Candlin, Kit. "The Empire of Women: Transient Entrepreneurs in the Southern Caribbean 1790–1820." *Journal of Imperial and Commonwealth History* 38, no. 3 (September 2010): 351–72.

———. *The Last Caribbean Frontier 1795–1815*. Basingstoke, England: Palgrave Macmillan, 2012.

Carretta, Vincent. *Equiano, the African: Biography of a Self-Made Man*. Athens: University of Georgia Press, 2005.

Clark, Emily. *The Strange History of the American Quadroon: Free Women of Color in the Revolutionary Atlantic World*. Chapel Hill: University of North Carolina Press, 2013.

Coclanis, Peter A., ed. *The Atlantic Economy During the Seventeenth and Eighteenth Century: Organization, Operation, Practice, and Personnel*. Chapel Hill: University of South Carolina Press, 1999.

Colley, Linda. *The Ordeal of Elizabeth Marsh: A Woman in Global History*. London: Harper, 2007.

Connell, Neville. "Hotel Keepers and Hotels in Barbados." *Journal of the Barbados Museum and Historical Society* 33, no. 4 (1970): 162–85.

———. "Prince William Henry's Visits to Barbados in 1786 and 1787." *Journal of the Barbados Museum and Historical Society* 25 (1958): 157–64.

Costa, Emília Viotti da. *Crowns of Glory, Tears of Blood: The Demerara Slave Rebellion of 1823*. New York: Oxford University Press, 1994.

Cox, Edward L. "Fedon's Rebellion 1795–96: Causes and Consequences." *Journal of Negro History* 67, no. 1 (Spring 1982): 7–19.

———. *Free Coloureds in the Slave Societies of St. Kitts and Grenada*. Knoxville: University of Tennessee Press, 1984.

Craton, Michael. "Proto-Peasant Revolts? The Late Slave Rebellions in the British West Indies 1816–1832." *Past and Present* 85, no. 1 (November 1979): 99–125.

———. *Testing the Chains: Resistance to Slavery in the British West Indies*. Ithaca, N.Y.: Cornell University Press, 1982.

Cumberbatch, Cynthia. "Amaryllis Collymore and Her Son Ren: Slaves Who Became Plantation Owners." *Journal of the Barbados Museum and Historical Society* 53 (November 2007): 140–57.

Dabydeen, David, John Gilmore, and Cecily Jones, eds. *The Oxford Companion to Black British History*. Oxford: Oxford University Press, 2010.

Dalton, Henry G. *The History of British Guiana: Comprising a General Description of the Colony: A Narrative of Some of the Principal Events from the Earliest Period of Products and Natural History*. Carlisle, Mass.: Applewood, 2009.

Daly, Vere T. *A Short History of the Guyanese People*. London: Macmillan, 1974.

Davis, David Brion. *The Problem of Slavery in the Age of Revolution 1770–1823*. New York: Oxford University Press, 1999.
Davis, Michael T., and Paul Pickering, eds. *Unrespectable Radicals: Popular Politics in the Age of Reform*. Aldershot, England: Ashgate, 2008.
Davis, Tracy C. *Actresses as Working Women: Their Social Identity in Victorian Culture*. London: Routledge, 1991.
Devas, Raymund P. *The History of the Island of Grenada 1650–1950*. St. George's: Justin James Field, 1964.
——— . *A History of the Island of Grenada 1498–1796: With Some Notes on Carriacou and Events of Later Years*. St. George's: Careenage Press, 1974.
Donaldson, G. *The Scots Overseas*. London: Robert Hale, 1966.
Draper, Nicholas. *The Price of Emancipation: Slave-Ownership, Compensation and British Society at the End of Slavery*. Cambridge: Cambridge University Press, 2010.
Drescher, Seymour. *Econocide: British Slavery in the Era of Abolition*. Pittsburgh, Pa.: University of Pittsburgh Press, 1977.
Dubois, Laurent. *Avengers of the New World: The Story of the Haitian Revolution*. Cambridge, Mass.: Harvard University Press, 2005.
——— . "Slavery in the French Caribbean 1635–1804." In Eltis and Engerman, *The Cambridge World History of Slavery AD 1420 to AD 1804*, 431–49.
Duffy, Michael. *Soldiers, Sugar and Seapower: The British West Indian Expeditions and the War Against Revolutionary France*. Oxford: Clarendon, 1987.
Dull, Jonathan R. *The French Navy and the Seven Years' War*. Lincoln: University of Nebraska Press, 2005.
Dunker, Sheila. "The Free Coloured and the Fight for Civil Rights in Jamaica 1800–1830." Master's thesis, University of London, 1960.
Edwards, Peter David. *Dickens' Young Men: George Augustus Sala, Edmund Yates and the World of Victorian Journalism*. Aldershot, England: Ashgate 1997.
Eltis, David, and Stanley Engerman, eds. *The Cambridge World History of Slavery AD 1420 to AD 1804*, vol. 3. Cambridge: Cambridge University Press, 2011.
Epstein, James. "The Politics of Colonial Sensation: The Trial of Thomas Picton and the Cause of Louisa Calderon." *American Historical Review*, 112, no. 3 (June 2007): 712–41.
——— . "The Radical Underworld Goes Colonial." In Davis and Pickering, *Unrespectable Radicals*, 47–165.
Equiano, Olaudah. *The Interesting Narrative of the Life of Olaudah Equiano, or Gustavus Vassa, the African*. New York: Penguin Classics, 2003.
Farley, Rawle. "The Shadow and the Substance." *Caribbean Quarterly* 4, no. 2 (December 1955): 132–53.
Felix, Joel, and Frank Tallet. "The French Experience 1661–1815." In Storrs, *The Fiscal Military State in Eighteenth Century Europe*, 147–66.
File, Nigel, and Chris Power. *Black Settlers in Britain 1555–1958*. London: Heinemann, 1981.

Foix, Alain. *Toussaint L'Ouverture*. Paris: Gallimard, 2007.
Fry, Michael. *The Scottish Empire*. East Linton, Scotland: Tuckwell, 2001.
Fryer, Peter. *Staying Power: The History of Black People in Britain*. London: Pluto, 1984.
Fuentes, Marisa J. "Power and Historical Figuring: Rachael Pringle Polgreen's Troubled Archive." *Gender and History* 22, no. 3 (November 2010): 564–84.
Gaspar, David Barry, and David Patrick Geggus. *A Turbulent Time: The French Revolution and the Greater Caribbean*. Bloomington: Indiana University Press, 1997.
Gaspar, David Barry, and Clark Hine, eds. *Beyond Bondage: Free Women of Color in the Americas*. Chicago: University of Illinois Press, 2004.
"George Augustus Sala and His Panorama." Newsletter of the Fryer Library, University of Queensland (September 2006): 13.
Gerzina, Gretchen. *Black England: Life Before Emancipation*. London: Allison and Busby, 1999.
Gillis, John R. *For Better, for Worse: British Marriages 1600 to the Present*. Oxford: Oxford University Press, 1985.
Gilroy, Paul. *The Black Atlantic: Modernity and Double Consciousness*. Cambridge, Mass.: Harvard University Press, 1995.
Ginzburg, Carlo, and Carlo Poni. "The Name and the Game: Unequal Exchanges in the Historiographic Marketplace." 1979. Reprinted in *Microhistory and the Lost Peoples of Europe: Selections from Quaderni Storici*. Baltimore, Md.: Johns Hopkins University Press, 1991.
Girard, Charlotte. "Sir James Douglas's Mother and Grandmother." *BC Studies*, no. 44 (Winter 1979–80): 25–31.
Green, William A. *British Slave Emancipation: The Sugar Colonies and the Great Experiment 1830–1865*. Oxford: Clarendon, 1976.
Greene, Jack, and David W. Cohen. *Neither Slave, nor Free: The Freedmen of African Descent in the Slave Societies of the New World*. Baltimore, Md.: Johns Hopkins University Press, 1972.
Gundara, Jagdish, and Ian Duffield, eds. *Essays on the History of Blacks in Britain*. Avebury, England: Aldershot, 1992.
Hamilton, Douglas. "Robert Melville and the Frontiers of Empire in the British West Indies 1763–1771." In Mackillop and Murdoch, *Military Governors and Imperial Frontiers*, 181–205.
———. *Scotland, the Caribbean and the Atlantic World 1750–1820*. Manchester, England: Manchester University Press, 2005.
Hancock, David. *Citizens of the World: London Merchants and the Integration of the British Atlantic Community 1735–1785*. New York: Cambridge University Press, 1995.
Handler, Jerome S. "Joseph Rachell and Rachael Pringle Polgreen: Petty Entrepreneurs." In Sweet and Nash, *Struggle and Survival*, 76–391.

———. *The Unappropriated People: Freedmen in the Slave Society of Barbados*. Baltimore, Md.: Johns Hopkins University Press, 1974.
Handler, Jerome S., ed. "Memoirs of an Old Army Officer: Richard A. Wyvill's Visits to Barbados in 1796 and 1806–7." *Journal of the Barbados Museum and Historical Society* 35, no. 1 (March 1975): 21–30.
Havard, Robert. *Wellington's Welsh General: A Life of Sir Thomas Picton*. London: Aurum, 1996.
Heuman, Gad. *Between Black and White: Race, Politics and the Free Coloureds in Jamaica 1792–1865*. Westport, Conn.: Greenwood, 1981.
———. "The British West Indies." In Porter, *Oxford History of the British Empire*, vol. 3, 470–95.
Higman, Barry. *Slave Populations of the British Caribbean 1807–1834*. Mona, Jamaica: The Press, 1995.
Hitchcock, Tim. *English Sexualities 1700–1800*. New York: St. Martin's, 1997.
Hoefte, Rosemarijn, and Jean-Jacques Vrij. "Free Black and Colored Women in Early Nineteenth Century Paramaribo, Suriname." In Gaspar and Hine, *Beyond Bondage*, 45–168.
House, Madeline, Graham Storey, Kathleen Mary Tillotson, Angus Easson, and Nina Burgis, eds. *The Letters of Charles Dickens*. Oxford: Oxford University Press, 2002.
Jacobs, Curtis. "The Fedons of Grenada 1763–1814." Paper presented at the Grenada Country Conference, January 2002, http://www.cavehill.uwi.edu/BNCCde/grenada/conference/papers/jacobsc.html (accessed April 28, 2013).
James, C. L. R. *The Black Jacobins: Toussaint L'Ouverture and the St. Domingue Revolution*. Secker and Warburg, London, 1938.
Jones, Hilary. *The Métis of Senegal: Urban Life and Politics in French West Africa*. Bloomington: Indiana University Press, 2013.
Kennedy, Paul. *The Rise and Fall of the Great Powers: Economic Change and Military Conflict 1500 to 2000*. London: Fontana, 1989.
Kerr, Paulette. "Victims or Strategists." In Shepherd et al., *Engendering History: Caribbean Women in Historical Perspective*, 197–212.
Knapp, Oswald G., ed. *The Intimate Letters of Hester Piozzi and Penelope Pennington 1788–1821*. New York: John Lane, 1914.
Knight, Franklin W., ed. *The General History of the Caribbean*, vol. 3: *The Slave Societies of the Caribbean*. Basingstoke, England: Macmillan, 1997.
Laidlaw, Zoe. *Colonial Connections*. Manchester, England: Manchester University Press, 2005.
Lambert, David, and Alan Lester, eds. *Colonial Lives Across the British Empire: Imperial Careening in the Long Nineteenth Century*. Cambridge: Cambridge University Press, 2006.
Lambert, Sheila, ed. *House of Commons Sessional Papers*, vol. 82. Wilmington, Del.: Scholarly Resources, 1975.

Landers, Jane. *Atlantic Creoles in the Age of Revolutions.* Cambridge, Mass.: Harvard University Press, 2010.

Lawson, Philip. *The East India Company: A History.* London: Longman, 1993.

Levine, Phillipa, ed. *The Oxford History of the British Empire Companion Series: Gender and Empire.* Oxford: Oxford University Press, 2007.

Livesay, Daniel. "Children of Uncertain Fortune: Mixed-Race Migration from the West Indies to Britain, 1750–1820." PhD diss., University of Michigan, 2010.

———. "Extended Families: Mixed Race Children and the Scottish Experience 1770–1820." *International Journal of Scottish Literature,* no. 4 (Spring–Summer 2008): 1–17.

Mackenzie, Judy. *The Letters of G. A. Sala to Edmund Yates.* St. Lucia: University of Queensland Press, 1993.

Mackillop, A., and S. Murdoch, eds. *Military Governors and Imperial Frontiers 1600–1800: A Study of Scotland and Empires.* Leiden: Brill, 2003.

Marshall, Bernard. "The Black Caribs: Native Resistance to British Penetration to the Windward Side of St. Vincent 1763–1773." *Caribbean Quarterly* 19, no. 4 (December 1973): 4–19.

McCalman, Iain. *The Radical Underworld: Prophets, Revolutionaries, and Pornographers in London 1795–1840.* Cambridge: Cambridge University Press, 1988.

McDaniel, Lorna. "The Philips: A 'Free Mulatto' Family of Grenada." *Journal of Caribbean History* 24, no. 2 (1990): 178–94.

McDonald, Roderick A., ed. *West Indies Accounts: Essays on the History of the British Caribbean and the Atlantic Economy in Honour of Richard Sheridan.* Kingston: University of the West Indies Press, 1996.

McLeod, Cynthia. "Celebrating the Extraordinary Life of Elisabeth Samson." *Encuentros Series,* IDB Cultural Center, no. 27 (August 1998): 1–14.

———. *Elisabeth Samson, Een Vrije, Zwarte Vrouw in het 18e Eeuwse Suriname.* Redshank, Netherlands: Uitgeverij Conserve, 1996.

———. *The Free Negress Elisabeth.* London: Arcadia, 2009.

Meteyard, Belinda. "Illegitimacy and Marriage Law in Eighteenth Century England." *Journal of Interdisciplinary History* 10, no. 3 (Winter 1980): 479–89.

Midgett, Douglas. "West Indian Version: Literature History and Identity (Grenada)." In Torrens and Whitten, *Blackness in Latin America and the Caribbean,* 337–65.

Midgley, Clare, ed. *Gender and Imperialism.* Manchester, England: Manchester University Press, 1998.

Millette, James. *The Genesis of Crown Colony Government: Trinidad 1783–1810.* Curepe, Trinidad and Tobago: Moko, 1970.

Mohammed, Patricia. *Gendered Realities: Essays in Caribbean Feminist Thought.* Mona, Jamaica: University of the West Indies Press, 2002.

Moogk, Peter. "Reluctant Exiles: Emigrants from France in Canada Before 1760." *William and Mary Quarterly,* 3rd ser., 46, no. 3 (July 1989): 463–505.

Morris, Robert. "Progenitors and Coloured Elite Families: Case Studies of the Belgraves, Collymores and Cummins." *Journal of the Barbados Museum and Historical Society* 47 (2001): 52–65.

Muir, Edward, and Guido Ruggiero, eds. *Microhistory and the Lost Peoples of Europe: Selections from Quaderni Storici*. Baltimore, Md.: Johns Hopkins University Press, 1991.

Mulcahy, Matthew. *Hurricanes and Society in the British Greater Caribbean, 1624–1783*. Baltimore, Md.: Johns Hopkins University Press, 2005.

Murdoch, D. H. "Land Policy in the Eighteenth Century British Empire: The Sale of Crown Lands in the Ceded Islands 1763–1783." *Historical Journal* 27, no. 3 (September 1984): 549–74.

Murray, Venetia. *An Elegant Madness: High Society in Regency England*. New York: Viking, 2000.

Myatt, Frederick. *Peninsular General: The Life of Sir Thomas Picton 1758–1815*. Newton Abbot, England: David and Charles, 1996.

Naipaul, V. S. *The Loss of El Dorado*. 1969. Reprint, Basingstoke, England: Picador, 2001.

Neely, Wayne. *The Great Hurricane of 1780*. iUniverse, 2012.

Nelson, James L. *Benedict Arnold's Navy: The Ragtag Fleet That Lost the Battle of Lake Champlain but Won the American Revolution*. New York: McGraw-Hill, 2006.

Newton, Melanie. *The Children of Africa in the Colonies: Free People of Color in Barbados in the Age of Emancipation*. Baton Rouge: Louisiana State University Press, 2008.

Nussbaum, Felicity. *The Limits of the Human: Fictions of Anomaly, Race, and Gender in the Long Eighteenth Century*. Cambridge: Cambridge University Press, 2003.

Ogborn, Miles. *Global Lives: Britain and the World, 1550–1800*. Cambridge: Cambridge University Press, 2008.

O'Shaughnessy, Andrew J. *An Empire Divided: The American Revolution and the British Caribbean*. Philadelphia: University of Pennsylvania Press, 2000.

———. "The Formation of a Commercial Lobby, the West India Interest, British Colonial Policy and the American Revolution." *Historical Journal* 40, no. 1 (March 1997): 71–95.

Patterson, Orlando. *The Sociology of Slavery*. London: London University Press, 1967.

Petley, Christer. "Gluttony, Excess, and the Fall of the Planter Class in the British Caribbean." *Atlantic Studies* 9, no. 1 (March 2012): 85–106.

Pitman, Frank Wesley. "Slavery on British West Indies Plantations in the Eighteenth Century." *Journal of Negro History* 11, no. 4 (October 1926): 584–668.

Pope-Hennessy, Una. *Charles Dickens: 1812–1870*. New York: Howell and Soskin, 1946.

Porter, Andrew, ed. *Oxford History of the British Empire*, vol. 3: *The Nineteenth Century*. Oxford: Oxford University Press, 1999.

Pybus, Cassandra. *Black Founders*. Sydney: University of New South Wales Press, 2006.

———. "Tense and Tender Ties: Reflections on Lives Recovered from the Intimate Frontier of Empire and Slavery." *Life Writing* 8, no. 1 (2010): 5–17. Reprinted in *International Life Writing: Memory and Identity in a Global Context*, ed. Paul Arthur, 5–17. Oxford: Routledge, 2013.

Quintanilla, Mark. "Mercantile Communities in the Ceded Islands: The Alexander Bartlet and George Campbell Company." *International Social Science Review* 79, nos. 1–2 (January 2004): 1–14.

Rothschild, Emma. *The Inner Life of Empires: An Eighteenth-Century History*. Princeton, N.J.: Princeton University Press, 2011.

Sainty, J. C. *Office-Holders in Modern Britain*, vol. 4: *Admiralty Officials, 1660–1870*. London: Institute of Historical Research, 1975.

Scott, Julius S. "The Common Wind: Currents of Afro-American Communication in the Era of the Haitian Revolution." PhD diss., Duke University, 1986.

Scott, Rebecca, and Jean M. Hébrard. *Freedom Papers: An Atlantic Odyssey in the Age of Emancipation*. Cambridge, Mass.: Harvard University Press, 2012.

Scully, Pamela, and Diana Paton. *Gender and Slave Emancipation in the Atlantic World*. Durham, N.C.: Duke University Press, 2005.

Sensbach, Jon. *Rebecca's Revival: Creating Black Christianity in the Atlantic World*. Cambridge, Mass.: Harvard University Press, 2005.

Shepherd, Verene A., ed. *Women in Caribbean History*. London: James Currey, 1999.

Shepherd, Verene A., Bridget Brereton, and Barbara Evelyn Bailey, eds. *Engendering History: Caribbean Women in Historical Perspective*. Kingston: Ian Randle, 1995.

Sheppard, Jill. *The "Redlegs" of Barbados*. New York: KTO Press, 1977.

Sheridan, Richard B. "The Condition of the Slaves on the Sugar Plantations of Sir John Gladstone in the Colony of Demerara, 1812–49." *New West Indian Guide/Nieuwe West-Indische Gids* 76, nos. 3–4 (2002): 243–69.

———. "The Role of Scots in the Economy and Society of the West Indies." *Annals of the New York Academy of Sciences* 292 (June 1977): 94–106.

———. *Sugar and Slavery: An Economic History of the British West Indies, 1623–1775*. Barbados: Caribbean Universities Press, 1974.

Sherson, Erroll. *London's Lost Theatres of the Nineteenth Century*. London: John Lane, 1925.

Shyllon, Folarin. "The Black Presence and Experience in Britain: An Analytical Overview." In Gundara and Duffield, *Essays on the History of Blacks in Britain*, 202–24.

Sio, Arnold. "Marginality and Free Coloured Identity in Caribbean Slave Society." *Slavery and Abolition* 8, no. 2 (1987): 166–182.

———. "Race, Colour and Miscegenation: The Free Coloureds of Jamaica and Barbados." *Caribbean Studies* 16, no. 1 (April 1976): 5–21.

Slade, H. Gordon. "Craigston and Meldrum Estates 1769–1841." *Proceedings of the Society of Antiquaries of London* 114 (1984): 481–537.
Smith, Raymond. *British Guiana: Issued under the Auspices of the Royal Institute of International Affairs.* Oxford: Oxford University Press, 1962.
Steele, Beverley. *Grenada: A History of Its People.* Oxford: Macmillan Caribbean, 2003.
Stoeltje, Beverly. "Ashanti Queen Mothers: A Study in Female Authority." In *Queens, Queen Mothers, Priestesses and Power: Case Studies in African Gender,* ed. Flora Edouwaye Kaplan, 41–71. New York: Annals of the New York Academy of Sciences, 1997.
Stoler, Ann Laura. "Tense and Tender Ties: The Politics of Comparison in North American History and (Post) Colonial Studies." *Journal of American History* 88, no. 3 (December 2001): 829–65.
Stone, Lawrence. *The Family, Sex, and Marriage in England 1500–1800.* London: Wiedenfeld and Nicholson, 1977.
———. *Uncertain Unions: Marriage in England, 1660–1753.* Oxford: Oxford University Press, 1992.
Storrs, Christopher, ed. *The Fiscal Military State in Eighteenth Century Europe: Essays in Honour of P. G. M. Dickson.* Farnham, England: Ashgate, 2009.
Straus, Ralph. *Sala: The Portrait of an Eminent Victorian.* London: Constable, 1942.
Sugden, John. *Nelson: A Dream of Glory.* London: Jonathan Cape, 2004.
Swann, Julian. *Parliaments and the Political Crises under Louis XV 1754–1774.* New York: Cambridge University Press, 1995.
Sweet, David, and Gary Nash, eds. *Struggle and Survival in Colonial America.* Berkeley: University of California Press, 1981.
Sweet, James. *Domingos Alvares, African Healing, and the Intellectual History of the Atlantic World.* Chapel Hill: University of North Carolina Press, 2011.
Taylor, Christopher. *The Black Carib Wars: Freedom, Survival, and the Making of the Garifuna.* Jackson: University Press of Mississippi, 2012.
Thompson, Alvin. *Unprofitable Servants: Crown Slaves in Berbice, Guyana, 1803–1831.* Mona, Jamaica: University of the West Indies Press, 2002.
Thornburn, C. C., ed. *No Messing: The Story of an Essex Man: The Autobiography of John Castelfranc Cheveley I, 1795–1870,* vol. 2. Chichester, England: Crosswave, 2012.
Tomalin, Claire. *Mrs Jordan's Profession: The Actress and the Prince.* London: Knopf, 1995.
Torrens, Arlene, and Norman E. Whitten Jr., eds. *Blackness in Latin America and the Caribbean.* Bloomington: Indiana University Press, 1998.
Vickery, Amanda. *The Gentleman's Daughter: Women's Lives in Georgian England.* New Haven, Conn.: Yale University Press, 1998.
Walvin, James. *An African's Life, 1745–1797: The Life and Times of Olaudah Equiano.* London: Continuum 2000.
Welch, Pedro. "'Crimps and Captains': Displays of Self Expression Among Freed

Coloured Women, Barbados, 1750–1834." *Journal of Social Sciences* 4, no. 2 (December 1997): 89–126.

———. *"Red" and Black over White: Free Coloured Women in Pre-Emancipation Barbados.* Bridgetown: Carib Research Publications, 2000.

———. "'Unhappy and Afflicted Women?' Free Coloured Women in Barbados 1780–1834." *Revista/Review Interamericana* 29, nos. 1–4 (1999): 9–12.

Wesley, Charles H. "The Emancipation of the Free Colored Population in the British Empire." *Journal of Negro History* 19, no. 2 (April 1934): 137–70.

Wheeler, Roxann. *The Complexion of Race: Categories of Difference in Eighteenth Century British Culture.* Philadelphia: University of Pennsylvania Press, 2000.

Williams, Eric. *From Columbus to Castro.* London: Deutsch, 1970.

Wilson, Kathleen. *The Island Race: Englishness, Gender, and Empire in the Eighteenth Century.* London: Routledge, 2003.

Winfield, Rif. *British Warships of the Age of Sail 1714–1792: Design, Construction, Careers and Fates.* London: Seaforth, 2007.

Woollacott, Angela, ed. *Gender and Empire.* Basingstoke, England: Palgrave Macmillan, 2006.

Zaceck, Natalie. *Settler Society in the English Leeward Islands 1676–1776.* Cambridge: Cambridge University Press, 2010.

Ziegler, Philip. *King William IV.* London: Harper and Row, 1973.

WEBSITES

Ancestry, http://www.ancestry.com
Guyana Colonial Newspapers, http://www.vc.id.au/edg/transcripts.html
Legacies of British Slave-Ownership, http://www.ucl.ac.uk/lbs
Oxford Dictionary of National Biography, http://www.oxforddnb.com
Peerage, http://www.thepeerage.com
Slaves and Highlanders, http://www.spanglefish.com/slavesandhighlanders

INDEX

Abercromby, Ralph, 50
Account of the Black Charaibs, An (Young), 183n27
Act of December 1797, 202n31
actresses, 163, 211n77, 211n79
Actresses as Working Women (Davis), 211n77
Act to Prevent the Further Sudden Increase of Free Negroes and Mulattos, An, 184n39
Address to Lord Bathurst, An (Philippe), 157
Adelaide of Saxe-Meiningen, Queen (wife of William IV), 163
African diaspora, 12
African heritage, 179–80
Africans. *See* free people of color; free women of color; race; slavery; slave trade
agency, 13, 36, 49, 173–74, 179–80
Age of Revolutions: gender, race, and power dynamics, 6–7, 14, 27–32, 178–79; impact on southern Caribbean, 7, 9, 15–31; treatment of free people of color, 157
Amedroz, Henry (father), 154
Amedroz, Henry (son), 154
Amedroz, Magdalene Judith (née Thornton), 153–55
American Revolutionary War, 20, 70–71, 105, 107, 108
Antigua, 16, 107
apprenticeship system, 60, 150, 161, 179
Ashanti women, 180
Ashe, Thomas, 139
Ashfield, Elizabeth, 115
Aslakson, Kenneth, 176, 200n99
Atlantic Creoles in the Age of Revolutions (Landers), 182n13
Atlantic economy: free women of color in, 14, 98–99, 110, 114, 119, 171, 178; historical references to, 8–10; impact of conflicts and wars, 6–7, 19–20, 74, 84–85; race and gender dynamics of, 3–4, 10–14, 172,

179; role of slavery, 39–40, 54, 173–74. *See also* ceded islands; slavery; Windward Islands
Austen, Jane, 129
Austin, Betsy, 38
Austin, Suzy, 113

Baddington Peerage, The (Sala), 163, 211n76
Bailey, Barbara, 9
Baillie, Campbell and Thornton, 68
Baillie, James, 77, 117, 147
Baillie family, 19, 105, 175
Bannister, Elizabeth Swain, 92, 99, 143–44, 207n39
Barbadian, 44
Barbados: free women of color in, 48–49, 97–99, 138–44; poverty in, 85–86, 175; race relations in, 30, 33–41; slavery in, 43, 80–82, 84, 178; stability of, 8–9
Barbados slave rebellion (1816), 84
Barker, Matthew Henry, 121, 142, 205n12, 206n26
Barrow, William, 105–6, 108
Bartlett and Campbell company, 19
Bates, Charles, 105
Bathurst, Henry (3rd Earl Bathurst), 103–4
Bayley, Frederick William Naylor, 35
Beckles, Hilary, 10
Belleran, Michel, 71
Bellgarde (leader of free people of color), 28
Bellini, Vincenzo, 165
Benjamin, Andrew, 55
Berbice, 27, 87–88, 93, 98–99, 143–44
Berbice slave revolt (1762), 99
Beresford, Gibson, 90
Berlin, Ira, 182n13
Besson, Stanislaus, 71
Best, Mary, 92
Best, Thomas, 92
Between Black and White (Heuman), 182n13

Beyond Bondage: Free Women of Color in the Americas (Gaspar and Clark), 9
Bhabha, Homi, 10
Biassou, Georges, 71–72
Black Atlantic, The (Gilroy), 9
black Caribs, 19, 26, 28, 72, 183n27
Black Jacobins, The (James), 182n13
Blackman, Christian: memorial to Dorothy Thomas, 102, 104, 199n81; property ownership and business success of, 82–83, 85, 196n12, 198n38; relationship to Priscilla Ostrehan, 92, 97
black studies, 36
Blair, Duncan, 77, 148, 151
boardinghouse keeper stereotype, 34–35. *See also* stereotypes of free women of color
Bolingbroke, Henry, 94–98, 199n65
bon ton culture, 98
Book of Common Prayer, 127
Boys, Daniel, 154
Boys, Ellen Ann Thornton, 153–55
Boys, Susannah Catherine, 154
Boys, Thomas, 154
Brabant, Christopher, 3
Brace, Jeffery, 34
Brade, Sabina, 35, 38, 92–93
Brathwaite, Edward, 182n13
Brayshaw, Thomas, 105
Brereton, Bridget, 9
Brett, Mary Ostrehan, 83, 90, 99–102, 104, 121, 171, 175
Bridgetown, 34, 44–45, 47–49, 87–89, 97–98, 113
Britain: assimilation of mixed-race descendants in, 11, 117–18, 133, 143, 147–61, 168, 175–76; conquests and conflicts over islands, 6–7, 15–21, 24–31, 49–50; religious discrimination by in islands, 19, 21, 70–71; slavery in, 15, 149–51. *See also* Seven Years' War
British Caribbean: historical studies of, 5–6, 10–14, 36, 142–43; marriage laws in, 129; racial dynamics of, 6–7, 28–31, 150. *See also* ceded islands; southern Caribbean; Windward Islands
British Columbia, 159
British empire: historical studies of, 5–6, 10–14, 36, 142–43; opportunities for free women of color in, 12, 93, 117, 159–60, 175, 178
British Windward Islands, 60. *See also* ceded islands; southern Caribbean; Windward Islands
Brizan, George, 183n31, 194n72
Broglio, Charles Victor de (prince), 162
Brontë, Emily, 150
Burke, Edmund, 16
Burton, Antoinette, 10
Butler, Jane, 69–70
Butler, Thomas, 69

Calderon, Louisa, 50–51
Cambridge, Duchess of (Princess Augusta), 163, 165
Cambridge, Duke of (Prince Adolphus), 163, 165
Campbell, Archibald, 17–18
Campbell, Carl C., 182n13, 210n49
Campbell, James, 21
Campbell, Margaret, 127
Campbell, Thomas, 77
Campbell family, 19
Candlin, Kit, 5, 190n1
Caribbean historiography, 5–14, 35–36, 142–43, 173, 177
Cathcart, Sarah Hunter Taylor, 149
Catholicism: discrimination against, 19, 21–22, 61, 70–72; and marriage laws, 69, 109, 140–41; practice of, 66–67, 106, 128, 140, 162, 201n10. *See also* religion
ceded islands, 6–9, 16–20, 182n10. *See also* southern Caribbean; Windward Islands
Cedulants and Capitulants (Campbell), 182n13, 210n49
Cells, Catherina, 106, 111, 124
Cells, John Coesvelt, 107, 111
Charbonne, Marinette, 59, 64
Charbonne, Pierre, 59
Charles, John, 58–59
Chatoyer, Joseph, 28
Cheverley, John Castelfranc, 169–73, 203n39

Children of Africa in the Colonies (Newton), 182n13
Church of England, 109–10, 126–29, 141, 154
clandestine marriage, 69–70, 140–41, 193n66. *See also* marriage
Clark, Emily, 176, 177, 200n99
Clarke, Nancy, 38, 91, 113
Cleland, John, 40
Code Noir, 62–63. *See also* slavery
Cohen, David W., 182n13
Coleridge, Henry Nelson, 35
Collar, Julia, 209n30
Collymore, Amaryllis, 38–39, 54, 90, 142–43
Collymore, Robert, 39, 43, 90, 177
Collymore, Susannah, 90
colonialism, 177, 178
Colonial Office, 4, 33, 75, 103–4, 157, 173–74
Combermere, Lord (Stapleton Cotton), 121
common-law marriage, 112, 138. *See also* marriage
concubines, 10, 43–44, 176. *See also* stereotypes of free women of color
Congnet, Madame, 54, 55
Cook (Captain), 45–46, 48
Cook, Ann, 92, 97
Cotton, Stapleton (Lord Combermere), 121
Cox, Edward L., 182n13
Coxall, Dorothy E., 102
Coxall, Elizabeth, 116
Coxall, John, 111–12, 116, 201n11
Coxall, John Cavalero, 111
Creoleana (Orderson), 41–45
creole marriage, 127
Creutz, Carl, 2–3, 177
Cromwell, Oliver, 106
Cuming, Thomas, 114

Dash, Betty, 120–21
Davies, Matthew, 79
Davis, Tracey C., 211n77
Day, Charles William, 34
Declaration of the Rights of Man and Citizen, 25
Defoe, Daniel, 40
D'Egville, James Harvey, 162, 164
Delph, Sara Ann, 102

Demerara, 16, 27, 30, 93–99, 101–4, 108, 113, 199n65
Demerara Gazette, 101–2, 104, 114
Demerara slave rebellion (1823), 101–4
Description of the Grenadines (Morse), 64
d'Estaing, Charles Hector (Comte), 182n15
Devas, Raymund P., 183n31, 193n71, 194n72
Development of Creole Society in Jamaica (Brathwaite), 182n13
Dickens, Charles, 164–65, 167–68
disease, 18, 24, 26, 93, 94, 96, 108, 124
Domingos Alvares, African Healing, and the Intellectual History of the Atlantic World (Sweet), 12
Dominica, 6, 7, 15–16, 18–19, 30–31, 81, 92, 105–9
Douglas, James, 97, 159–60
Douglas, John, 97, 159
Douglas, Mary Ann Ritchie, 159
Draper, Nicholas, 149, 195–96n108
Dundas, Henry, 25, 28
Dunker, Sheila, 182n13
d'Urban, Benjamin, 101
Dwyer, Bartholomew, 54

education: and legitimacy and respectability, 11, 70, 117, 155–56; of mixed-race descendants, 99, 118–19, 150, 158, 161
Elphinstone, James, 162
Engendering History: Caribbean Women in Historical Perspective (Shepherd et al.), 9
English Sexualities (Hitchcock), 188n56
entertainment, 44, 100–102, 121, 171, 173
entrepreneurial free women of color: Atlantic economy role, 4, 7–9, 14; business relationships with white men, 10–11, 55, 171, 180; business skills of, 47, 52–53, 82–83, 85–87, 113–15, 175–76, 179; financial independence of, 110–11, 115–17, 134, 142–46, 176; historical studies of, 39, 47, 138–39, 142, 180; mixed-race descendants of, 117–19, 147–68, 175–76, 178, 204n63, 213n16; plantation management by, 2, 57, 69, 76–77, 116, 149; political agency of, 6, 173–74, 178–79; property ownership by, 36–38, 48–49,

entrepreneurial free women of color (*cont.*) 64–65, 76–78, 89–90, 114; slave ownership by, 38–40, 57–61, 65–66, 78–85, 91–92, 143, 173–75. *See also* Ostrehan, Susannah; Philip, Judith; Polgreen, Rachael Pringle; Samson, Elisabeth; Smith, Rosetta; Thomas, Dorothy
Equiano, Olaudah, 12
Errol, John, 124
Essequibo, 27, 93
Evan Baillie Sons and Company, 117

Fairfield, Henry, 163
Family, Sex and Marriage in England (Stone), 193n66
Fanny Hill (Cleland), 40
Farley, Rawle, 205n4
Fedon, Julien, 21–24, 29, 71–76, 141
Fedon, Marie Rose Cavelan, 21–24, 27–29, 75, 141, 173–74, 179
Fedon, Pierre, 183n34
Fedon Rebellion, 23–24, 27–28, 71–76, 110, 112, 174, 184n42
Fedons, The (Jacobs), 183n34
feminine importation, 98
Fenner, Walter, 190n3
filial manumission, 82–84, 92, 106, 109, 111–12, 174–75, 178–79. *See also* manumission; slavery
Firebrace, William, 38, 49
Fitzclarence, Augusta, 163
Foden, Charlotte, 112, 113
Foden, William, 105–8, 112–13, 142
Fotheringham, Jean-Jacques, 68
Fotheringham, Jeanne-Rose, 68
Fotheringham, Patrick, 68
France: Caribbean settlement, 61–63, 67, 69, 76, 140–41, 156; conquests and conflicts over islands, 6–7, 14–21, 24–31, 69, 70–72, 95, 107; impact of French Revolutionary Wars, 20, 24–29, 31, 71–72. *See also* Seven Years' War
Fraser, Alexander, 88, 105, 108, 113
Fraser, Anna Maria, 144, 207n45
Fraser, Elizabeth, 143–44
Fraser, George, 143–44
Fraser, Jane, 99, 143–44
Fraser, John, 143–44
Fraser, William, 99, 143–44, 177, 207n44
"Free Coloured, The" (Dunker), 182n13
Free Coloureds (Cox), 182n13
Freedom Papers: An Atlantic Odyssey in the Age of Emancipation (Scott and Hébrard), 12
Free Mulatto, A (Philippe), 157
free people of color: contradictions of power and race in slave economy, 39, 86–87, 172–73; financial success in ceded islands, 16–17, 98; legal status of, 17, 21–24, 40, 81, 150, 157, 184n39; political loyalties of, 25, 27–31, 71–72, 74, 85, 156–57, 172; racial identity, 149, 168, 169–70
free women of color: business interests of, 98–99, 110, 114, 119, 170–71, 175; discrimination against by British, 22–23, 75, 80–82, 101–4, 112; marriage and intimate relationships, 128, 131, 134, 151, 176, 177; sexual objectification of, 32–36, 177; and slavery, 31, 39–40, 178–79; social and cultural role of, 11–14, 32, 99–101; stereotypes of, 34–36, 43–46, 56, 70, 115, 140, 141; wealth of, 4–5, 10, 20, 36, 142–43, 155, 176. *See also* entrepreneurial free women of color
French Revolutionary Wars, 20, 24–29, 31, 71–72
Fullarton, William, 50–53
Fullerton, Charlotte, 114, 116, 119, 138
Fullerton, Gavin, 113, 124–25, 160–61, 202–3n37, 205n83
Fullerton, John, 112, 113, 124–25, 138, 202n37
Fullerton, Mary, 101
Fullerton, Sarah, 115

Gage, Captain, 164
Garraway, Ann, 130, 133, 144–46
Garraway, D. G., 194n72
Garraway, Frances, 144–45
Garraway, John, 105, 126, 144
Garraway, John Gloster, 112, 116–17, 124–27, 144–45, 177
Garraway, Joseph, 145, 161, 207n50

INDEX   235

Garraway, Robert, 126–31, 144–45
Gaspar, David Barry, 9, 184n47
Geggus, David Patrick, 184n47
Gender and Empire (Wollacott), 10
Gender and Imperialism (Midgley), 10
gender roles: and agency, 13, 36, 49, 173–74, 179–80; in Caribbean history, 4–14, 35–36, 176–77; and dynamics of race and power, 3–4, 6–7, 10–14, 27–32, 172, 173–75, 178–80; sexuality, 32–36, 177; stereotypes of free women of color, 32–36, 44, 56, 70, 98, 115, 138–40
George III, King, 45, 75
George IV, King, 121–22
Gill, Hannah, 38
Gilroy, Paul, 9
Ginzburg, Carlo, 5
Goodwin, Betsey, 33, 38, 49, 53
Gordon, Edward Strathearn (Baron Gordon of Drumearn), 160
Gordon, Huntly, 132–34, 136, 160, 206n16
Gordon, John, 131–37, 160
Gordon, Thomas, 134
Grant, James, 18
Grantham, Julia, 160
Green, Charles, 75
Green, Mary-Bella, 38, 91–92
Greene, Jack, 182n13
Grenada: Fedon Rebellion, 21–24, 27–28, 71–76, 110, 112, 174, 184n42; imperial conflict over, 6, 15–17, 24–28, 61–62, 68–69, 108, 183n31; marriage laws in, 69, 109, 137, 138, 141; opportunities for free people of color, 7–8, 28–31; political polarization, 70–72; slavery in, 57, 112, 203n52
Grenada (Steele), 183n31, 194n72
Grenada, Island of Conflict (Brizan), 183n31, 194n72
Grenada House of Assembly, 112
Grenada National Museum, 191n14
Gretna Green, 128, 193n66. *See also* marriage
Griffiths, Rebecca, 55–56
Grimaldi, Stacey, 147

Hall, Catherine, 10, 149
Hamlet (Shakespeare), 165

Handler, Jerome, 149–50, 182n13, 196n6
Hardwicke, 1st Earl of (Philip Yorke), 127–28
Harwood, Sarah, 152
Hastings, Warren, 53
Hay, John, 23–24
Hayes (judge), 59–61
Haynes, Susan Ostrehan, 91
Hays, John, 184n42
Hébrard, Jean M., 9, 12, 178
Heuman, Gad, 182n13
Higman, Barry, 8
Hine, Darlene Clark, 9
History of Barbados (Poyer), 33
History of the Island of Grenada, 1498–1796, A (Devas), 194n71
History of the Island of Grenada, 1650–1950, The (Devas), 183n31
History of Trinidad, A (Joseph), 56
Hitchcock, Tim, 188n56
Holmes, Joseph Henry, 121
Holmes, Marianne Pemberton, 121, 204n72
Hopkinson, Benjamin James, 169–72, 212n2, 213n5
Hopkinson, Joanna, 170, 175, 213n5
hotels and hoteliers, 34, 85, 91–93, 98, 100, 174
Houston family, 19
hucksterism: as livelihood for free women of color, 8, 32, 54; taxation of, 104; use of slaves for, 98, 110, 114–15, 119–20, 170–71
Hughes, Victor, 25–27, 30, 71–72
hurricane of 1780, 107–8, 201n15

Iles, Edward (Ned), 107–8, 110
Iles, Ellis, 107–8
India, 181n2
Inner Life of Empires, The (Rothschild), 12
interracial marriage, 1–3, 28, 62–63, 65, 129, 138, 205n4. *See also* marriage
Inverness Royal Academy, 117, 204n63
Is She His Wife? (Dickens), 164

Jacobs, Curtis, 183n34
Jamaica, 7, 16–18, 28, 84
James, C. L. R., 182n13

Joanna (slave), 38
Johnstone, Alexander, 12–13
Johnstone, George, 18
Jones, Hilary, 180
Jose (slave), 58–61, 78
Joseph, E. L., 56

Kennedy, John, 124–25
Kensington House school, 117, 123, 161–62, 205n78
Kerr, Crawford Davison, 153
Kerr, Paulette, 9
Kerrison, Edward, 164
King, Matthew, 89
King, Thomas, 115
King, William, 115, 125
Kirwan, Andrew, 106–8, 142
Kirwan, Dorothy. *See* Thomas, Dorothy
Kirwan, Elizabeth, 106, 111, 112, 126, 201n11

Lady's Monthly Museum, 163
La Grenade, Louis, 72–73, 184n47
Laidlaw, Zoe, 213n16
Lambert, David, 213n16
Landers, Jane, 182n13
Lang Chauncy and Lucas, 117
Last Caribbean Frontier, The (Candlin), 190n1
Lauder, William, 41–42, 48
Lee, Caroline, 38
Leeds, Norah, 171
Legacies of British Slave-Ownership, 195–96n108
legitimacy, 117, 149–51, 156–61, 177–78
Lemon, Betsy, 38, 91, 101, 113, 213n6
Lemon, Molly, 170, 213n6
le Plat, Louis, 119
Lester, Alan, 213n16
Letters from the West Indies (Lloyd), 201n10
Lewis, Hannah, 38, 45
Life and Adventures (Sala), 212n92
Lilburne, Grace, 55–56
Lionel Parks, 90
Livesay, Daniel, 149
Lloyd, William, 47, 123–24, 201n10
Long, Edward, 35, 118
Lords Commissioners for New Lands, 15

Louis XV, King, 62
L'Ouverture, Toussaint, 28, 72
Lushington, William, 55

Madden, Richard, 45, 47
Magee, Henry, 90
malaria, 26, 94, 96. *See also* disease
manumission: costs and obstacles to, 80–84, 202n31; filial, 82–84, 92, 106, 109, 111–12, 174–75, 178–79; frequency for women, 31; payment for by enslaved women, 92, 105–6; slave owners' strategies to obtain, 32, 43, 82, 92, 111–12, 139, 197–98n38. *See also* slavery
Map of Carriacou, 190n3
"Marginality and Free Coloured Identity" (Sio), 182n13
maritime trade, 6–7, 19, 62, 95, 107–8, 110, 113, 115. *See also* slave trade
Maroons, 2, 28
marriage: and Catholic Church, 69, 70, 109, 140–41; clandestine form of, 69–70, 140–41, 193n66; colonial laws, 1–3, 62–63, 69, 109, 127–28, 131; common-law marriage, 112, 138; creole form of, 127; interracial, 1–3, 28, 62–63, 65, 129, 138, 205n4; property implications of, 110, 128, 134, 145–46; and respectability, 134; Scottish law, 128–29, 134–37, 160; by white settlers to white women, 68, 141, 144, 159, 177
Marriage Act (Britain, 1753), 109, 127–28, 140–41
Marriage of Figaro, The, 163
Martinique, 17, 25–28, 62, 72
Mary Ann (slave), 92
Mary Rose (slave), 111
matrifocal family, 83–84
matrilineal inheritance, 79, 83–84, 90–93, 102, 144, 145–46, 177–78
McCallum, Pierre Franc, 50, 52–53
McDaniel, Lorna, 190n1
Mcdowell and Millikin company, 19
McGarel, Charles, 161–62
Mckenzie to the Duke of Portland (National Archives of the United Kingdom, 1795), 184n42

McLeod, Cynthia, 4, 181n1
Melvill, Robert, 16, 17–18, 22
Métis women, 180
micro-biographies, 4, 9, 12–14, 176, 178–80. *See also* Caribbean historiography
Middlemore, George, 60–61, 191n19
Midgley, Clare, 10
migration, 29–30, 61
Milton, John, 41
Mingo, Jenny, 92
miscegenation, 11, 22–23, 28–29, 63, 142. *See also* marriage
mistress stereotype, 51, 56, 137, 139–41. *See also* stereotypes of free women of color
Mitchell, George Abercrombie, 77, 148, 151
mixed-race descendants of entrepreneurial free women of color, 117–19, 147–68, 175–76, 178, 204n63, 213n16
Moll Flanders (Defoe), 40
Mongre, Louis, 64, 67
Montserrat, 16, 106–8, 142
Moore, Henrietta, 113
Moore, Susannah Charlotte, 113
Moreton, J. B., 35
Morse, S. V., 64
multiculturalism, 6–9, 14, 19–20, 28–31, 108, 178
Murray, James, 18
My Diary in America in the Midst of War (Sala), 168

Nanoe (slave), 2, 179
Napoleonic Wars, 84–87
Narrative of the Insurrection (Hay), 184n42
National Archives of Scotland, 129
Neither Slave, nor Free (Greene and Cohen), 182n13
Netherlands: ceded colonies, 6, 14, 20, 27, 93–95, 99; colonial settlers and travelers, 12, 108; marriage laws, 1–3, 131, 138, 173
Nevis, 16
New and Accurate Map of the Island of Cariacou, A (Fenner), 190n3
New Orleans, 139, 176–77
Newton, Melanie, 150, 182n13
Nogues, Charles, 71, 73, 194n88

"Notes on Demerara" (Holmes), 204n72
Notes on the West Indies (Pinckard), 199n65
Nunes, Elizabeth, 127

Ogborn, Miles, 12
Orderson, J. W., 41–46
Ostrehan, Elizabeth, 88–90
Ostrehan, Lydia, 88, 90
Ostrehan, Mary, 88–90, 92–93, 97–102, 104
Ostrehan, Priscilla, 81–84, 90, 92, 179
Ostrehan, Susannah: Atlantic economy influence of, 175–76; business success, 85–87, 93; estate of, 90–93; family and slave origins, 87–89; manumission of family members, 112, 207n39; property ownership, 89–90; as self-made entrepreneur, 141–42; slave ownership by, 80–85, 91–92, 143, 174–75, 197–98n38
Ostrehan, Susannah (niece), 87–88, 90, 99, 101
Ostrehan, Thomas, 87–89
Ostrehan, William, 88–90, 92
Owens, Frances, 108, 111, 113, 140
Owens, John, 108, 113
Oxford History of the British Empire: Gender and Empire (Levine), 10

Paisley Grammar School, 143, 204n63
Paradise Lost (Milton), 41
Parker, Charles, 116, 118–19, 138
Parry, Edward Francis, 153
Paton, Diana, 179
Patterson, Orlando, 187n55
Pattinson, John and William, 169
Pauline (slave), 66
Payne, Katherine, 38
Penny, Thomas Ostrehan, 88–89
Penny, Thomas Woodin, 88
Perpignon, Hannah, 55
Petite Martinique, 62–65, 67, 71–74
Philip, Catherine, 61–63, 65
Philip, François, 23, 61–62, 65, 76, 148
Philip, Honore (junior), 63–64, 67, 148
Philip, Honore (senior), 61–63, 76, 148, 191n25
Philip, Jean-Baptiste, 76, 157–58

238 ∾ INDEX

Philip, Jean Baptiste-Louis, 57, 64–65, 67–68, 76–77, 148, 157–58
Philip, Jeanette, 61–67, 83, 148, 179
Philip, Jean-Pierre, 61–62, 65
Philip, Joachim, 64, 72–76, 79, 148, 156, 194n82
Philip, Judith: business success and property ownership, 64–66, 76–78, 175; estate of, 78–79; family origins, 61–64, 179; marriages of daughters, 67–70, 140–41, 176; political positions of family, 70–76, 174; as self-made entrepreneur, 67, 143; slave ownership by, 57–61, 65–66, 78–79, 174–75, 190n2, 195–96n108; success of descendants, 147–58
Philip, Magdalen, 64, 67–68, 72
Philip, Marie-Magdalaine Vigi, 65
Philip, Michel, 64, 67, 74, 148
Philip, Michel Maxwell, 157–58
Philip, Nicholas Regis, 64, 67, 77, 148
Philip, St. Luce, 76, 157
Philip, Susannah, 57, 64, 67–68, 73–76, 148
Philip family, 148–49, 154–55
Philippe, Jean-Baptiste (Jean-Baptiste Philip), 76, 157–58
Philips, The (McDaniel), 190n1
Picton, Augusta, 158
Picton, Edward, 158
Picton, Frederick, 158
Picton, Richard Rose, 158, 189n84
Picton, Thomas, 36, 50–53, 55–56, 140, 157–59, 176
Picton, Thomas, Jr., 158–59, 210n59
Piero (free woman of color), 64
Pietry, Maria, 158
Pinckard, George, 34, 47, 91–92, 141, 199n65
plantations: and agricultural expertise, 18, 107; decline of golden age of, 148–49; impact of political events on, 107–8, 110; management by free women of color, 2, 38–39, 54, 57, 64–65, 76–77, 116, 149; ownership by free people of color, 2, 69, 73–74, 76, 104, 114, 157, 160–61; role of slavery, 64–66, 79
planter assemblies, 19
Poisson, Jeanne Antoinette (Madame de Pompadour), 62

Polgreen, Edward, 43, 48, 188n61
Polgreen, James, 188n61
Polgreen, John, 188n61
Polgreen, Rachael Pringle: business success and property ownership, 36–38, 48–49, 85, 89; estate of, 36; family origins, 47, 48; historical and literary references to, 40–47, 56; as self-made entrepreneur, 141–42, 176; slave ownership by, 38–40, 174–75, 213n6
Political Council of Suriname, 1–3
Polly (slave), 199n61
Pompadour, Madame de (Jeanne Antoinette Poisson), 62
Poni, Carlo, 5
Portland, 3rd Duke of (William Cavendish-Bentinck), 33, 184n42
Portland, 5th Duke of (William John Cavendish-Scott-Bentinck), 152, 209n25
Port of Spain, 54, 150, 158
poverty, 54, 85–86, 175
Poyer, John, 33–34, 49, 51, 87
Price of Emancipation, The (Draper), 195–96n108
Princess (slave), 120
Pringle, Thomas, 38, 42–43, 48, 49
prostitution and sexual services, 8, 33–34, 41, 46–47, 110, 188n56, 211n77
public woman, 211n79
Pybus, Cassandra, 5

quadroon mistress, 151
"'Quadroon-Plaçage' Myth, The" (Aslakson), 200n99
Queen's Royal Regiment of Foot, 205n11
Quite Alone (Sala), 167

race: and dynamics of gender and power, 3–4, 6–7, 10–14, 27–32, 172, 173–75, 178–80; racial hierarchy, 3, 34, 85, 117, 156–57, 171–73; racial identity, 11, 149–51, 161. *See also* entrepreneurial free women of color; free people of color; free women of color; interracial marriage; slavery
"Race, Colour and Miscegenation" (Sio), 182n13

Rainey, George, 118
rate books (taxation books), 48–49
Rebecca's Revival: Creating Black Christianity in the Atlantic World (Sensbach), 12
religion, 19, 22, 72, 112. *See also* Catholicism; Church of England
research methods and scope, 4–14
respectability, 49, 69, 70, 109, 127–28, 134, 151
Rice, Thomas Spring, 61
Richards, E., 102
Ricketts, George, 33, 38, 49, 140
Ritchie, Mary Ann, 97
Ritchie, Rebecca, 97, 102, 121, 159
Roach (Mrs.), 38
Robertson, Charles, 118
Robertson, Daniel, 118
Robertson, Eliza, 115–16, 138
Robertson, George, 118, 124–25, 203n43
Robertson, Gilbert, 113, 114–16, 118, 138, 202–3n37, 203n43, 206n20
Robertson, Gilbert, Jr., 118
Robertson, Harry, 118, 125
Robertson, Henry "Harry," 161
Robertson, John, 118, 204n59
Robertson, Sandbach and Parker, 115, 118, 203n43
Robertson of Kindaece (chief of clan), 118
Rochambeau, Jean-Baptiste, 28
Rolland, Jane Dellor, 55
Rosalie (slave), 9
Ross, Elizabeth A., 102
Rothschild, Emma, 12
Rowlandson, Thomas, 40–41, 45, 46
Royal Naval Hotel, 36–37, 44, 47, 89

Sala, Albert, 166
Sala, Augusta, 166
Sala, Augustus John James, 162–63
Sala, Charles Kerrison, 164, 165
Sala, Frederick, 166
Sala, George Augustus, 122–25, 150–51, 161, 166–68, 211n71, 211n76, 211n80, 212n92
Sala, Henrietta Catherina Florentina Simon, 116–17, 122–23, 161–68
Sala, Henrietta De Egville, 164, 166
Sala, Susannah, 162

Sally (slave), 119–20
Salterelli, Antonio, 162
Samson, Elisabeth, 1–5, 172–76, 179
Scotland: Caribbean settlers, 12–13, 16–19, 22, 28–29; education of mixed-race descendants of free women of color, 99, 118–19, 150, 158, 161; marriage laws, 128–29, 134–37, 160
Scots Magazine, 16, 17
Scott, Rebecca, 9, 12, 178
Scott, William, 74–75, 77
Scully, Pamela, 179
Sensbach, Jon, 12
service industry, 47, 54–55, 98, 101–2, 110, 113, 171
Seven Years' War, 6–7, 15–21, 61, 63, 69, 182n15
sexuality, 32–36, 177
sexual services. *See* prostitution and sexual services
Shadow and the Substance, The (Farley), 205n4
Shepherd, Verene, 9
Short Account, A (Garraway), 194n72
Simon, Catherina, 113, 115–16, 124, 138
Simon, D. P., 111, 115–16, 138, 161
Sio, Arnold, 149–50, 182n13
skin color, 10, 32, 156
Slave, The, 165
Slave Consolidation Act (1826), 81
slave economy, 4, 39–40, 60, 84, 172–74
slave rebellions, 19, 29, 84, 98–99, 101–4, 172
slave registers, 39, 203n52
slavery: abolition of, 60, 104, 149–51, 173; compensation commission, 8, 60, 78, 104, 121, 172, 196n108; conditions of, 43–44; economic role of, 54, 84, 98; ethical questions in historical research, 173; impact of imperial conflicts on, 25, 31, 72, 93–94; ownership of by family members, 80–83; ownership of by free women of color, 2, 7, 39–40, 46–47, 55, 57, 78–79, 119–21; and political agency of free women of color, 173–74; political loyalties of slaves, 24–25, 66; rights of free people of color to own slaves, 157;

240 ∾ INDEX

slavery (cont.)
  self-emancipated slaves, 142, 173, 174–75.
    See also manumission
Slaves Without Masters (Berlin), 182n13
slave trade, 15, 93–94, 105, 108, 174
Smith, George, 117
Smith, John, 205n85
Smith, John Lurie, Jr., 124–25, 205n85
Smith, Lionel, 60–61
Smith, Rosetta: business success and wealth
  of, 52–56, 174–76; family of, 53; literary
  and historical references to, 50–53, 56;
  and mistress stereotype, 36, 140; success
  of children, 158–59
Smith Payne and Smith, 117
Snagg (lawyer), 59
Society for the Encouragement of Arts,
  Manufacture and Commerce, 85
Sociology of Slavery (Patterson), 187n55
Soldier's Recollection, A (St. Clair), 199n65
southern Caribbean: barriers of race and
  legitimacy, 156–57; colonial settlement,
  16; impact of imperial conflicts, 7,
  14, 19, 20, 24–28; multiculturalism, 6,
  29–31; transition from slave economy to
  emancipation, 60. See also ceded islands;
  Windward Islands
Spain: colonial settlement and
  administrative policies, 7, 28, 66, 67, 75,
  157; conflicts over islands, 6, 7, 14, 27, 29,
  94, 107
St. Clair, Thomas Staunton, 199n65
St. Domingue, 17, 24–28, 61, 85, 182n15
Steele, Beverley, 183n31, 194n72
Steele, James, 59
stereotypes of free women of color, 32–36,
  44, 56, 70, 98, 115, 138–40
Stevens, William, 38
Stewart, John, 149
Stewart, Mary (Polly), 207n45
St. Kitts, 16, 17, 106
St. Lucia, 17, 25–28, 72
Stoeltje, Beverly, 180
Stoler, Ann Laura, 11
Stone, Lawrence, 193n66
Strange Gentleman, The (Dickens), 164

Strange History of the American Quadroon,
  The (Clark), 200n99
Strickler, Melchier, 162
Stuart, John (Lord Bute), 17
St. Vincent: conflicts with black Caribs, 19,
  26, 28, 72; conquests and land acquisition,
  6, 15–16, 20, 27; ethnic profile, 7, 30;
  opportunities for free people of color, 31
subscription balls, 100
sugar, 15, 63, 94, 107
Suriname, 1–4, 6, 7, 178
Sweet, James, 12

Tain Academy, 204n63
taxation, 48–49, 87–88, 101–4, 112, 174
Telford, Norton and Co., 19
Thackeray, William Makepeace, 118
Thiel, Nicholas Francis de, 162
Things I Have Seen (Sala), 212n92
Thomas, Ann (Nan), 105, 112, 116–17, 124–26,
  138
Thomas, Doll. See Thomas, Dorothy
Thomas, Dorothea Christina, 110–12, 117,
  126–38, 160, 206n26
Thomas, Dorothy (née Kirwan): business
  success of, 4–5, 113–15, 171, 205n12; estate
  of, 124–25, 145–46, 166, 203n43, 206n26;
  financial independence, 110, 115–17,
  139–40; literary and historical accounts
  of, 121–24, 142, 199n82; political activity
  to overturn discriminatory tax, 102–4,
  173–74; property ownership, 203n39,
  206n21; relationship with Joseph Thomas,
  109–11, 137, 176; slave origins and family
  of, 105–12, 126–31, 134, 142, 201n7; slave
  ownership by, 119–21, 174–75; success of
  descendants, 117–19, 160–68
Thomas, Eliza, 109, 113, 115, 116
Thomas, Harry, 109, 124–25
Thomas, Joseph, 105, 106, 108, 109–12,
  127–29, 137, 142, 206n37
Thomas, Joseph, Jr., 109, 114
Thomas, Mary, 111
Thornton, Ann Rachel, 68, 77, 147–49, 152
Thornton, Edmund, 68–71, 77, 140–41, 143,
  193n63

Thornton, Elizabeth, 152
Thornton, Ellen Ann. *See* Boys, Ellen Ann Thornton
Thornton, Frances Catherine, 153, 155
Thornton, Jeannette Rose, 153–55
Thornton, Judith, 68, 70, 147–49, 151–53, 155–56
Thornton, Louis Edmund, 68, 78, 147, 152
Thornton, Magdalene, 68, 147–49, 151–53, 155–56
Thornton, Magdalene Judith, 153–55
Thornton, Philip, 68, 70, 78, 147
Thornton, William Wheeler, 153–56, 209n30
Tobago, 6, 7, 15, 17–18, 20, 30, 31
Tramezzani, Diomiro, 162
transcolonial mobility, 6, 9, 11–12, 14, 71, 78, 107, 178
Travels in America, Performed in 1806 (Ashe), 139
Treaty of Paris (1763), 15–21, 69. *See also* Seven Years' War
Treaty of Paris (1783), 108
Trinidad: conquest and conflicts over, 6, 16, 27, 29, 50, 94; policies and administration of, 50–51, 66, 67; settlement of, 5, 7–8, 30, 31, 75, 210n49
Trollope, Anthony, 34, 155
Turbulent Time, A (Gaspar and Geggus), 184n47

Unappropriated People, The (Handler), 182n13

Vanity Fair (Thackeray), 118
Velden, Lucy Van Den, 171–72
Velluti, Giovanni, 162
Ventour, Etienne, 71
Verdet, Joseph, 23
Veseprey, Henrietta, 64
Vestris, Lucia Elizabeth, 163

Victoria, Queen, 159, 165
Victory, The (Barker), 205n12
Village Coquettes, The (Dickens), 164
Vincent, Rosalie, 178
Voyage in the West Indies (Waller), 33
Voyage to Demerary (Bolingbroke), 199n65

Waller, John, 33, 139
Warner, Henry, 89
Warner, Margaret Ostrehan, 89
War of the Austrian Succession, 62
Webster, Benjamin, 111
Welch (Captain), 82–83
Welch, Pedro, 9, 149–50, 197n33, 207n39
Western, Elizabeth Charlotte, 147
Western, Mary, 152
West India lobby, 15
White, James, 92
white women, 10, 33, 63, 85–86, 175
William IV, King, 163
William Henry, Prince, 44–45, 122–23
Willoughby, William, 90
Windward Islands, 16–17, 24–31, 60, 71. *See also* ceded islands; southern Caribbean
Women in Caribbean History (Shepherd), 9
Woodford, Ralph, 157
Woollacott, Angela, 10
Woolsey, John, 90
Woolsey, Susan, 90
www.ancestry.com, 203n52
Wyvill, Richard, 86, 91

yellow fever, 26, 95, 124. *See also* disease
Yellow Rose, The, 165
Yorke, Philip (1st Earl of Hardwicke), 127–28
Young, William, 183n27

Zobre, Hermanus, 3

RACE IN THE ATLANTIC WORLD, 1700–1900

The Hanging of Angélique
*The Untold Story of Canadian Slavery and
the Burning of Old Montréal*
BY AFUA COOPER

Christian Ritual and the Creation of
British Slave Societies, 1650–1780
BY NICHOLAS M. BEASLEY

African American Life in the Georgia Lowcountry
The Atlantic World and the Gullah Geechee
EDITED BY PHILIP MORGAN

The Horrible Gift of Freedom
Atlantic Slavery and the Representation of Emancipation
BY MARCUS WOOD

The Life and Letters of Philip Quaque,
the First African Anglican Missionary
EDITED BY VINCENT CARRETTA AND TY M. REESE

In Search of Brightest Africa
Reimagining the Dark Continent in American Culture, 1884–1936
BY JEANNETTE EILEEN JONES

Contentious Liberties
American Abolitionists in Post-emancipation Jamaica, 1834–1866
BY GALE L. KENNY

We Are the Revolutionists
German-Speaking Immigrants and American Abolitionists after 1848
BY MISCHA HONECK

The American Dreams of John B. Prentis, Slave Trader
BY KARI J. WINTER

Missing Links
*The African and American Worlds of
R. L. Garner, Primate Collector*
BY JEREMY RICH

Almost Free
A Story about Family and Race in Antebellum Virginia
BY EVA SHEPPARD WOLF

To Live an Antislavery Life
Personal Politics and the Antebellum Black Middle Class
BY ERICA L. BALL

Flush Times and Fever Dreams
A Story of Capitalism and Slavery in the Age of Jackson
BY JOSHUA D. ROTHMAN

Diplomacy in Black and White
John Adams, Toussaint Louverture, and Their Atlantic World Alliance
BY RONALD ANGELO JOHNSON

Enterprising Women
Gender, Race, and Power in the Revolutionary Atlantic
BY KIT CANDLIN AND CASSANDRA PYBUS

Eighty-Eight Years
The Long Death of Slavery in the United States, 1777–1865
BY PATRICK RAEL

Finding Charity's Folk
Enslaved and Free Black Women in Maryland
BY JESSICA MILLWARD

The Mulatta Concubine
Terror, Intimacy, Freedom, and Desire in the Black Transatlantic
BY LISA ZE WINTERS

The Politics of Black Citizenship
Free African Americans in the Mid-Atlantic Borderland, 1817–1863
BY ANDREW K. DIEMER

Punishing the Black Body
Marking Social and Racial Structures in Barbados and Jamaica
BY DAWN P. HARRIS

www.ingramcontent.com/pod-product-compliance
Lightning Source LLC
Chambersburg PA
CBHW011745220426
43666CB00018B/2897